D1297291

Heifetz As I Knew Him

Heifetz
As I Knew Him

by Ayke Agus

AMADEUS PRESS
Portland, Oregon

Every reasonable effort has been made to contact copyright holders and secure permission. In any instances where this has not proved possible, we offer apologies to all concerned and ask that any omissions be brought to our attention.

"If" by Rudyard Kipling reproduced with permission of A. P. Watt Ltd. on behalf of The National Trust for Places of Historic Interest or Natural Beauty (United Kingdom)

ISBN 1-57467-062-X

Printed in Singapore

Published in 2001 by
AMADEUS PRESS (an imprint of Timber Press, Inc.)
The Haseltine Building
133 S.W. Second Avenue, Suite 450
Portland, Oregon 97204 U.S.A.

Library of Congress Cataloging-in-Publication Data

Agus, Ayke.
    Heifetz as I knew him / by Ayke Agus.
        p.   cm.
    Includes bibliographical references (p.   ).
    ISBN 1-57467-062-X
    1. Heifetz, Jascha. 2. Violinists—Biography. I. Title.

    ML418.H44 A48 2001
    787.2'092—dc21
    [B]
                                                            00-056932

*This book is dedicated
to Michael and to our daughter, Ada,
for their unconditional love
and for the freedom they gave me
to devote my days and years to Mr. Heifetz.*

Contents

A Message to the Reader

W hat I wish for each reader of this book is to come away with an understanding of the truly unique relationship that existed between Ayke Agus and Jascha Heifetz.

Who was this young woman who came into Heifetz's life as his violin student but whose piano virtuosity enabled her to become the most important accompanist of his last fifteen years? We know that all the accompanists during his professional career were great; they had to be or they could not fulfill his constant insistence on perfection. But Ayke's instinctive accompanying skills became the very reason she was able to succeed not only in their musical bond—which at times would so overwhelm Heifetz that he would stop in the midst of a passage and ask, "Ayke, how did you know I was going to do that?"—but also in their everyday lives.

Ayke was the perfect companion. She attributes this, in great part, to her cultural upbringing, a tough-love environment that prepared her for the difficult taskmaster that Heifetz was. I say, only maybe! It certainly helped, and Heifetz would toast in appreciation with his glass of vodka at dinner, not to Ayke but to her mother. I leave it to the reader to decipher the meaning behind this left-handed compliment.

Heifetz tested each of us who spent time with him. We had to bend and sway to his demands, and most of us broke in the bending, some sooner than others. He had a great need for order in his life, but oh how he loved to play games. Heifetz reveled in orchestrating the unexpected, which kept those who cared about him on their toes. Here Ayke was the quintessential accompanist-companion, always responding to his whims and fancies.

She would anticipate the way Heifetz might phrase any particular day just as she listened to the way he phrased a passage of a violin sonata.

She walked side-by-side with him, always in perfect step. Perhaps a bit of genius of her own allowed her to be one step ahead.

Their relationship was a collaboration of heart and mind. And certainly another title for this book could have been *Accompanying Heifetz*.

ADELE GLICKMAN SHAPIRO

Adele Glickman Shapiro, a long-time friend of both Jascha Heifetz and Ayke Agus, worked for Heifetz briefly in the late 1970s.

Acknowledgments

*T*his book has been more than ten years in the making. Jascha Heifetz died on 10 December 1987, and I needed encouragement to keep both pleasant and unpleasant memories fresh. I owe thanks to Adele Glickman Shapiro, who gave me the incentives and courage and who knows from experience what it was like to be Jascha Heifetz's companion: she was one for a short while. I also thank her husband, Dr. Edward Shapiro, Heifetz's internist for many years, for his emotional and psychological support during my years with Heifetz and after his passing. Thanks are due to Laila Nilles, the producer-editor of my CDs, for her counsel, and to her husband, Jack, for photographs and for his help with the computer, and for the moral support that they both provided. Thanks to my family, my sister Laili and her husband, Jonathan Glassman, for their never-ending support and assistance with computer and emotional problems. And last but not least, thanks to Michael Palotai, the father of my daughter, Ada, for his indefatigable help in verbalizing my story and editing the manuscript. I consider it my responsibility to cultivate Jascha Heifetz's legacy until my last breath, but I have also come to realize the importance of self-discovery and will forever be grateful to my family for encouraging me on this path as well.

1

Fanfare

Magicians of music leave a lasting mark not only on the history of performance but on the collective memory of humankind as well. In the past the magic of Niccolò Paganini and Franz Liszt left such lasting marks for us—Paganini died before his powers had diminished, and Liszt retired from the stage as a pianist in time to leave his record untarnished. Of those who may claim a similar universal fame in the twentieth century, none was closer to the mark than Jascha Heifetz, who also retired from the stage before his powers ebbed. Like his two famous predecessors, Heifetz, too, raised performance standards to heights that before him were not even considered possible.

Following the time-honored tradition of past masters, in the last twenty-five years of his life Heifetz concentrated his energies on teaching the art of violin playing. By his own admission he felt obliged to pass on a special kind of violin playing as he had received it from his famous master, Leopold Auer. In the Jascha Heifetz master class, selected talented students could observe and learn how to make magic. Few, if any, could absorb it all—Heifetz was infinitely more than just a magician full of tricks. His students found that just learning some of his technical secrets didn't add up to comprehending his art.

I had hardly passed the age of twenty when I first met Jascha Heifetz. At that time he was already seventy. I first became his violin student in the master class, then the pianist for the class, and eventually his private accompanist and musical collaborator for his transcriptions. By that time I was already fulfilling the duties of hostess of his house, and he felt that a title was necessary to justify my being around so much. He didn't like the sound of "house manager," and so we left it as unofficial private accompanist, a euphemism for indispensable factotum. Coming at the age of eighteen from Indonesia or, as he preferred to say, "from the jungles of Java," I had to learn quickly how to cope with a complicated person whose problems were aggravated by his basic, simple view of the world. He looked at things as black or white, and people were either for him or against him. Things had to be done immediately if not sooner, and there were no excuses for failure. Heifetz prided himself on being difficult even at relatively normal times, and "You are bloody no good" came easily from him when I thought I had done something quite well. When the dark demons took over his mind, I learned to resort to *Thousand and One Nights* devices by telling him stories from my life in mysterious Indonesia. My stories were always followed by a short silence, then by a half-believing "You are lying." Nevertheless, they opened the floodgates of his memory, and my role was to be a good listener who asked no questions. To him questions meant that I was prying.

Yet one day I learned that his stories were not just idly told. After a long one he made the surprising remark, "Now, you make sure that you do not forget to put all this in the book you are going to write after I am dead and gone." From the careful emphasis on the "do not" instead of the colloquial "don't," I was to understand that Heifetz meant what he said.

He let me know that he did not want to write his memoirs because he was loath to join the crowd of every "has-been" who had used a last chance to cash in on vanishing fame. Furthermore, his principles also got in the way. He quite often sternly admonished, "Don't write anything down because once it's written, it could be held against you." He justified his limitations on conversational topics with his friends and guests with the principle "Don't tell your friends anything that you don't want your enemies to know." I can only explain his desire to have a book written about him by comparing it to everyone's desire to be better known and to see whatever good could come of the effort. Nevertheless, he could not bring himself to sit down with a ghost writer and publish under his name another person's version of his life, containing some truth, some half truths, and a great deal of bending of the truth.

The question "What's in a name?" had special significance for Jascha Heifetz. He gave people permission, explicitly or implicitly, to use a certain version of his name. The name "Heifetz" was used strictly in the business of music, in his relationships with managers, publicists, and critics. He expected his students and the personnel in his house to call him Mr. Heifetz; a step further, "Mr. H." was used by people with whom he preferred to be on a more intimate level. The "Mr. H." level was close enough to make him feel free to expect more services from its users than he expected from others, yet distant enough to safeguard him from familiarity's breeding contempt. Using "Jascha" was discouraged, and only old and very close friends dared to use it to his face. Friends whom he saw socially on a regular basis were permitted to call him Jim, which came from the pseudonym Jim Hoyl, under which name he had written popular songs in his younger years. To top off the list, his real name was Joseph Heifetz, which nobody used and few knew about. Furthermore, some bumpkin visitors from his Russian homeland called him Geifetz; the *H* does not exist in Russian so that this version, which he immensely disliked, appeared in the Russian literature. In this book I will use "Heifetz" for simplicity's sake, but on occasion I will allow myself to call him Jim as I often did in his lifetime when the situation demanded it. Heifetz also used a logo with the letters *J* and *H* fused, which was also his musical signature on every transcription, whether published or in manuscript. He had this logo embroidered on most of his garments, and it was even printed on paper napkins.

Finding a way to portray this complex yet simple person ("simply complex," as he would have played with the words) felt enormously difficult at first, but eventually I found inspiration in his last testament. He left two objects for me, the significance of which eluded me for years. One was a Steuben glass prism, the other a solid gold scabbard with his initials engraved on its casing, containing both a letter opener with a magnifying glass at its end and a pair of scissors. Heifetz must have attributed great importance to these objects; he mentioned few specific items in his will and left no clear provisions for most of his multimillion-dollar estate, yet these two gifts were singled out. I interpreted the prism as a hint about how to write my book. A Steuben prism is a work of art; its surface has irregular angles and planes, each of which shows the same object differently to the person who looks through the glass. Some views are magnified while others are distorted and recede from the "real" view. Viewing Heifetz through such a prism could help us comprehend his "simply complex" personality. He always claimed that there was more than one side to a story or to music, so each chapter in this book considers a different side of Heifetz in turn, the prismatic magnification leaving his other characteristics at a distance, sometimes at the unavoidable expense of somewhat distorting these other views.

At the head of each chapter are a few lines from the poem "If" by Rudyard Kipling, chosen to suit each chapter and therefore out of their original order. The poem held great significance for Heifetz; it became his shield and buckler when he was about twenty-one, a basis for his moral code and self comport. He always carried his handwritten copy of this poem in his pocket and thought of it as a sort of talisman that had saved his life in a crisis that he considered life threatening. I considered myself lucky that he showed me this poem early enough in our relationship and told me its story, because it helped me to understand what made him tick, which in turn guided me at times of baffling disasters.

Following his customary advice I have omitted names as much as possible—mentioning names, he often said, "will only get you in trouble." He dreaded being misquoted and would rather drop conversations altogether if he felt that he was being trapped into gossiping: he didn't want to give anyone the chance to say something that began with "Heifetz said." He knew the value of his opinion and the weight his name carried. Since this book contains only my personal experiences with him during the last fifteen years of his life and is neither a history, a collection of gossip, nor his hagiography, the reader should be able to forgive me for such omissions.

To recapitulate the basic facts of his life, Jascha Heifetz was born on 2 February 1901 in Vilna, in Russian Lithuania. He was given the name Joseph at birth. His mother, Annie, probably was responsible for the later change to Jascha, which seems to be a Yiddish version of Yashup, the Hebrew for Joseph. He took his first lessons from his father, Ruben (Ruven or Reuven), at the age of three and soon was enrolled in the local music academy. From my own experience I know that parents don't make very good music teachers, regardless of their own playing standards.

At the age of six he played Felix Mendelssohn's Violin Concerto in E minor, Op. 64, to a large audience in Kovno, with great success; he claimed to have made his debut at age seven. His childhood was that of a prodigy, and his studies in St. Petersburg under the celebrated violin teacher Leopold Auer were often interrupted by concert engagements in Russia and Europe, starting perhaps at an early age. The tours were primarily to support his parents and his two younger sisters, Pauline and Elsa. He made his phenomenally successful debut in Carnegie Hall on 27 October 1917 in the presence of the most famous violinists of the time. He made four world tours in his life and played in practically every major city on the globe. Heifetz left behind a large number of recordings, most of them reissued posthumously on compact disc, and enriched the violin repertory with some 150 transcriptions. In the mid 1950s he practically gave up concertizing and in 1962 took up teaching a master class in Los Angeles which he continued almost to the end of his life.

Since I knew him well only for the last fifteen years of his life, I have tried to exclude everything that happened before 1972 except stories that

Heifetz narrated for me or references that are essential to the flow of events. Though I met him late in 1971, sixteen years before he died, I have spoken of our time together as fifteen years, which is the time during which I was close to him. Sometimes I felt that I had to repeat well-known stories about him because the way he told them to me differed from their generally known versions; other times the reader's ability to understand my story would suffer had I not reached into the past. In these cases sometimes I had to rely on secondary sources. All in all, the story is about Heifetz as I saw him and does not reflect others' thoughts of him. I interviewed no one. I'm sure that more scholarly and perhaps more "factual" biographies will come some day from competent historians.

An account of my Indonesian-Chinese background seems necessary to explain my high tolerance of Heifetz's often irrational behavior. My upbringing, based on an unquestioning respect of my elders, played a considerable role in my ability to stick it out with him when others were unable to do so. Despite our coming together from distant corners of the world, Heifetz and I had a great deal in common in education, family background, and appreciation of values in life. As I recount in some detail in chapters 5 and 6, we were both primitives in the sense that he never attended schools except for short studies in the St. Petersburg Music Academy. His interest was in the violin, its history and makeup, and he read artists' biographies avidly. Otherwise he read *Reader's Digest* faithfully and some classical Russian novels, which suited me fine. In spite of my college degrees, I did not consider myself an intellectual, which also worked in my favor. Heifetz was my mother's violinist hero, and she did everything in her power to instill his way of violin playing in me from the time I was a babe.

Perhaps the chapter titles need some explanation. All have musical significance, some more obviously than others, although their sequence is determined by the chapters' content rather than by musical meaning. "Recitativo Accompagnato" (accompanied recitative) is a baroque operatic term evoked in chapter 3, as Heifetz, in need of an accompanist for his master class, artfully changes me from a violin student into a pianist. "Intermezzo" is a rather vague term describing lighter musical entertainment performed between acts of classical dramas. "Passagework" as a musical expression describes transitional material between important sections of a musical form.

For the better part of this century the name Jascha Heifetz was synonymous with perfection. "Musica Disciplina," chapter 9, borrows a Renaissance musical term used to describe strict counterpoint. This chapter deals with Heifetz's tremendous self-discipline in musical matters and his conflicts with the ordinary ways of life. Perfection is a jealous mistress and comes at a high price, which Heifetz paid in more than one way. The rare moments of serenity and domesticity in his life are described in chapter 10, "Sinfonia Domestica," which is the title of Richard Strauss's only symphony. Richard Strauss was among Heifetz's favorite composers. "Dies Irae," the name of a Sequence or hymn from the Latin Requiem Mass, means literally Day of Wrath or, by implication, Judgment Day. Chapter 12 presents the dark side of Heifetz's personality and my struggles to stay sane facing it. The Greek title of the penultimate chapter, "Threnody," means lament. Professional mourners in ancient villages still recite the merits and the life of a worthy person during wakes in this loose form; the chapter contains the story of the accident that took his life, including his last days and a reflection on the influence he exercised over me as a musician and as a person. "Postludium," Chapter 14, refers to the exit music in church after the service. Here it serves as my own personal closure.

An appendix of works by Heifetz lists his published and unpublished transcriptions for violin and piano and the works from which they were taken, as well as his original transcriptions and compositions.

If I had to live again through any of my fifteen years with Jascha Heifetz, I would choose the last five. During these years he had finally come to terms with himself—with his persistent self-doubt and with the people who really loved him. And most importantly, Heifetz had learned to trust me and therefore to trust himself.

Heifetz had built an impenetrable barrier around himself as protection for his innermost uncertainties about his worth as a human being. Because of that, he was the target of personal and impersonal criticisms, often deeply rooted in jealousy. His personality was so complex that it obscured understanding of his motives, his actions and reactions, and even his art.

2

Overture

If you can make one heap of all your winnings
And risk it on one turn of pitch-and-toss,
And lose, and start again at your beginnings
And never breathe a word about your loss

RUDYARD KIPLING

*M*y first memory of hearing music played by Jascha Heifetz is lost in the obscurity of my infancy. My mother, Ada Oei Hok Nio, played his records all the time when she wasn't away from home helping my father, Liem Tiong Hien, with his building projects. A piano teacher herself, when she was home she took over my care, at least musically, from our Javanese servants and did her best to instill in me her idea of perfection in violin playing. I must have heard Heifetz's recordings countless times even before I became conscious of my own existence. I cannot possibly remember how I decided that the player of such unearthly sounds must have died long ago, but I believed that what I could only hear and not see could not be present among real people walking on the earth. His pictures on the dust jackets of his recordings must have helped me to arrive at this conclusion. I associated Heifetz with the heroes of our Javanese shadow-puppet plays, the Wayang Kulit. Watching these plays, I observed that the heroes lived in an unreal world in which only their shadows could perform heroic deeds, an unseen narrator droning their stories from the old Indian epic, the Ramayana. I must add that news from the outside world travels slowly to a small Indonesian town, and this isolation played no small part in my not knowing, during the first twenty years of my life, that Heifetz was still alive. I'm not sure my mother would have changed my misconception even if she had known about it.

The truth was not revealed to me until 1971 during my second summer as a violinist in the student orchestra of the Tanglewood Music Festival in Massachusetts. As a scholarship student I served in a training orchestra for the few conductor candidates chosen from hundreds of applicants from all over the country.

Leon Barzin mentored the student conductors at that time, but they also could work under Leonard Bernstein, Seiji Ozawa, Aaron Copland, Michael Tilson Thomas, and other eminent conductors who were invited to lead the festival's main orchestra, the Boston Symphony. These great conductors gave some time to the student conductors and to the student orchestra. Besides playing in the orchestra, most of us were assigned in groups to chamber music coaches, and the more promising chamber ensembles performed during student recitals.

During my second summer there, dear old William Kroll, a violinist and composer (he wrote the famous "Banjo and Fiddle" for violin and piano), coached my group in the Frank Bridge Sextet, which we duly performed one warm afternoon in the theater building. I played first violin, and I remember Mr. Kroll telling me before the performance, with love and emotion in his voice, "Ayke, I know you will play this piece with romance in your heart, as it was intended by the composer." I did my best to live up to Mr. Kroll's expectations, and after the performance he gave me a big hug, moisture gleaming in his eyes.

I packed my violin away and left the theater. The grounds at Tanglewood were quite lovely; huge sycamores lined the sides of the gravel road and enveloped me in their late afternoon shadows. I glanced at several groups of people picnicking on the beautifully kept lawn, waiting for the evening concert. I was in a hurry for a most prosaic reason: my stomach was making the most unmusical noises because that day, as every day the whole summer, I had only an undistinguished breakfast of tea and powdered eggs made with water, and a peanut butter and jelly sandwich for lunch. The fellowship I received didn't include lunch, and I had to save money for more important things.

Understandably I was a bit annoyed when a middle-aged gentleman blocked the way to my well-deserved dinner. He congratulated me on my playing, then asked rather curiously, "Are you a student of Jascha Heifetz?" If a thunderbolt had struck me out of the blue, I couldn't have been more surprised. Suddenly I even forgot that I was starving. I was not sure I heard him correctly and, a little tremulous, asked the man for a repeat performance: "How was that? Did you say Jascha Heifetz?"

"Well, I suspected from the style of your playing, from your slides, fingerings, and bowing, that you must be one of his students."

I stared at the stranger, probably with my mouth open.

"Are you all right?" he said. "You have a funny look on your face."

I couldn't explain to him that Jascha Heifetz's being dead had been an unshakable article of faith for me ever since I first heard his recordings. For how could anybody be alive—the childhood logic was still in full force—and produce such heavenly sounds? I realized that the man was looking at me with concern, and I could hardly squeeze a reply from my throat: "No, sir, I never studied with Heifetz. As a matter of fact, I thought he was dead long ago. Where does he live and does he still teach?"

All the kind stranger knew was that Jascha Heifetz was living somewhere in southern California, and the names of some of his students.

At that time I had finished two years at Rosary Hill (now Daemen) College in Buffalo, New York, and was about to embark on my third year, which I expected to be my last. I had taken courses at an accelerated pace to finish in three years instead of four. After the summer and the festival at Tanglewood, I returned to Buffalo and loaded myself up with extra courses for the semester, never quite forgetting about Heifetz.

My mother's dream was that I should return to Indonesia and teach, a profession that she considered the ultimate goal for anyone. Even before I finished my studies I had received an offer from the Indonesian government to be headmistress at a village school on the island of Sumatra, a position that would pay a grand sum of one hundred dollars a month in addition to free lodging and as many cheap servants as I wanted to have. However, my three years in America had taken the sheen from such grand offers.

Back in Buffalo I practiced my instruments and earned my room and board by working in the library, but I couldn't help thinking about what that stranger had told me in Tanglewood. I found it surprising that so far no one, not even Ivan Galamian, with whom I had lessons at his home once a month, nor my violin teacher in Buffalo, a former Galamian student, had ever told me that my style of violin playing suggested that I had trained with Jascha Heifetz. It took me the better part of that semester to decide that I should track down Heifetz and resurrect him from the dead. I made inquiries about him, and a local newspaper helped me to find out where he taught. I sent a letter about my desire to meet him and soon received an answer from the University of Southern California, informing me that auditioning was the only way to meet him. I was asked to send in my program and a curriculum vitae in case I should decide to go ahead.

An Indonesian girlfriend of mine who studied English at a nearby college was about to marry someone in San Jose, and her wedding gave me further reason for a trip to southern California. I wrote back to USC to ask for an audition, taking the plunge on mere impulse and courage rather than following any focused preparation or thoughtful decision. I could not imagine how to prepare to play for Jascha Heifetz and was afraid that even with the best of preparation I could not come close to the standards that Heifetz's playing signified for me. But I wanted to see my idol at least once in my life. I also sent quite an ambitious program which included, among other pieces, a Paganini caprice, Maurice Ravel's *Tzigane*, Bach's Chaconne from the Partita No. 2 in D minor, and Franz Waxman's *Carmen Fantasy*, all of which I had previously played in a student recital. I was invited to audition at USC during the fall of 1971.

To protect himself from unpleasant surprises and curiosity seekers, Heifetz had established a rigorous routine for these auditions. I had a pre-audition session with his assistant, Claire Hodgkins, and then a run-through of the program with the class pianist. I played the whole program for the two of them and was pleasantly surprised by the assistance they gave me. I passed this first audition, except for the scales. I didn't know that scale playing was an absolute necessity for a Heifetz audition. I had never studied scales, but I was told not to panic—if I wanted to learn them overnight, I could try just a few of them and tell Heifetz the truth at the audition.

How I got myself to the audition itself is a blur in my memory. All I remember is that Heifetz's assistant opened the door, inviting me to come in. Over the years of my Heifetz admiration I had built up an image of him in my mind, based on his pictures on the jackets of his recordings. I hated to admit to myself that when I finally was in his presence I liked the picture in my mind better than the actual person in front of me. I found out much later from Heifetz himself that show business has little to do with reality, and the fact that I had a fantasy picture of him in my mind was exactly what publicity intended to achieve. When I came in, Heifetz was sitting at his desk and got up to shake my hand. There was something resembling a smile on his face that seemed rather artificial. He was also painfully polite, which didn't fit the picture of the superior hero I had in my mind: legends were supposed to be distant, aloof, somewhat disinterested, and floating six feet above the ground. Taking a quick look around, I sensed only the professional, businesslike atmosphere—the pianist ready at his place, Heifetz sitting at his desk browsing through my papers, and his assistant standing by waiting expectantly for his instructions. My sentimental hero-worship turned into the realization that these people meant serious business for which I wasn't quite prepared. I had had a successful audition at the Juilliard School of Music the previous spring and with Mr. Galamian's encouragement and recommendation had received an offer of a four-year scholarship to study there once I graduated from Rosary Hill. But the pressure at the Juilliard audition, even with all those important people sitting there, didn't come close to what Heifetz was able to create with his mere presence.

Suddenly he looked up from the papers, and without letting me warm up, he asked me to play the first and the last pages of Ravel's *Tzigane*. I dug in my heels and did my best. Toward the end of the piece, he began to beat the tempo on the desk with a metal stick, faster and faster, apparently wanting to see if I could keep up with him. I kept calm and followed his beat; having played in various orchestras under some crazy conductors I had acquired enough professional routine and experience not to panic in such situations. Next Heifetz asked me to play bits from other pieces on my program, a bit from here and a bit from there, ending with the *Carmen Fantasy*. I felt as though I was in a torture chamber because he kept asking me to play everything in ways that were different from what was written in the score and for which I wasn't prepared. He wanted me to change long-practiced fingerings, shift to unusual positions, then change the tempo to slower or faster, shouting orders to play dynamics that made no sense to me. I don't remember how I played the *Carmen Fantasy*, only that I was in a daze most of the time, my eyes closed for fear of looking at my tormentor. By this point in the audition I couldn't have cared less how I played. I just wanted to get out of there as soon as possible, but I wasn't finished yet.

After I played my pieces, Heifetz asked me to play scales. I had heard from my teachers that playing scales is a waste of time, that they are meaningless in improving one's playing. I bravely improvised and thought I didn't do too badly, but he wasn't impressed with my extemporizing and didn't mince words about it. To complete my humiliation, he turned to his assistant, and talking only to her as if I weren't even there, he said, "This girl must have been very impressed with her own playing; she kept her eyes closed during the whole time."

By the Chinese etiquette I was brought up with, it was unthinkable to object to his statement even to defend myself, because he was much older than any of us in the room, consequently the only one entitled to an opinion. I wasn't quite sure about the local etiquette, but to be on the safe side I said nothing and just stared at the floor with the violin and bow still in my hands. Heifetz didn't let me get away with it and repeated his accusation, still speaking only to his assistant, but this time a little louder, all the time watching me out of the corner of his eye. I kept on staring at the floor and still said nothing. Heifetz repeated the statement for the third time, this time shouting but still to his assistant, apparently believing that I was hard of hearing. By now my Chinese etiquette had lost out, I felt heat rising in my body, and I replied softly that I wasn't impressed with my own playing. I thought Heifetz went crazy when he repeated himself for the fourth time, even louder and still to his assistant—he was apparently testing my boiling point. By that time I didn't care for him or for his master class, and feeling my face hot, turned to him, looked him straight in the eyes, and responded in a loud voice: "No, Mr. Heifetz, I was not impressed with my playing. I closed my eyes for fear of being disturbed by you; if I were impressed by my own playing, I wouldn't be here auditioning and wanting to study with you."

I was ready to be shown to the door after this outburst, but to my greatest surprise, a faint but this time genuine smile passed over his lips as if he were finally satisfied for getting what he wanted, my response. He then excused his pianist and his assistant as well, and interviewed me in private. He asked me the questions that I would so often hear years later during interviews with other prospective students, "What do you think I can do for you?"

"I would like to improve with your help my violin playing and music making," I answered with some difficulty.

The answer apparently satisfied him because he picked up my curriculum vitae and noted that I was attending a college in Buffalo. "What is your goal in life?" he asked next.

I didn't expect this question from him, as I wouldn't have expected it from anyone else. I was brought up in Indonesia with the notion that you shouldn't advertise your goals in life, for they were nobody's business. Besides, I was accustomed to my mother's telling me what my goals should be. Accordingly, my answer to his question was what my mother would have expected me to say: "I would like to finish my studies, earn a degree, and eventually go back to Indonesia to teach."

When Heifetz heard the word *degree*, he slowly got up, politely shook my hand, looked me straight in the eyes, and said with compassion, "Since you want a degree, I wish you all the best, and—good luck, Miss Agus."

After I put my violin away, he led me to the door, opened it for me, and gave me a smile as I walked out with tears in my eyes.

Strangely enough, after all the torment he had put me through, I felt sorry and disappointed that our meeting ended so abruptly. I was crushed that he didn't accept me in his class, but kept consoling myself that at least I had met the hero of my dreams. Deep down I felt genuine pain and hurt because I had never before failed a test. At that time I didn't know his hang-up about degrees; I didn't know he didn't have any, not even from a grammar school, and had refused a number of honorary doctorates out of spite for all such academic distinctions. I felt exhausted, sad, humiliated, and above all dissatisfied with myself that I didn't have the courage to ask him why I had failed the audition. The next day, all the way back on the plane to Buffalo, I cried in my heart and felt as if my beloved hero had just passed away.

I had four very close friends in the college. They had taken me under their wings from the time I entered the school and helped me with my difficulties with the English language. In my first college year, because of my troubles with English, I was unable to take notes in the lectures and always sat next to one of my friends. Instead of listening to the teacher's lecture, I was busy copying my friend's notes. Upon my return from California, my four friends were anxious to hear how the audition went. For a while I was unable to discuss my adventure with them, but eventually I told them everything. They tried to comfort me, but in the end one of them, my big, Polish-American friend, said the most sensible thing: "Ayke, now that you have met the man of your and your mother's dreams and your dreams proved disappointing, let's forget the whole thing and concentrate on our first-semester examinations."

For two weeks after my return to Buffalo, I was too busy with my studies to have time for thoughts about Heifetz and his master class during the day, but at night I went to sleep with the tormenting question of what I had done wrong at that audition. If I was good enough for the Juilliard School of Music, why wasn't I good enough for Jascha Heifetz? In fact, I mused to myself, he didn't criticize my playing, except for those scales, and he never said that I failed to meet his standards: I must have done something else, but I just couldn't figure out what.

Toward the end of the second week after my return while we were chattering away in the cafeteria after dinner, the telephone rang in the telephone booth. One of my friends eagerly ran to answer it. The call was from California, and it was for me. The operator told me to stand by and wait for a call from Los Angeles. The caller was the secretary to the dean of the School of Music at the University of Southern California, informing me that Mr. Heifetz had accepted me as a student in his master class. An airplane ticket would be sent to me, and my lodging and tuition would all be taken care of. Mr. Heifetz was expecting me as soon as possible. She also told me that Mr. Heifetz would be willing to make an exception and let me take courses at USC toward whatever degree I wished.

Off the top of my head, without giving it a second thought, I answered the secretary without the slightest hesitation: "Thanks, but no thanks. Please tell Mr. Heifetz that I appreciate his offer very much, but I would like to finish my studies here, which will take only one more semester." The secretary seemed a bit surprised and told me to call back operator number six in case I changed my mind.

I stood there in the booth for a while as the importance of what I had just said began to dawn on me. Did I really say those words, or was it someone else speaking through my mouth? As I looked at my friends out there in the dining room, I suddenly knew how much they meant to me; they were the first real friends I had ever had in my life, and perhaps Heifetz did me a big favor by not accepting me in his master class at my audition. Had he accepted me then, my thoughts ran, I would have left them without a second thought, without realizing what kind of cruel, competitive, unfeeling world I would have had to face in California. Here I had a circle of happy friends, a school, and an audience at the monthly school recitals, all of whom very much appreciated what I could offer them in music making. Heifetz and his cold, cantankerous, and ever-challenging audition left a bitter aftertaste in my mouth, and I wasn't sure any more that I could be happy in his kind of world and live up to his musical expectations. At that moment I doubted that studying the violin with Jascha Heifetz was worth the price, and I doubted even my ability to meet the standards he apparently set up for his students.

I walked back to my place at the dinner table and continued finishing my meal as if nothing had happened. My friends stopped eating and looked at me, expecting me to say something; I put on my best stony Chinese face and asked one of them to pass the salt. I didn't get the salt but rather a question from all of them speaking at the same time: "Ayke, who called?"

"It was from California," I said casually.

"From whom in California?" They all sat at the edge of their seats and looked at me expectantly.

"It was from the secretary to the dean of the School of Music at USC. She had a message for me from Mr. Heifetz."

"From whom?" they all asked again in disbelief.

"From Heifetz. *Mister* Jascha Heifetz. And I still want that salt shaker."

"And what did Mr. Heifetz want from you?"

They were all excited, and I felt pressured to tell them the truth. When they heard that I had just refused a scholarship offer in the Jascha Heifetz master class, they jumped up as one and screamed at me, "Ayke, are you crazy?" Their eyes opened up big, the way no Chinese girl can do, and even their mouths stayed open.

I said very calmly, "I'm happy here. I don't want to go anywhere, especially not back to Los Angeles. I had enough of Jascha Heifetz to last a lifetime."

The smallest among them, a real live-wire girl of Italian descent, was the first one to regain her normal speaking voice; she grabbed me by the arm, pulled me up from my chair, made me face the telephone booth and solemnly declared: "Ayke, you go back to that booth, call back that operator number six right now, and tell that secretary to send you that airplane ticket immediately. We all love you very much and want you to stay with us, but you are out of your mind if you are planning to sacrifice a chance to study with Jascha Heifetz for this crummy school with its phony courses. Besides, who knows how much longer Jascha Heifetz is going to live? This may be the last train that you have a chance to get on."

All four of them surrounded me lest I attempt to escape; they escorted me to the telephone booth and waited outside to make sure I did as I was told. I reached the secretary and told her that I had changed my mind and to please inform Mr. Heifetz of my acceptance of his offer. She told me to leave for Los Angeles as soon as possible, and she sent a one-way ticket with the date open. Not knowing what lay ahead for me, I decided first to spend Christmas with my family in Indonesia. And then I was on my way to California.

3

Recitativo Accompagnato

If you can bear to hear the truth you've spoken
Twisted by knaves to make a trap for fools,
Or watch the things you gave your life to, broken,
And stoop and build 'em up with worn-out tools

RUDYARD KIPLING

*A*rriving from Indonesia via the frontier town of Buffalo to the expansive maze of Los Angeles, for the first few weeks of the new year I felt lost in the venerable proving ground of the Jascha Heifetz master class. I felt like a child attempting her first steps as I learned to use the unreliable buses of the city and started the violin again from the beginning, with the scales the way Heifetz wanted them played. He gave me a week to get rid of my shoulder pad, which I always considered an indispensable accessory to violin playing, and when I felt almost settled, his assistant told me to change the two middle strings on my violin to pure gut strings, a very unusual request. I was fighting the scales during all my free time, my neck hurt from losing my shoulder pad, my fingers were sore from having to press the gut strings harder than the steel strings, and my violin sounded strange and different with the new strings. Oddly enough, though, I was happy with these challenges, and for the first time in my life I felt that I was getting somewhere with my violin playing. I missed the heart-to-heart talks with my friends, but soon enough I acquired new ones, though I could never duplicate the closeness I felt to my first friends in Buffalo who truly were the mothers of my American infancy.

My eventual eclipse as a violinist came about as a result of Heifetz's interest in his students' advancement on the piano. Rumors reached his ears that my piano playing was more than just dabbling at the keyboard. And his answer came back to me in the same roundabout way: he believed that all violinists sound the same at the piano—dull and amateurish.

Curiosity, however, got the better of him, and toward the middle of my first semester in the master class, he asked me, when we all had returned from a lunch break, if I played the piano. "Yes, I play the piano, just a little bit," I said modestly. Heifetz gave me a sidelong glance and said with feigned indifference, "Prove it!" Then he turned away, puttering at his desk and apparently looking forward to a few dull moments.

I went to the piano, thinking hard how to get myself out of this ordeal as fast as possible. I had scarcely practiced the piano since I had entered his class, only occasionally amusing myself with it late at night to relax. I have a good musical memory and firm control over my nerves, but to play unprepared for Jascha Heifetz was something else. On my way to the piano, I decided to play Ernst von Dohnányi's "Capriccioso" from his *Six Concert Etudes*. It is a very fast piece, and I was thinking that the faster I got through this unexpected testing the better. The piece was still well enough in my fingers since I had played it in Buffalo at a recital just before I left. It is not played often, and I don't think Heifetz knew it, a showy work in which the right hand plays thirds in triplets while the left continuously moves across the top in duplets in a fluid, half-circular motion, jumping from the left to the right side of the right hand.

When I finished there was not a sound in the class. I couldn't even hear my classmates breathing. I caught sight of Heifetz sitting motionless, bolt upright at the edge of his chair, just the way he wanted his audiences to sit when he was playing. I felt isolated in the silence as if enclosed in a capsule. Heifetz didn't move for a while; then I heard him saying very softly and slowly, separating each syllable with his Russian accent, "My com-pli-ments."

I felt too numb to react. I was still enclosed in my capsule of isolation and wasn't sure that I should say anything at all. I also felt that what he said was incomplete, as if a "but" would follow with some criticism. However, there was no "but," and he repeated, this time straightforwardly and a little louder, his "My compliments." It escapes me even today why I didn't react to his second statement, yet I didn't. Suddenly I heard him shouting at me: "You know, I don't compliment anyone lightly."

I slowly came out of the fog, realizing that he liked my playing. "Thank you," I said as lightly as I could to conceal my happiness that he didn't criticize my playing. "Well, well, that's much better," I heard Heifetz saying. He sounded almost relieved that I finally reacted to his compliment. For a while he didn't move, just sat at his desk seemingly absorbed in his thoughts, looking a bit distracted. Eventually he got up from his chair—he could make such a show of just getting up that it was worth watching—and came over to the piano. He stood with his elbow on the flat side of the music stand, facing me and the keyboard, and asked me to play parts of various works from the standard piano literature: the "Revolutionary" Etude by Frédéric Chopin, a partita by Johann Sebastian Bach, a movement from a Beethoven piano concerto, the slow movement from the Chopin Piano Concerto in E minor, and the beginning of a few other pieces. He was quite surprised that I knew them all, as a pianist should.

I was also surprised at his knowledge of the piano repertory; I sensed that he was thoroughly familiar with all the pieces he asked me to play. I also began to feel uncomfortable that he spent so much class time just with me, but eventually he let me go. When he continued with his class, he seemed to have lost some of his usual concentration. At the end of the class I observed him standing at the end of the grand piano with his violin case in front of him where he always put it, staring at it for an unusually long time.

I HAD COME to the master class from Buffalo with the stipulation that at USC Heifetz would let me finish my studies for the bachelor's degree in music. I hadn't realized what this would take. When the credits from my previous college were evaluated, I learned that so many of them were unacceptable at USC that I would be set back by two years. Fortunately as long as I was enrolled as a violinist in Heifetz's master class, my scholarship covered all my coursework, and I could even study over the summer.

By the end of my first semester, rapid changes had taken place in the part of the class that Heifetz somewhat grandiosely liked to call the Piano Department. His pianist quit, having set his mind on a solo career. Heifetz was sorry to see him go because he was a competent accompanist. A search was set in motion for a new pianist, and soon a young woman was found who was willing to tackle the job. She came ahead of time, and we met at USC during the summer classes that I took toward my degree. We became friends, and I gave her some information about how the class was conducted. I even remember that her first major project was Anton Arensky's Piano Trio in D minor, Op. 32, which she mastered just in time for the beginning of the master class sessions.

She was in for quite a surprise if she was looking for a quiet, amiable job with an agreeable elderly gentleman, for Heifetz could never resist a chance to find the breaking point of anyone who came in contact with him professionally. It wasn't past him to tell her one day to play a certain passage of a sonata more aggressively to give support to the violinist, and berate her the next day for doing exactly what she had been told the day before. Her excuse, "But Mr. Heifetz, you just told me two days ago to do this passage this way," wouldn't wash with him. Yesterday was another day and perhaps another violinist or the same one but playing differently; with Heifetz one had to seize the inspiration of the moment, for every performance was unique even if it was a mere rehearsal. The new accompanist was temperamental, somewhat self-righteous, and eventually defensive. By Christmas she saw the light and found a job elsewhere.

Meanwhile, though I was still a member of Heifetz's violin master class that fall, he had decided for me that I would study piano with Lillian Steuber, with whom he had recorded the sonatas of Howard Ferguson and Aram Khachaturian. (The other students in his class studied with a different teacher whose students were not pianists.) His meddling turned out for the best, for Miss Steuber was a good teacher in her rather pedantic way. She had wonderful technique but her interpretations were just as rigid as her teaching—to my taste, she lacked freedom, imagination, technical dare, and fire. I later discovered that most teachers become that way, I presume from the tedium that goes with the job. Still, Lillian put discipline in my playing, which I rather lacked since up to that time I had considered the piano as my fun instrument in comparison to the violin. I had lessons with Miss Steuber once a week, usually during the lunch breaks of the Heifetz class sessions. Her studio was also in Clark House where Heifetz held his classes, and that helped matters.

To my greatest surprise Heifetz showed up several times for my lessons with Miss Steuber. He listened to my playing, made comments to Lillian and to me, and added something to her teaching with which most teachers are not concerned at all. He examined how I looked at the piano from all corners of the room, gave advice about how to approach the instrument, how to sit down and get up, the proper way to put my hands on the keyboard before playing, how long to wait before starting to play, and how to finish with a flourish without being ostentatious. While doing all this Heifetz explained to Miss Steuber and to me in his haphazard way that a performer should not only play well but also give the best impression she can in stage appearance. A mousy-looking and -acting performer will be perceived as the one who plays mousily, often regardless of the musical merits of the performance, while an aggressive personality would have difficulty pulling off a dreamy Chopin nocturne without the danger of looking ridiculous. Arrogance and spiteful appearance, he declared, would turn off any audience. (Obviously he had not heard, let alone seen, rock music performances; he would have had difficulty adjusting his stage-manner theories.) The fact that he was interfering with Miss Steuber's lessons didn't bother him at all, though occasionally he mentioned that he had no intention to disturb her teaching.

During this time I began to feel a noticeable change in his attitude toward me. Whenever he called on me to play the violin I noticed a certain distraction in his demeanor, and he made me sight read a great deal more of the violin literature than other members of the class had to do. Once he asked me to play a Louis Spohr duet with him; he played the first violin and I the second. I knew from the manner in which he played that he wasn't interested in my violin playing at all; he always liked to play games, but this time it was obviously more than just games. He played fortissimo when pianissimo was indicated in the score and vice versa, slowed down when the indication was accelerando, made big accents whenever he felt like it, and just kept on doing whatever was not in the score, whether possible or impossible. He was apparently testing whether I was prepared for the most unexpected. I had enough routine left from having played in the Buffalo Philharmonic while I was a student in that city that I could follow him in whatever he did. When we finished the piece, he gave me a look of approval, then turned to the class and said with appreciation, "Not bad for a pianist." I didn't like his comment, but by then I knew that making a fuss about it would have been useless.

A week or two later he made me read another Spohr duet with someone else as my partner. Heifetz turned pages for me, but as I found out soon enough, not without a design. When I reached the bottom of my page, he deliberately held off turning it. I had never seen the piece before, but from its somewhat predictable patterns, I correctly divined the first few bars on the next page and kept on playing while screaming at him, "Turn!" He slowly turned the page, looked at the class, and said, "This girl must have a musical sixth sense. She knows what's on the next page before seeing it." I figured out only later that he wasn't testing my powers of musical divination but was looking for some qualities of an accompanist who wouldn't panic when pages aren't turned, or two pages are turned at once, and wouldn't stop playing when by accident or clumsiness the music falls off the stand.

Until a new, suitable pianist could be found for the master class, I was made the temporary pianist for the class. The appointment didn't come as a total surprise because I had already substituted at the piano a few times, but making my position official, *pro temp* alas, made me realize the seriousness of the situation. As soon as Heifetz noticed that he could squeeze more from me than from most of his accompanists, he gradually tightened the screws and set the standards higher and higher. He was voracious by nature, and the more he got, the more he demanded; Heifetz surely knew how to unnerve any pianist who was willing and able to play ball with him. Here are some of his tricks.

In the process of demonstrating a passage to his students, he would pick up his violin and with a passing remark of "Catch me" start to play without the slightest indication where he was beginning. He would expect me to be with him from the first note, and if I sometimes missed a note or two, he would give me a cold, uncomprehending stare. Thanks to my violinist past, most of the time I was familiar with the problem he was about to correct and usually guessed his starting point quite accurately. Just to test me, he would change the tempo to rubato, accelerando, the dynamics from *forte* to *piano*, from crescendo to diminuendo, and vice versa, put in accents, sudden sforzatos, sudden pianos, and all sorts of dynamic changes just to catch me off-guard. He fully expected that I should be able to make all the changes as he did. The toughest test came when he would make a sudden change of key in the middle of a passage and I would have to transpose with him immediately in the new key. To "develop" my sight-reading ability, once he gave me the whole Beethoven "Kreutzer" Sonata to learn in two days, and another time he assigned me the piano part of the Brahms Piano Quartet, Op. 25, No. 1, for the next session. The ultimate test not only of my sight-reading ability but of my self-control and willpower was the time when he told me just at the beginning of class that I would have to play the Dohnányi Piano Quintet No. 2, Op. 26, that day. This piece is full of double sharps and flats on top of the six-flat key signature of E-flat minor (which appears in the third movement), but he forbade me even to look at the score when I had a chance to do so. Strangely enough, I didn't mind these tests at all but took them as signs of his confidence in me, that he thought me capable of accomplishing what he expected from me. In the process I trained myself to read a whole line ahead with one comprehensive glance and then jump back to the spot where I was playing. To be fair, Heifetz didn't expect a perfect note-for-note reading, only that I would recognize and play the essential parts of the score, but always in the proper tempo, using the proper dynamics, and always making music, never just reading notes. I felt good that I could take it all without complaint, for I soon realized that he recognized only two kinds of musicians: the ones who could do it and the rest who could not. The latter always complained, explained, and justified why something was impossible to do, which all amounted to nothing with him.

Once Heifetz went into testing mode, testing musical abilities alone didn't quite satisfy him. The greatest test for everyone, but especially for musicians, is that of nerves. Freelance musicians have to cope not only with the pressure of preparation and with taking it on the chin as well if they receive unfavorable reviews, but also with a greater measure of job insecurity than permanent employees are exposed to. Unless someone is playing under contract in a well-established orchestra, jobs and engagements often come in boom or bust cycles. I was only the temporary pianist of the class, but it didn't escape Heifetz's attention that I began to like my job and all the pressures that went with it. Without apparent reason he often darkly hinted that he was still looking for a permanent accompanist, and my job depended on my ability to make further improvements. He actually put the job on the market and let me know that there were quite a few applicants perhaps better qualified than I was. I knew I wasn't doing badly, but in retrospect I think he only wanted to gain more control over me, as he liked to do to everyone in whom he was interested. He made his threat even more realistic by auditioning a few applicants, but none seemed to meet his standards. I think the reason for their downfall was not incompetence but that they gave excuses and explanations when Heifetz set them up against seemingly impossible tasks. The proper attitude toward his demands was, in music and in everything else, to try the impossible and see if you could beat the odds. "Do it or else" was his principle in professional matters, and not everybody was willing to accept his rigid attitude. As he expected from himself the utmost and nothing less than the maximum of which he was capable, he applied the same almost brutal principle to all others. Even though he couldn't find another accompanist, he still managed to make me feel that I was not indispensable and that there was still the possibility of hiring someone better.

As time went on and we became better acquainted with one another, something must have clicked between the two of us. The more challenges he put before me, the more I liked working with him, and he never tired of dreaming them up. I had never had a teacher of his magnitude before, and I began to feel that he was no longer treating me as an employee or a student but rather as a fellow musician whom he could shape as he wished. I was eager to learn from him, and to please him I fought off my own willfulness. I disciplined myself technically and emotionally, disregarded his threats and abrasive remarks, and was eager to see how much more I could learn from him without breaking down emotionally. I had to forget in a hurry my Asian sensitivity about losing face, for Heifetz

never stood on ceremony. Instead of being afraid of him, I came to look
forward to his new challenges every time we met.

Although I was doing all the work of the regular class pianist, including rehearsals with students in preparation for their lessons, Heifetz still
didn't dismiss me as his violin student. Perhaps he wasn't sure what he
wanted from me or what my main instrument should be, but just possibly
he enjoyed the control that the insecure situation held over me. He even
felt he should teach me the violin privately because in the class I was so
busy and could not do two things at the same time. He invited me to his
house to give me private lessons, but eventually these lessons became
occasions when he played the violin and I accompanied him at the piano.
While in the class he usually used a copy of a Seraphin model, at the
house he usually played his Guarnerius or Tononi, and sometimes he
handed me whichever he was using to make me prove that I still could
play the violin. On those occasions he accompanied me at the piano. As
for the accompanist's job, he kept me on tenterhooks for almost a whole
semester.

One day toward the end of the fall semester, he asked me to stay after
class. He ceremoniously asked me to sit down and got right to the point:
"I came to the conclusion that you're a pianist with a future. First of all,
you look better at the piano than with the violin in your hands. Looks are
sometimes as important as your actual playing. Also, you obviously had a
better training at the piano than on the violin. If you want to continue
with your violin studies, it would be up to you, but I would have to dismiss
you from my class. As a violinist the most you can hope for is a position in
a very good orchestra or in a chamber music group. For that you don't
need my teaching; you have all that you need, including the repertory
and the training. If that's the case, I wish you good luck, and I'll speed up
my search for a permanent pianist for my class. You'll be free to do whatever you want to."

Here he held a dramatic pause and looked at me as if waiting for an
answer, but I could only stare back at him, speechless. He looked out the
window, then at me again with those penetrating blue eyes that made
me shrivel up inside, and continued. "On the other hand, if you want to
abandon your studies as a violinist, I'll see to it that your status as the
pianist of the class would be confirmed, and you'll be on my staff with full
pay. In the bargain, as a faculty member, you may even continue your
studies free at USC in pursuit of your piano degree, and I'll guide you in
that, too, the best I can. These are your choices. You don't have to give
me an answer right now, but think it over. However, just to be sure, I

would like to consult with Lillian to see if she agrees with me concerning your future as a pianist."

By the end of this unusually long speech, I could see his face only vaguely because my eyes were filled with tears—tears of anger and disappointment, but also tears of being overwhelmed by my own indecision. Heifetz pretended not to notice my emotions and said that he would set the date for my final testing as a pianist as soon as he could agree on it with Miss Steuber.

Heifetz never did anything in a rush, especially if it concerned an important decision, as this was. He never acted irresponsibly, and his decisions were always very carefully thought out. He knew well that I didn't wish to leave the master class and that I had become attached to him and to his challenges. Yet deep down I still wanted to fulfill my mother's wish that I would finish my studies in America and become a violinist. Her other wish, for me to return home and teach violin somewhere in the jungles, was rapidly fading away together with any desire to return to Indonesia. However, in order to finish my studies, I needed financial support that my parents were unable to provide. I had left my full scholarship in Buffalo, and my scholarship at USC was contingent on my enrollment in the Heifetz master class. To make matters worse, changing to a piano major would mean that I would need additional courses to earn my degree. Accepting Heifetz's offer would keep me associated with him and bring financial stability, but it also meant total dependence on his good will and on the sincerity of his intentions. Should he find my performance wanting for any reason or discover someone else more suitable, I would be out of luck. I had already learned so much from him on the violin and the piano that I felt I shouldn't lightly throw away my chances to learn even more from him. The remark he made when I first played the piano for him—"I don't compliment lightly"—still echoed in my mind and gave me a sort of assurance that he took his job offer seriously.

At the same time it dawned on me that by his artful manipulations I was already inextricably entangled in the job and that getting out of it would be difficult even if I wanted to. Since his students had been coming to my house to practice for the class, I had to buy a decent piano. This investment alone was enough to force me to accept his offer if I wanted to keep up with my payments on it. I already practiced most of the time at the piano, rather than the violin, to prepare myself for his class and for my piano lessons with Miss Steuber. As for Heifetz's satisfaction with my piano playing, I was never completely sure how I stood with him —the most one could expect was a "not bad" or a "not too bad." Occa-

sionally he awarded a "pretty damn good" for somebody's playing, but
that usually came at the next lesson and not even to the person who did
the pretty damn good job. Yet I consoled myself that only children need
constant praise to encourage them to stay on the path of virtue; for adults
the knowledge of a job performed well should be sufficient reward.
Praise, I rationalized, has a tendency to deteriorate into cliché; eventually
only vanity would keep you from doubting its sincerity.

At any rate, Heifetz didn't verbalize well and didn't even feel the
need to communicate; most of his instructions to the person playing with
him consisted of a word or two: "too loud," "too timid," "too soft," "give
more," "too much bow," and the like. Yet when we played together there
was no need for words. His violin spoke eloquently enough, and if he got
excited he just shouted, "Give!" or "More!" or "Less!" and I knew what he
meant. Even if the climax of a piece had to be accompanied by full fortissimo from the piano, his violin could soar over the loudest sound without even forcing his violin. We got so used to one another's playing that
I always knew what he wanted even before he came to its execution; I
presume that I sensed instinctively how he felt the music and how he
built up his phrases. Heifetz was capable of conveying a message without
words, just through his playing. I soon came to recognize how the phrases
should flow and what kind of nuances, shades, and colors he wanted.

A standard violin coaching technique is to skip lengthy piano inter-
ludes as well as the introductions to piano reductions of orchestral compositions and tutti as irrelevant for the violinist, and to have the piano
play only one or two measures before the violin passage begins. When I
became the accompanist, Heifetz made me play all the lengthy introductions and all the orchestral tutti, not only to make the students familiar with these parts but also to teach me how to emulate orchestral sounds
on the piano. He once spent quite a long time on the two introductory
bars of Max Bruch's Violin Concerto in G minor, where the timpani open
the piece with a tremolo solo. I had to simulate the timpani on the piano,
playing through the bars evenly without the slightest accent anywhere,
yet give the feeling of two beats in a measure for the violinist who had to
enter without the benefit of a conductor's giving the beat with the baton.
Sometimes this was hard on the violinist standing by and waiting for his
entry while Heifetz made me repeat a long introduction again and again,
as for instance the one to Ernest Chausson's *Poème*, until it sounded just
right to him.

A Heifetz specialty was Richard Strauss's Violin Sonata in E-flat major, Op. 18, a piece that seemed to be his own. It had gotten him in trou-

ble when he played it in Israel during his 1953 tour of that country. He had been warned by the minister of education not to play it since Strauss was considered a Nazi sympathizer. Heifetz characteristically did not heed the warning and played the piece twice, once in Haifa and once in Jerusalem to a dead silent audience. After the Jerusalem concert when he was leaving his hotel at night carrying his violin, a young man rushed up to him and tried to smash his hand with an iron bar. Heifetz raised his right arm to protect his violin and got hit in the arm. He was only slightly hurt and the assailant was never found, although the incident left a scar which one could still faintly see on his lower right arm.

I played this sonata with him for the first time in his house, and he made me sight read the whole piece. I still remember the horror as my heart leapt into my throat in the second movement. I suddenly faced pages black with sixty-fourth notes needing to be fit against the violin's improvisatory melody with more feeling than simply following a rhythmical pattern. Somehow I survived, and he went on to drill me for hours in the piano solo of the Andante that opens the third movement. "This Andante sets the mood for the following Allegro, which uses the Andante's thematic material. If you cannot play the Andante properly, it's not worth playing the Allegro; you will have already ruined the whole movement," he warned me. He expected me to memorize this movement, and once when he was in the mood to play Strauss, he took his violin out, saying, "Strauss, third movement. I'm going to play it only if you play the Andante correctly." If I wanted to hear him play the Allegro I had to do the piano part by heart and the way he wanted it.

First-time conductors and soloists often feel "blown away" by the sudden impact of an orchestra's full sound. For a while they are unable to distinguish among the sounds pouring over them, and they may need time to become accustomed to hearing a mass of sound at close range. To avoid such shocks, Heifetz had his students acquire a pocket-size edition of the full score for the piece they were working on so that they could become aware of the orchestral sound they would be facing in an actual performance. To help them further, he expected me to simulate the instruments of the orchestra on the piano. Heifetz must have studied how this could be done, because at the keyboard whenever he wanted to show me, he could sound like a flute, a trombone, a choir of violins, or any other group of instruments. Soon, with judicious use of the pedals and by varying the touch on the keyboard in the most unorthodox ways, I was also able to bring about a reasonable approximation of orchestral sounds. He taught me how to produce sound effects by novel fingering and touch techniques that made the piano sing or thunder, effects that ordinary pianists and piano teachers never dreamed of.

While Heifetz was preparing me with his tricks for the job, I was still waiting for his final decision about whether I should be a violinist or a pianist. When at long last he made an appointment for Lillian Steuber to come to the master class for my final test and his ruling, a whole month had passed since the crucial moment after class when he had told me his thoughts. To make a fair judgment, Miss Steuber was first supposed to observe me as a violinist. She had never heard me play the violin. For the test I played a Bach violin partita and a Mozart violin sonata, and when Heifetz asked her how my violin work compared to my piano playing, her astonished reply was that I did both equally well. That, however, wasn't what Heifetz wanted to hear from her, and he looked a bit disappointed in her musical judgment. They had lunch together, and then Heifetz informed his assistant and me that after class we were going to Miss Steuber's studio to make a final decision about my status in the master class.

In Lillian's studio Heifetz took command of the situation and first asked me to play a few pieces of his choice. After I finished he again politely asked Miss Steuber's opinion of me as a pianist. I don't remember what Lillian said, but it didn't much matter because he wasn't listening anyway. He asked me to play the Beethoven Piano Concerto in C minor, with Lillian playing the orchestral part at the second piano, while he walked around the room and watched me from various angles. When we finished he kept silent, apparently forgot to ask Lillian for her opinion, and sent me out of the room. I went back to his classroom and sat frozen with apprehension. Finally Heifetz walked in and to my amazement sat down at his desk and announced to me, to his assistant, and to a few students who had stayed after class out of curiosity that from now on I was a pianist and that I would officially take over the duties of the class accompanist. He never asked my opinion, not even a polite "What would you think if"; he simply took upon himself the power to make a decision concerning my future. I was angry and tempted to tell him that I just wanted to be a good, decent fiddler, to get out of his class, and to be allowed to mind my own business. However, my better judgment prevailed, and I never said anything of the sort.

That decision marked the beginning of years of hard work to learn the art of musical collaboration the Heifetz way, for he wanted not only an accompanist but a musical collaborator as well, and not only for the class but also for himself. The task of learning music from him was marked by the axiom that nothing was good enough, and whenever I felt that I had accomplished something, Heifetz served notice that I was only at the bottom of a very high mountain. I also had to discover some tricks of the trade for myself, which is the most precious and satisfactory part of the learning process, tricks that were essential for my survival with him but which he took for granted.

I DISCOVERED soon enough that even the simplest accompaniment leaves no room for coasting; one must always be ready for the unexpected, whether for lapses of memory or attention on the soloist's part or for the inevitable changes that happen during a performance. Every good artist should become inspired during a performance and even carried away by things that were not agreed upon during rehearsals; only the most rigid and unimaginative artist performs a piece exactly the same as it was rehearsed. The accompanist cannot stop a performance and say, "Hey, maestro, this wasn't the way we rehearsed it," or "You skipped a bar or two or perhaps a whole page." One has to find the place and continue as if nothing had happened. For other kinds of disasters, as when the wind blows the music off the stand or the page-turner turns to the wrong page, there are no remedies other than knowing the piece fairly well or being able to fake a few bars until help arrives. Another commonly occurring disaster has to do with the way music is often printed so that the page must be turned in the middle of a fast-running passage, typically an awkward procedure even with the help of a page turner. If I had no time to memorize the beginning of the next page, I would photocopy the part I would need before the page turn and glue it to the top or the side of the preceding page.

It took me longer to figure out how to avoid being a hair ahead of, or behind, the soloist. This is a problem that regularly plagues even the best accompanists. Sometimes it is a matter of fatigue, coupled with a lack of concentration or mental preparation, but most often it comes from not knowing the soloist's instrument well enough if at all. Aside from being mentally ahead of the soloist, the accompanist should understand the mechanical process involved in the soloist's sound production. If the accompanist strikes the keys on her piano exactly at the moment when the soloist strikes the string with the bow, usually the accompanist is already too late. A good accompanist must anticipate the soloist's actions and know how much time the violin, say, will take to produce a sound. Perhaps the word *know* is not the proper one; one has no time to "know" anything in such situations; rather one must feel it, based on well-grounded knowledge. An extreme example is the first movement of Antonio Vivaldi's Suite for Violin and Piano in A major, an arrangement by violinist Adolf Busch of the Sonata for Violin and Harpsichord, Op. 2, No. 2. It begins with a single sixteenth-note upbeat by the violin alone and continues in sixteenths. For the pianist to come in on the second sixteenth-note, exactly on the downbeat, often takes luck, unless he or she is familiar with the mechanical process of preparing that sixteenth note. Only then would the pianist know how to be slightly ahead of that downbeat and catch it exactly in time.

Rehearsals and discussions between soloist and accompanist are rather standard procedures for getting an idea of what to expect in style, tempo, and dynamics, even though all that may be forgotten and cast overboard in the heat of a performance. To anticipate such events, to avoid disaster, soloist and accompanist must open other lines of communication. It was a great pleasure to play with Heifetz because he cared for the accompaniment and could immediately establish several lines of communication. Foremost was eye contact; his eyes sparkled with mischief and communicated passion, excitement, peace, relaxation, or drama as the music required. I could read in his eyes a sudden change of mood if that struck him in the middle of a performance. He could also relay to me that the piece was getting too long, the audience was getting restless, and we would have to "move it"—the tempo, that is, subtly, without destroying the music.

Though my violinist past helped me a great deal as an accompanist, I now became more conscious of the physical and mechanical process of violin playing. Upon a little analysis I discovered that it wasn't so much my musical instinct that kept me together with the violinist but rather my close attention to how the violinist appeared. I realized that the violinist cannot make a sound on the strings without some sort of bow preparation; for a fortissimo passage or note he will need a great deal more preparatory movement than for a pianissimo. Watching the bow carefully, one can always anticipate the dynamics the soloist is about to produce, and the bow preparation is preceded by other warning signs. Striking the string with greater force requires a greater physical effort; therefore the violinist will take a deeper breath, slightly twist his body, or move his violin in one direction or another in preparation.

Even Heifetz, who had a superior and flawless technique and was famous for his immobility onstage, wasn't above these signals because they are part of the physical process of sound production on the violin. Some of his students telegraphed everything they were about to do with body gyration, swaying, and deep lowering and lifting of the violin. Heifetz tried to discourage such useless motion which he considered a sign of lack of self-control, yet he couldn't forbid it. Presumably such gymnastics conveyed musical excitement by extramusical means, perhaps contributing an "understanding" of the music for some listeners. Heifetz often told his students not to show emotions through physical means: "Try not to express your emotions through external means, but convey them through your music, and let the audience emote." He knew well that such histrionics do not affect the sound one way or another, and they are just a nuisance from the accompanist's point of view. Too much movement, and all the time, tends to become meaningless and obfuscate any significant movement, while showing a little movement at a crucial time should be essential for the accompanist. Heifetz's statuelike playing with an immobile upper torso, together with his deadpan face, contributed to the allegations that he was cold and that his playing lacked emotion. Nothing could be further from the truth, as has been amply proven, but some people, including professional reviewers, apparently could not perceive excitement without a physical show. Others found his immobility fascinating; I once read a short story in which the main character, an amateur violinist, attended a concert in which Heifetz played the Mendelssohn violin concerto. The hero of the story spent his time at the concert by keeping track of the number of times Heifetz blinked or moved his body. He couldn't count too many but seemed to enjoy himself.

Knowing that the soloist has a consistent habit of bow usage is a great help to the accompanist, because following the movement of the bow is a way to recognize when the soloist is ready to begin a new line or phrase. "Running out of bow" is a danger not to be taken lightly. Even some seasoned violinists are inconsistent in bow usage, often using only the upper half or three-quarters of it; Heifetz strictly demanded that his students use a full bow when needed. This may sound like a simple rule, but for those who were not used to it, it was difficult to follow. Half-bow usage may have something to do with nerves; some violinists may feel unsafe and unable to control their arm pressure as soon as their stroke reaches the lower part of the bow where it is held. Controlling the upper half of the bow is easier. If someone in the master class was unable to use a full bow, Heifetz had his own funny remedy. He had in reserve a very short bow, about twelve inches long, that he produced at the appropriate moment with the remark, "Here, use this one; you don't need that clumsy long stick for what you are doing."

Among the hardest lessons he had to teach his young virtuosos was that most accompanied pieces were written for the violin and the accompanying instrument, the piano, not for the violin with background noise from the piano. Students found it difficult to accept that some of their hard-practiced, brilliant passages were nothing more than an accompaniment to an important theme in the piano and that those passages should support the pianist's theme instead of overpowering it. In Heifetz's recordings, one can hear his playing in the nature of an accompaniment when the piano or orchestra has the important melodic lines. For Heifetz the music and its content mattered first; showing off virtuosity for virtuosity's sake he took as a sign of musical arrogance. At any rate, he didn't think much of virtuosos; he had seen enough of them come and go in his time.

Few great pianists are automatically great accompanists, for aside from having a natural gift for it, few are willing to fulfill a role considered secondary to that of the soloist. Yet most classical sonatas offer equally important roles to the violin and the piano. For the piano to be relegated to the background in a César Frank sonata, or the Richard Strauss, is unthinkable, yet it is done. Ideal musical collaboration takes a great deal of humility toward the music itself and an ability on the part of each instrumentalist to forego the desire to outshine the other. It is indeed rare to find soloists of Heifetz's stature who could afford the generosity of letting the music speak for itself without ill-conceived self-interest.

4

Exposition

If you can talk with crowds and keep your virtue,
Or walk with Kings—nor lose the common touch

RUDYARD KIPLING

Jascha Heifetz took pride in his teaching, believed in what he was doing, and always gave his students all he thought they were able to absorb. He was dedicated to the cause of passing on a certain tradition, and most remarkably for an artist of his caliber, he was not discouraged by getting back less than he put in. He was as patient with his students as a gardener with his plants, but when he saw no hope in the seedling, he threw the student out without false sentimentality. He had no need to hang onto those whom he considered deadbeats just to have a certain number of students to keep his class going. His disappointments came much later, after a student left his class and was on his own, and the results didn't quite justify the amount of energy Heifetz had invested in that person. When he was disappointed in a student, past or present, his most often repeated remark to me was "You can't squeeze blood out of a turnip." This he didn't mean in a disparaging way, but that even very good technique could not substitute for depth and artistic temperament.

Heifetz enjoyed his authority over a bunch of young adults who loved, feared, respected, and were in awe of him. To be a dedicated Heifetz student meant a great deal more than just participating in his master class. His real aficionados knew every record he had ever made, including the ones pirated from his live performances. They could precisely "quote" the way he played every important phrase in life or on his recordings; they memorized his fingerings, his slides, and his dynamics in every piece of music the master ever laid his hands on. They also could quote his funny statements, knew all the jokes about him, and took an odd pleasure in discussing the jealous and disparaging remarks uttered by other violinists, his hopeless competition. For many of them reciting the lore of Jascha Heifetz was as much a way of life as quoting the Bible is for other zealots.

The thought of becoming a teacher didn't come all of a sudden to Heifetz. It went back to the time when his teacher, Leopold Auer, was still alive. Auer had planted the thought of teaching in Heifetz's mind during one of his regular visits with the old master after Auer had moved to New York. The story took some time for me to piece together from bits and scraps tossed my way during my years with Heifetz.

For years I had observed that on his walks Heifetz sometimes took along a hardwood cane that showed much wear and tear. The cane had a crook fashioned of a transparent material. I also noticed that the crook had a few cracks in it, and when it finally broke, Heifetz became very upset. For me it was just an old, beaten-up cane, and when I asked him what he was so upset about, he told me the cane's story. The cane originally belonged to Leopold Auer, he said, and to prove it he showed me a little silver plaque embedded in the crook; he also pointed out the fading, ornate letters *L. A.*, Leopold Auer's initials, engraved in the plaque. Heifetz wanted me to find a reliable cane shop to make a new crook of a similar material and to reinsert the plaque as it was before. The repairman should not repair or touch up any other part of the cane. I was duly impressed with his concern and went to several cane shops until I found the one that I thought would meet his approval. He even visited the shop with me to make sure that my judgment was not mistaken.

When I brought the cane back with the new crook, Heifetz told me how it came into his possession. Not long before Auer died, Heifetz visited him in his New York home as was his custom when he was in town. Already a famous violinist, he still came to the old man and played pieces he was preparing for a concert, perhaps seeking Auer's approval or maybe just trying to make the old man feel good. Just before Heifetz left this particular time, Auer brought out the cane, handed it over to him, and pronounced the famous words in his thick Hungarian accent, as Heifetz remembered them, "Jascha, some day you will teach, and you will be a good teacher."

Heifetz may have taken this little ceremony as a symbolic gesture to pass on to him the authority to teach violin in the tradition he had learned in the Auer class, as a shepherd passes his crook to the one who follows him on the job. I was aware of Heifetz's deep-set inclination toward symbolic interpretation and his compulsion to preserve tradition. He could have seen such implications in the passing of that cane. Heifetz also knew that by taking over responsibility from Auer he became part of a famous artistic and teaching tradition: Heifetz, student of Auer, student of Joachim, student of Ferdinand David, student of Spohr. How could he refuse to continue such a famous and proud lineage? Heifetz wasn't much of a scholar, but there was very little he didn't know about the violin, violinists, and their history, though he rarely talked about this knowledge.

Before settling down to teach at the University of Southern California, Heifetz held master classes for a while at the University of California at Los Angeles. He was appointed Distinguished Professor, a title which after his resignation he liked to twist to "Extinguished Professor." Apparently the circumstances accompanying his job there weren't exactly to his liking, and his demands were higher than the students applying for his class could cope with. To illustrate his case, Heifetz had great fun telling a favorite story.

Some time before he resigned from his Distinguished Professorship, Heifetz gave the usual auditions for aspiring new students. One applicant was a rather corpulent elderly lady who, upon request, produced a five-dollar violin and enthusiastically played a poor, scratchy C major scale. Heifetz, amazed at her gall, asked, "My dear lady, is there anything else you could play for me?"

"This is it," she proudly said. "That's all I know."

"But why do you want to join my master class?"

"Nothin' doin'," she answered. "I don't wanna join no master classes. All I wanna do is tell my friends that I've played for Jascha Heifetz."

Heifetz, ever curious about human nature, didn't let it go at that. "May I ask you, how did you learn that scale?

"I figgered it out all by m'self" was the proud answer.

Whether this audition or problems with the administration over selecting students was the straw that broke the camel's back, he did not say. Before teaching at UCLA, Heifetz had taught for a while at USC, which also did not work out to his satisfaction. Later, when Grant Beglarian was appointed dean of the School of Music at USC, he reestablished the music chairs and asked Heifetz and Gregor Piatigorsky to give master classes. Dean Beglarian also saw to the necessary financial arrangements.

When I first met Heifetz at my audition in 1971, I was surprised by his physical appearance. I had always imagined him as a strapping giant with broad shoulders, tall and muscular. Now, at seventy, he was a bit rotund but in reasonable shape, about five feet seven inches tall. His complexion was unusually smooth, which he attributed to often washing his face in ocean water, and his cheekbones slightly elevated, which he liked to

At the dedication ceremony for the Heifetz and Piatigorsky music chairs at USC in November 1974 are (left to right): Gregor Piatigorsky; John R. Hubbard, USC president; Grant Beglarian, dean of the School of Music, and Heifetz. Courtesy University Archives of the University of Southern California

believe came from the genes of a mysterious Mongolian ancestor. When he took off his jacket, which he never did during the master class, his shoulders appeared rather narrow and thin, his spine a bit curved in the shape of an S. He kept an X ray of his spine, and when he showed it to me, he called the curve the result of his "occupational hazard." It could have come from the way he held the violin, a trademark that only a violinist would notice, which was more to his left while other violinists usually hold the instrument more toward a straight angle in front of them. His feet were small; his shoes were size seven-and-a-half and of fine quality, all custom made. His most striking feature was his eyes—clear, light blue with large pupils, piercing or gentle according to his mood, which could change at the drop of a hat. I had the feeling that he could see through me, penetrate my soul and mind, and read my secrets as from an open book. He had the habit of looking straight into the eyes of the person he was talking to, as if searching for a favorable or unfavorable first impression. Heifetz, indeed, was inclined to judge people from the first impression he received. This first look was always supplemented with a second one from the corner of his eye, obliquely, to see how that person behaved while believing that he was unobserved.

Heifetz set great store in the impression he derived from people's smiles. He hated the insincere, artificial smiles of movie-star and politician publicity pictures. He could not bring himself to crack one in his own photographs. He would have great fun imitating these standard, superficial smiles and the vacant eyes and facial expressions that go with them. "The smile is in the eyes," he often said, "and if you can't smile with your eyes, saying 'cheese' won't do any good for you."

When I later told Heifetz about my first impressions of him based on his pictures on the sleek record-sleeves, he told me that the illusion that he was a giant came from the camera angle and the broad shoulders from the padding in his jacket. The noble look on his face was manufactured by taking his pictures from a right angle, turned three-quarters away from the camera, in the exact position his audience saw him onstage. All of this was carefully rehearsed and photographed during photo sessions with first-class photographers, to please his picture-hungry public. As for a smile, he could manage only the grin that he was willing to display to his friends and visitors when he was in a facetious mood. For this same obvious reason, on his publicity pictures he preferred not to smile at all and only presented a sort of pensive expression on his face. He was too self-conscious to act, as became painfully apparent in *They Shall Have Music* and *Carnegie Hall*, the two movies featuring him as a sort of actor.

The year I joined his master class he was teaching twice a week in a stately old building, Clark House, outside the University of Southern California campus. Clark House had been a private mansion. The building and its small park provided a quiet and inspiring background to various musical activities. Heifetz liked the place; he had his own classroom on the second floor, and while a student played a piece, he often stood at the window looking out at a grand old tree that stood only a few feet away from his window. He liked to listen to the mockingbirds in the spring mating season, their imitations of the violin pouring in through the open window.

As Heifetz stated publicly, he had no formal "Heifetz method" for teaching violin or producing virtuosos. In this he resembled his own teacher, for whom he expressed almost boundless admiration. Heifetz, like Auer, basically treated each student individually according to his or her own talent, developing the individuality of each musician.

The Jascha Heifetz master class was filmed in 1962 as part of a series of videos, about a decade before I entered the class. Unfortunately such projects contain a great deal of artifice, and these documentaries do not reflect the way Heifetz was teaching ten years later. All those who took part in his class realized that only the most outstanding students were filmed and only those who were already well-prepared, while his most fascinating teaching really took place when he started out with a new student who played for him for the first time in class. Even though the student got to play a piece of music that had been assigned ahead of time, Heifetz would usually begin to challenge the newcomer right away by asking him to read something he had never seen before, thus trying to discover how adaptable the new student would be.

When Heifetz demonstrates in these movies, even a professional will have difficulty perceiving the subtle differences between his demonstrations and the student's performances. The true nature of his teaching was lost in the understandable effort to make a showcase of only the best of what went on in his class, an effort that also made the demonstrations somewhat stale and lifeless. In fact, in real life Heifetz was able to retain a sense of freshness with each student, prepared or unprepared, and managed to keep his class on its toes all the time.

HEIFETZ SPENT a great deal of time and energy selecting his students. Prospective candidates had to fill out a two-page questionnaire, listing educational institutions attended, languages spoken or read, secondary instruments played, and need for scholarship, in addition to answering the usual questions about former teachers, awards, and recommendations. He also wanted to know why they wanted to enroll in his master class; he asked this question of every applicant regardless of what they might have already written elsewhere in the questionnaire. He looked for mature students whom he considered young enough to be still pliable, but he rarely accepted prodigies. Having been one himself, he considered prodigies as suffering from a disease that required considerable luck to survive, but he knew well that luck was not on everybody's side. He wanted no part in ruining and perhaps even emotionally crippling these children in the best years of their lives for the vague hope of a brilliant future. He wanted from his students a certain amount of maturity and willingness to devote themselves to the hard work he imposed on them. The students also had to postpone their anxious desire to appear in public and to show off their abilities until Heifetz gave them the green light. Experience had taught Heifetz that postponement of public performance was not at all acceptable, not so much to the hopeful prodigies but rather to their parents, most of whom he felt were anxious for fame and greedy for money.

Musical talent and outstanding technique were certainly indispensable for acceptance in the Jascha Heifetz master class, but these were not all he was looking for. He was a keen judge of human nature, and during his interviews with prospective students he immediately recognized those who showed dedication and commitment to their own talent and in whom he detected a sense of discipline and self-respect. Heifetz could recognize during the audition whether an applicant was teachable or had already become inflexible in his or her ways of making music. Nevertheless, he was always willing to give the benefit of the doubt to those whom he had accepted against his better judgment. If any of these proved unteachable, either he got rid of them in a short time, or the students themselves soon recognized the futility of trying to impress Heifetz with their ability to play the violin. Some who were dismissed or quit sooner than expected were quite talented but just couldn't be helped. A few of them had a meteoric start to a career which soon petered out, perhaps because they were just as unable to accept the rigors of an artistic career as they had been to accept or tolerate the pressure of Heifetz's seemingly nit-picking ways of conducting his class.

As every student soon learned, Heifetz's assistant would help prepare them for his class, helping with any technical problems and even exercising a certain authority over whether a student was ready to play a new piece for Mr. Heifetz. Although his assistant and pianist were on the university payroll, Heifetz considered them his own fulltime employees and would not accept excuses for anything—especially other engagements—that would keep them from fulfilling their obligations. His relationship with his employees was a bit out of sync with latter-day employment practices; when he needed company or help in his own home, he called on them, using one pretense or another, and he always got what he wanted. The usual pretense was an invitation to his house or to the beach "to talk about something very important" which often turned out to be something of a trifle or even less.

The function of his assistant went way beyond that of an ordinary employee or administrative assistant. In many ways Heifetz expected his assistant to mother his students; she had to make sure that financial or health problems would not get in the way of preparing properly for his classes. She also had to take care of the students' housing if they needed help and deal with any problems with the U.S. Immigration Service concerning student visas and their extensions. She was expected to notice if a student needed clothing or better food or help with personal appearance, and she even had to try to deal with family problems. Once in the Jascha Heifetz master class, the student was under Heifetz's sort of paternal care until he or she left or was asked to leave.

Unless he was in the mood to drive his own car to the university, Heifetz was picked up by his assistant or by his pianist in his Beverly Hills home. A student routinely waited for them at the university parking lot, took his briefcase, which sometimes contained some music but usually only his lunch, and they came together to his classroom. He walked straight in while his students waited outside for the assistant's invitation to enter. The assistant sometimes whispered a few words to them at the door about Mr. H.'s mood. These warnings sometimes served the opposite of their purpose, making the students feel uneasy if Heifetz was not in a particularly good mood, but perhaps she was trying to be helpful.

The classroom had a large desk with a straight chair for Heifetz, a cabinet with his own music library in it, standard school chairs and music stands for the students, and a grand piano. He never went out for lunch but always brought his own or expected someone to bring it for him. He usually ate in the company of his assistant. On rare occasions an old friend from the faculty or a guest from out of town would join him for lunch. Guests were usually permitted to visit the class either during the morning or the afternoon session but only for a limited amount of time.

The master classes took place twice a week, from eleven in the morning to four in the afternoon with an hour lunch break. Teaching eight hours weekly would not be easy for anyone over seventy, especially if the job involved a great deal of physical activity. Heifetz certainly worked harder for his salary than most of the invited or distinguished visiting professors of any age and reputation who were in a similar situation. An integral part of his teaching "method" was a metal stick, which really was an expandable piece of a radio antenna. This stick was at hand all the time, and I think he considered it a symbol of authority over his students, perhaps even a substitute for the Auer cane. With it he struck the desk in front of him whenever something was going on that displeased him or if he needed attention. Sometimes he resembled a schoolmaster as he banged on the desk, accompanied by an authoritative "Hello!" The desk bore plenty of marks testifying to the number of times that he felt this need for control. He raised his voice to an unusual volume only during performances when the student otherwise could not hear his normal speaking voice.

Heifetz always came well prepared to his class, knowing exactly what he was going to do, but his plans changed quickly if his students' preparedness didn't live up to his expectations. His assistant saw to it that the scores of all basic violin studies and etudes as well as the Bach solo violin sonatas and partitas were always on his desk, ready to be used if he needed references. In spite of his incredible musical memory, he never hesitated to verify his statements by consulting the printed music. He also used these scores to show his students the different versions of a piece in various editions. For this reason and just to be sure before accusing anyone in class of having made a mistake, he always asked, first, what edition the student was using. Heifetz liked to use certain editions that he considered authentic and asked his students to use the same ones for the sake of uniformity.

Heifetz remembered everybody's progress or regress—a Heifetz saying—from the first day of the student's entry in his class. He was prone to make notes on bits of paper during class and to pass them on to his assistant as a reminder of something that had to be done, such as an exercise to help a student solve a technical problem, or even just a silly remark to amuse himself.

At the beginning of his class, he always made small talk with his students to put them at ease by letting them observe the fearful master as another human being whose words weren't always put in the proper order and whose sentences sometimes made no sense. He let them laugh for a moment before serious work began. A standard question was about the breakfasts they had had that morning. I remember, once, a younger student confessed that she always threw up her breakfast just before she got into her car, she was so afraid of him. As simple and sometimes corny as his questions were, they always accomplished their intended purpose of easing the initial tension. Next he always tuned his violin quickly and efficiently, before anybody else did. Then he sometimes called for a volunteer to be first, or he continued any unfinished business with the last student from the previous class or asked his assistant to suggest who should be first.

Heifetz didn't like to teach his students technical things but rather left such matters to his assistant if there was a need. However, he took his time to teach one of the most elementary steps in violin playing, the proper technique of tuning, especially for his new students. As a first step he admonished them to do it softly and with as little fuss as possible. Contrary to standard practice Heifetz liked to tune the A string to the accompaniment of a D major chord on the piano instead of the traditional D minor one. The major chord would give the tuning a feeling of brightness, he said, and one should instinctively pull the strings up just a hair higher, which would make the violin sound brighter so that it would shine over the piano. He taught us how to tune the violin without the assistance of the pianist; standing at the piano, with the violin in his hand, he would strike the middle A on the piano, hold its sound with the pedal, then softly add to it the F-sharp and the D. As he took his hand off the keyboard he would use the pedal to keep the sound going until he finished tuning. "This is the proper way of tuning the fiddle to a piano, and there should be no need for assistance," he would say.

Heifetz expected all his students to play all the scales in all their major and minor forms, including modal scales, at a reasonably moderate tempo, not at breakneck speed. The students had to know straight scales; scales in thirds, sixths, tenths, and in fingered and parallel octaves; and all arpeggios, performed with legato and staccato bowings and reasonably in tune. They were expected to have these scales ready at any time upon request; Heifetz often said that regular scale-practicing contributes to good intonation. How difficult these exercises are is known only to violinists who have tried and given up in despair. Yet they were Heifetz's daily diet in his concertizing days and even after, and they gave his playing its much-admired technical foundation. Scale-playing in the class often caused more tension than the major piece of the day did. Heifetz tried to take the tension out of these moments, and when he noticed the jittering bow of a student struggling with an unusually difficult scale, his favorite saying was "Don't be afraid of those scales; make the scales be afraid of you."

Heifetz knew well what nerves can do to a performer, though judging by his relaxed appearance and deadpan face onstage one could easily come to the conclusion that he had nerves of steel and stage fright was unknown to him. Not so: when he noticed a case of nerves in one of his students, he sometimes asked, "Are you nervous?"

"Yes, Mr. Heifetz!" was the usual answer.

To our surprise Heifetz would respond, "I certainly hope so; it's good to be nervous."

What he meant was that nervousness is part of our emotional makeup and that at least some of it is necessary for an exciting performance. Once he told me in private that he always had a certain amount of fear before a performance, which usually passed as soon as he started playing. Then he mentioned the case of a famous singer—I think it was Lily Pons—who always threw up before going onstage and then gave a beautiful performance.

After the student passed through the torment of scale playing, Heifetz sometimes wanted to hear an etude, other times a Bach partita or a Paganini caprice. All students had to be ready all the time with at least one movement from these pieces, from memory. For most raw recruits in his class, the idea of knowing something by heart meant that they could play the piece even in their sleep, mechanically, without giving it a second thought. To guard against such thoughtless knowledge, Heifetz often asked the student to play a recurring phrase with different fingerings, phrasing, or dynamics. For those who knew the piece only mechanically, so that it was in their fingers rather than in their minds, such a request was impossible to fulfill, for mechanical playing does not allow thinking. To test the student and to help him or her break such mechanical habits, he sometimes stopped the performance in the middle of a phrase to request, "Go back four bars and try to play that passage again, but this time use different fingerings." Those who knew the piece only mechanically never could find that place. The acid test of knowing a piece was when he asked the student to go to just six bars from its end and play it again from there; surprisingly enough, even some of his seasoned students couldn't do it without a well-marked measure as a cue.

When Heifetz noticed that a student played a virtuoso passage too carefully, he first complimented the student on his or her playing: "It was nicely done, but it was too careful, too safe. Play it with flair, with dash." To make sure that he was understood, he would change the fingerings in the student's music with the result that it had to be played by taking risks. Heifetz was against safe playing in the sense that he didn't like to play too much in the same position; playing safely in the same position usually results in breaking up the phrases because string crossings become necessary which alter the timbre of the sound. Such technique is common only for those who prefer to be safe rather than sorry. Heifetz insisted on playing one phrase or even the whole melody on one string, fingering higher and higher on the same string if proper phrasing required it.

To make an unremarkable phrase memorable, Heifetz sometimes suggested to the student to take the bow off the string just before coming down with it, especially in a fast, showy passage. This way the performer not only had to take chances but would give the audience the impression of dashing originality. While musical excitement was always a major goal in his interpretations, Heifetz considered such show elements necessary to reinforce this excitement. Heifetz hated nothing more than a perfect-but-dull performance.

After the major piece of the day and sometimes even before it, all students were expected to "surprise" him with a small piece, which he liked to call an "itsy-bitsy." Playing these small pieces on his programs was an essential part of Heifetz's phenomenal success; many of them were his own transcriptions of pieces that were already known to his audiences in their original forms. He also made popular other, lesser-known original pieces. Small pieces were usually scheduled in the second part of his programs, and being short and lighter, they didn't demand too much of the audience's already flagging attention. Heifetz made his students understand that the shortness of these pieces didn't mean that they were technically or musically negligible. In fact, they represented a real challenge inasmuch as the performer had only a short time at his disposal, a few minutes, to establish a mood and carry out a range of emotions. Playing short pieces was a Heifetz specialty, and he developed it to utmost perfection.

Short pieces have a checkered history in the violin literature. Performers and critics once considered them indispensable, but for a time they were often thought of as nonmusic that reputable violinists should not consider putting on a program, and the chance of receiving a sneering review was discouragement enough. Perhaps the time is now turning again.

The majority of these short pieces are either original character pieces or transcriptions, mostly by violinists who wanted to lighten their programs or as vehicles for showing off virtuosity as a welcome relief from heavy sonatas. Heifetz transcribed some 150 finished and unfinished songs, dances, piano, and orchestral character pieces. To perform these pieces successfully, the artist would benefit from having some familiarity with the words of the songs, some knowledge of the nature of the dances, or even some ability to play their original piano versions for an impression of their character. Heifetz had a motley crew of students from all over the world. Some came from the Far East, mostly from Japan and Australia, the majority from Europe and the United States. There was little advertising of his class, and most students learned about it from other students, from their teachers, or from members of a jury when they played in a competition. My own story is typical of the haphazard way information circulated among musicians and amateurs. Given this international makeup of the master class and his students' varied intellectual and musical backgrounds, it was often an up-hill struggle to instill in the minds of his students from other cultures the spirit of a *Porgy and Bess* transcription or of a Negro spiritual, not to mention Spanish flamenco dances or a song by Stephen Foster.

In comparison to other violinists' works, the Heifetz transcriptions have something special and unique. In other violinists' arrangements the piano is usually regarded as a secondary instrument and relegated to the background to play a typically insignificant secondary role. Heifetz gives a prominent role to the piano; in fact, the piano plays as an equal partner to the violin whether the piece is very short or lengthy. If an arrogant and insensitive violinist tries to give prominence only to the violin in a Heifetz transcription, the interpretation seems somehow truncated and half its effect lost. In many Heifetz transcriptions the piano sets the mood with a short introduction, and upon this introduction, according to Heifetz, rests the success or failure of the whole piece. After I became the class pianist, he often made me play these introductory bars over and over again until he was satisfied that I had caught their proper spirit by appropriately introducing the violin's main motivic idea.

When Heifetz was about to demonstrate one of these pieces, a hush fell over the class and an electrifying tension of anticipation vibrated in the air. We all knew that what we were about to hear was something unique that only Heifetz could produce. It was magic indeed as he came through brilliantly with the most difficult passages at an age past seventy. His intonation, tempo, rhythm, rubatos, and sense of timing were always impeccably perfect, and he always knew how to create excitement within a few seconds. He always played these pieces by heart, yet he never prepared for them; they were, after all, "surprises," and most of the time he didn't even know what short pieces the students were going to play.

Although Heifetz had no rigid teaching method, certain steps recurred often enough to allow some general observations of the way he conducted his class and of what he considered important in his teaching. Sometimes Heifetz let a student playing a major piece sweat it out all the way to the end before he made a comment; other times his stick came down on the desk to stop the performance after the first few bars. To make amends and corrections, he first would try to explain verbally and vocally what improvements he wanted to hear, but if the student didn't catch on, and only then, he would pick up his violin and demonstrate a passage. His demonstrations never were in an arrogant "This is the way to play it" manner. I never ceased to be surprised at his humble approach to music. His and his students' egos were always secondary to the only important task of penetrating the depths of the piece under discussion. His demonstrations were those of a craftsman revealing all the secrets of his trade to his apprentice, showing the student how to handle the material he had to work with and teaching the student everything that he or she should absorb. He called attention to better and easier fingerings that usually were less complicated than what the students had used. He demonstrated ways to avoid crossing strings and thereby breaking a phrase, and how to move the thumb as little as possible when shifting or changing positions. He encouraged the student to make repetitive phrases more interesting by using different fingerings and dynamics regardless of what the score said. He pointed out the importance of bringing out nuances and slight rhythmical changes to make a piece move but always within the framework of the original tempo. Heifetz never forced his musical ideas on the students but rather helped them to find their own solutions. He always made us understand that his interpretation was only one of many possible interpretations and that his solution for a problem wouldn't necessarily suit others' personalities. Unfortunately, many students found it easier to attempt to imitate a Heifetz interpretation than to try to be original. I remember a very talented student, a really stubborn one, doing a marvelous performance of a concerto movement, but one full of technical clumsiness that Heifetz could have easily corrected or criticized. Instead his only comment was "You did some things the hard way, but it worked for you, and you made it sound convincing."

His most often repeated remark to his students was "Say something with your playing." This didn't necessarily mean that the student had said nothing with his or her performance, though sometimes that was the case; often it only meant that the student's playing didn't sound sincere enough to Heifetz or didn't suit the student's temperament and musical personality. Heifetz liked to use the metaphor that the student was wearing someone else's clothing, either too loose or too tight. Sometimes the spirit of a piece eluded the student because the work was one he had always wanted to learn and he thought he should learn it with Heifetz. Heifetz sometimes had trouble guiding his students away from these pieces that didn't suit their personalities. If he felt that the piece was beyond their technical ability or temperament, he tried to discourage them by saying, "You may like this piece, but for now, I don't think the piece likes you. Why don't you pick something else?"

Although Heifetz was known to change dynamics and sometimes to edit pieces if he thought his performance would be more effective, he insisted that his students pay meticulous attention to all markings in the score. He never stopped calling the students' attention to nuances and tone colors; he was an unsurpassed master in painting shades and light through music, and he did his best to make his students recognize their importance and their effect on the audience. To help the students create a more intense sound, Heifetz insisted that they use gut strings except for the E string; the G string was gut wrapped with aluminum. "Press your fingers very hard on the strings no matter what the dynamic marks are," he often admonished. He had fingers of steel which never trembled, all the way to the end of his life.

After the first few weeks in his master class as a violinist, I began to wonder why his demonstrations sometimes didn't achieve the intended effect. I observed that no matter how differently he demonstrated a passage, the student often would keep on playing it in the same old way. Obviously some of these students just could not absorb his teaching, but others were bright and willing to learn yet never succeeded no matter how hard Heifetz tried. I came to the conclusion that the reason for our lack of comprehension was that we were overwhelmed, even intimidated, by his demonstrations. Instead of watching for the technical elements of his playing and benefiting from Heifetz the teacher, we came under the hypnotic spell of Jascha Heifetz, the supreme magician of the violin. Later when I became the class pianist and he occasionally asked my opinion, after class, about how the class was progressing, I became brave and pointed out this problem to him. At first he refused to accept my opinion, which was a standard procedure with him, but eventually he eased up a bit with his demonstrations and was more willing to repeat a difficult passage if the baffled student asked him, "How was that again, Mr. Heifetz? I didn't get it. Could you repeat it, please?" Before, he would have refused to comply with such requests, expecting everyone to observe and grasp everything at the first hearing. Evidently he had difficulty understanding that some students were unable to do so. However, something good came from my remark because after repeated demonstrations he became more insistent on results, as he said jokingly yet with a serious intent, "I expect that I should have not worked so hard for nothing." Now the students themselves had to work harder on the demonstrated passages until they came closer to what Heifetz expected from them, although he always recognized the technical and musical limitations of his students and didn't push them beyond their ability.

To test flexibility and adaptability, Heifetz sometimes asked a student to tune a string just a bit off the proper pitch. "It may happen during a concert," he explained, "that one of the strings goes out of tune in the middle of a piece and you have no chance to retune it. One has to be ready for all kinds of emergencies, and this is one of them." To prove his point, once he tuned a string nearly a half-tone off and played almost a whole movement of a sonata absolutely in tune. He had such technical facility that he could rearrange his fingerings in a pinch and nobody was the wiser that a string was out of tune.

Not all his students were equally musically gifted; some were excellent technicians but lacked musical sensitivity. To these Heifetz suggested listening to recordings of the piece they were working on, not only by one but by several artists, hoping that these students would acquire some musical ideas since they didn't have any of their own. He never suggested his own recordings but hoped that by imitating somebody they would eventually acquire a more personal musical sense. "It is better to imitate someone else's feelings than playing with no feelings at all," he used to say. He also said that "one cannot change the spots on the leopard": such procedures would never substitute for genuine musical talent.

While he encouraged imitation for his less talented students, he considered it an affront if a musically gifted student tried to imitate the Heifetz style. Once a talented auditor played a movement of a concerto in an almost perfect imitation of the Heifetz recording. Heifetz listened to the performance from beginning to end with a stony face. The student was obviously very pleased with his performance and expectantly looked at Heifetz for his approval. Heifetz looked at him for a few dramatic moments, then coldly growled at him in a low voice, "Copycat!" He never called on that student to play for him again.

The worst punishment he ever meted out to a poorly prepared auditor or student was to let her play her piece all the way to the end, while it was obvious to everyone that the agony should have been stopped after a few bars. When it was all finished, Heifetz would look distractedly in the air and only say, "Next." It was an embarrassment almost beyond endurance. On the other hand, if someone tried to be original but it just didn't come out right, Heifetz would pick up his fiddle and imitate with gross exaggerations what he had just heard. He had great fun with such mockery and was very good at imitating any style or no style at all; he could play consistently and gratingly out of tune or play a classical piece in Gypsy style or even in country music style. One talented student was actually a Gypsy, but his beautiful, suave playing always slipped into his inevitable Gypsy rubato. Once this student played a Bach partita with his usual mannerisms. When it was over, Heifetz picked up his fiddle and said, "If you want to play Bach in Gypsy style, let me show you how to do that, too." Then he played the partita with such comical Gypsy exaggerations and embellishments that everybody cracked up. Unfortunately, no matter how hard Heifetz tried to instill discipline in our Gypsy friend's style of playing, it didn't work.

He could easily recognize if a not-so-perfect performance was caused by nervousness or by poor preparation. Heifetz didn't let anybody get away with anything and thoroughly detested any students, especially the talented ones, who tried to fake their way through a lesson hoping that he wouldn't notice their lack of serious preparation. He considered such fakery a lack of responsibility toward one's talent, and when a very talented student played the Mendelssohn violin concerto for him just a week before its actual stage performance, he said in disgust, "You know, at this moment I don't know whether I should tell you 'God bless you' or 'God help you' as a send-off to your concert." After class, in private, he expressed his disappointment to me and said, "What a waste of talent."

Heifetz accepted no excuses for coming unprepared to his class. He had no sympathy for such standard apologies as "I could do better if I had a chance to do it again." Sometimes, though, he let the student repeat a performance, and if it turned out better the second time, he would just say wryly, "You could have done it just as well the first time around." He told us that he had the same sort of feeling after concerts of his own that he considered not so good, but that eventually he had disciplined himself to begin all his concerts with the thought that there are no second chances and that every performance happens only once. Indeed, even if one could redo a performance, the results may be no better than the first time around. I learned from Heifetz that you should play each performance truly as if your life depended on it. If you wanted to be even near his league, trying your best wasn't good enough; with him there were no "ifs" and "buts," for excuses do not count with the audience; they come to hear a good performance, not excuses.

Among the gravest mistakes a student could make was to show off his or her virtuosity in the master class. Heifetz considered virtuosos to be a dime a dozen, and unless virtuosity came with some musical content, he wanted to have no part of it. I remember a performance by one of his better students that got faster and faster, going out of control all the way to the end. When it was over, Heifetz put his hand on the student's bow-arm and said with a deadpan face, "I was worried about you for a while," and asked him to play the slow movement of the same concerto but really slowly and espressivo. Heifetz set the tempo and made sure that the student stayed with it. It was like hobbling a racehorse.

At rehearsals some musicians are preoccupied with explaining their plans of execution for certain places in the music. They like to enlarge on what the composer meant with a certain passage and give lengthy discourses on the merits and style of the piece, all of which usually comes to naught in the actual playing. Heifetz never wanted to hear explanations, theoretical, historical, musical, personal, or otherwise. If a student began with an explanation, Heifetz gave him his best cold-fish look and said, "No explanations please, just play!" He called those who liked to explain music "the learned ones," pronouncing the word *learn-ed* to emphasize its two separate syllables; he took the behavior as a sign that they were trying to talk themselves out of playing. For him music spoke for itself in its own language, and those who spoke that language needed no verbal explanations. Words, in his view, were necessary only for reviewers, critics, historians, amateur music lovers, and theoreticians whom he called "musicriminologists." He was also convinced that being "brainy," that is, thinking too much about what and how one is going to play, including consideration of textbook rules on style, destroys feelings in the player and results in a calculated, cold, unemotional performance. His favorite statement after a brainy, calculated rendering was "It was wonderful—but I didn't feel anything."

Although Heifetz spent little time teaching technique beyond suggesting better fingerings and bowings, if he noticed that someone had technical problems, he knew exactly what studies or etudes to recommend. His accomplished students often resented being sent back to restudy etudes of their beginner years. Perhaps they didn't know that Heifetz practiced the same standard etudes regularly and kept them in his fingers all the time.

Heifetz had some surprises for those students who had never learned to appreciate the importance of the accompaniment. He sometimes made his students accompany one another at the piano, and even beginners at the piano had to do this, especially if the piano parts were not too demanding. He wanted them to experience firsthand how the pianist feels when the violinist "cuts corners," that is, rushes his or her parts so that the pianist hasn't enough time to finish difficult passages. Such carelessness usually comes from the violinist's unfamiliarity with the piano part, or just an unwillingness to listen to what the piano has to say. These demonstrations may have had little more than shock value for most violinists with minimal, if any, ability at the piano, but even so, some would hear their own music for the first time from the accompanist's point of view. Heifetz often stopped speedy, corner-cutting students with the remark, "Do you know what the piano has to play?" The answer quite often was an embarrassed "No."

Heifetz sometimes checked a student's familiarity with the piano part by asking the pianist to pick a spot near the middle of a piece and begin to play the accompaniment. The student, meanwhile, was supposed to find the appropriate place in his violin part. If the student was at loss in this test, Heifetz would ask him or her to produce the piano accompaniment, which the student quite often couldn't do, not even possessing a copy. Heifetz wanted all his students not only to have a copy of the piano part of each violin piece but also to spend time studying it. He knew well that too many violinists never even look at the accompaniment or know it only by ear if they know it at all. He wanted his students to understand that the accompaniment keeps a piece together; it provides color and backbone for the soloist as an indispensable part of the fabric of the music against which the solo part is set off. Often soloists consider accompanists as their employees who are paid for staying in the background and for not competing with the soloist's playing, even to the detriment of the music.

To be sure that the students paid attention to each other's playing, Heifetz sometimes asked them to provide constructive criticism. He took this seriously and once passed out the largest fine, ten dollars, to someone who criticized another student facetiously and arrogantly but was then unable to show how the piece should be played. Fining his students, from a nickel to several dollars, was one of his "improvements" over other teachers. It was a sort of punishment, but the biggest punishment was to be dismissed for failing to show proper interest during class and for such offenses as habitually staring at the ground while others had a lesson or Heifetz was offering a demonstration.

Heifetz was fascinated by the piano and envied its broad range of power, especially in comparison with that of the violin. He took piano lessons regularly as a child and told me that he often filled in as accompanist in the Auer class when the pianist was absent. He insisted that his students take piano lessons at USC and made arrangements for them to do so; some were rank beginners who had never studied the piano before. Heifetz even listened to their playing at least twice a year to observe their progress or to see whether those who didn't take lessons because they were advanced players had maintained their competence. All students had to take viola lessons for at least one semester to be able to play that instrument when the class had its monthly chamber music sessions.

Heifetz knew well that many of his students would end up playing in an orchestra or perhaps in a chamber music group or would be making a living by playing in the studios. To prepare his students for that, too, he sometimes held sight-reading sessions, making everybody read the violin and viola parts from the standard orchestra repertory. As part of this exercise, he made us read violin and violin-viola duos; he especially liked those by Spohr. To challenge our sense of rhythm, he made us read Bohuslav Martinů's *Rhythmic Etudes* for violin and piano. Reading these etudes was also a requirement in the audition for his master class.

Heifetz was a born disciplinarian and ran his class as a one-man institution. The students had to learn how to turn pages properly for the pianist or for other players and how to clean their violins. He taught them what parts of the violin were the most sensitive to deterioration and consequently needed the most attention; he showed them how to clean and rosin their bows and the proper way of securing their violins in their cases to avoid possible damage. Nothing escaped his attention. If someone got a rash or skin bruise under the chin from practicing, his advice was not to baby it too much and just to keep it clean. He wanted his students to keep their music clean and wouldn't let them mark up the sheets, not even with his suggestions, except for a few important ones. "Don't write anything down; try to remember it," he used to say, presuming that we all had the kind of memory he had. If he demonstrated something unusual on the violin, he would tell his students, "Don't write it down and don't tell anybody, just play it that way," as if it were a secret that only his students should know, just as magicians don't tell the secrets to their tricks.

A student entering the Jascha Heifetz master class had to be ready to adjust to a great deal more than just his unorthodox ways of teaching. He didn't like to be called Master, Maestro, Professor, Distinguished or Extinguished, or by any other terms commonly used by famous artists. He was just plain Mr. Heifetz for his students, and that is the name by which they automatically remember him for the rest of their lives. Upon entering the class all students were hit with the same request that he had made of me, and it was never easy to satisfy: he wanted them to discard their shoulder pads. The shoulder pad is a small pillow, worn between the shoulder and the violin, that helps to hold the instrument in place and relieves strain on the violinist's neck. Only students with very long necks were permitted to wear one, and only a very thin one. Heifetz claimed that the shoulder pad buffeted the sound of the violin, and its use was only self-indulgence, not permissible to a true Heifetz student. If a student tried to explain to him why he or she had to wear a shoulder pad, his standard reply was "In that case, I am not sure that you should continue playing the violin. The way we hold the fiddle is already such an unnatural and uncomfortable position that a shoulder pad shouldn't make any difference. I suggest that you take up playing the cello or the double bass where such problems don't exist."

Heifetz seemed to have the notion that he was responsible for the education of an artist in toto, not just for teaching a brute who happened to play the violin. Toward this end he gave us short lectures on how to get on and off the stage, how to stand correctly with two feet planted firmly on the ground without being too stiff or moving too much, that is, without swaying from left to right and down and up. He showed us the right way to bow before and after the numbers and never stopped emphasizing the importance of being properly dressed not only for the stage but also in our private lives. He couldn't remind us often enough of the importance of the first impression an artist gives onstage and how that impression enhances the receptiveness of an audience. He told us how to go about an audition with a conductor and mentioned basic financial aspects of making a living as a performer, such as fee scales, contracts with managers and promoters, and their fair share of an artist's fees.

To introduce his students to the rigors of an artist's life, Heifetz set up a dress and behavior code in his classroom that would have astounded anyone familiar only with the classroom standards of today's schools of higher education. Boys had to wear coats and ties, long pants, and clean shoes (sneakers or other "contraptions," as he called them, would not pass as footwear). Girls had to dress attractively (by Heifetz's taste and standards), had to have high-heel shoes that were neither too low nor too high, no miniskirts, and especially no pants, lest one wanted to be greeted by him in the class by a "Hello boy!" He suggested that those who had to wear glasses get used to wearing contact lenses if the glasses were not becoming; those with a pale or poor complexion were taught by his assistant how to put on makeup properly. Neither gender was allowed to wear "funny" haircuts, exceedingly long hair, nor an excessive amount of jewelry. In addition, a certain level of cleanliness was expected: the boys wiped their shoes on the back of their pants before entering class, and everybody checked his or her nails, which had to be kept short. Some boys with bad breath, either from drinking too much beer or having a bad stomach, carried an ample supply of throat spray and applied it generously before entering his class. Deodorant sprays were also in vogue, a blessed difference appreciated by everyone who ever attended a standard university class. By nature Heifetz was very observant and nobody got away with breaking any of his rules. He noticed unusually long hair immediately, and when one pupil (who later became quite famous) tried to hide his inordinately long hair under a wig, Heifetz walked over to him, inspected the wig in great detail, and then unceremoniously pulled it off. All in all, for many a raw recruit he seemed prehistoric in his ideas

of education, but their choices were limited to putting up with them or
to leaving his class. When he felt the need, Heifetz would ask a male student to stay after class and discuss some problem he noticed, including
bad breath, dirty shoes, or sloppy dress. For female students he left such
discussions to his assistant.

His system of penalization was not limited to the relatively serious
offense of offering unconstructive criticism; his students were fined for
smaller offenses and dismissed for repeated disobedience. Dirty, unkempt, neglected violins called for a fine starting at twenty-five cents; the
same fine was meted out for minor violations of the dress code, such as a
skirt an inch too short, heels too high, spots on a coat or blouse, or hair
that was too long. For more serious violations, such as coming unprepared or not remembering his instructions from a previous class, he
wouldn't listen to the offender's playing for a certain amount of time;
after repeated offenses he made the offenders pay a heavier fine into his
piggybank. The money thus collected went to purchase strings, rosin, or
music for those students who had limited financial resources. If all warnings and penalties failed, Heifetz would ask the obstinate offender to
leave the class, his talent or musical progress notwithstanding. He excused such persons from studying further with him by saying, "They did
not offend me as much as they offended my class."

It would be easy to call Heifetz an old-fashioned, finicky, and cranky
old school master who wanted his way by any means, but he had an
underlying purpose. To persist through long hours of hard and often
boring practice, aspiring artists must keep in mind a certain goal. For
most of them it is the goal of success and perhaps some financial gain.
Heifetz attempted to bring them down to earth by putting obstacles in
their way similar to those they would incur during their career. He knew,
if anyone did, that even success is not all a bed of roses, and even when it
seems to be, its thorns can make an inexperienced artist wonder if it was
worth the effort. Though he wanted to make us sensitive musicians, he
knew that one must be tough enough to face criticism, just or unjust,
and be able to face restrictions that managers and promoters force upon
their charges. To toughen us up, he expected us not to display emotion
toward his criticism, even if it sometimes seemed beyond our comprehension. He had no favorites in his class, though he obviously liked to
work with those who took to his teaching. He also believed that a certain
universal justice was applicable to all members of his class, guilty or not
guilty. Once, on a very bad day when everybody performed below par, he
gave hell to all students for their unpardonable and inexcusable laxity in

fulfilling their duties toward themselves and his class. At that time I was already the pianist of the class. After he was through with them, he turned to me and bawled me out for having done an awful job, for not following previous instructions, and for playing to soulless performances with soulless accompaniment. This time I had to summon up both my musical and my Chinese family training because I believed that I had done nothing wrong. I had only followed his general instructions, that the pianist shouldn't try to upstage the soloist by showing in the accompaniment that she knew better. Heifetz had instilled in my mind that it was something like bad-mouthing your partner if the accompanist did better than the soloist.

I held my horses and said nothing in my own defense except for a short "I am sorry." However, the next day he brought up the subject in private conversation. Heifetz didn't like to apologize and rarely did so, but this time he felt he owed me one. "I'm sorry about yesterday," he said. "Actually you were very good, but praising you and knocking down the rest of them would not have been good for the morale of the class." I had to think for a while to understand what he meant. Eventually it dawned on me that by elevating me above the rest of the class, he would have set me apart as an outsider, but by putting us all together in the same boat, guilty or not guilty, we remained one. He was right, for I never lost the trust and friendship of the members of the class.

Most of the time Heifetz had difficulty approaching a subject directly; he often used metaphors, similes, and parables, and sometimes he twisted his meaning and said just the opposite of what he intended to say. It was all part of his predilection for secrecy and, perhaps, his unusual upbringing in which he never mingled and communicated with children his own age. His conversations often resembled the well-known Russian-Jewish joke in which two Jewish gentlemen get on the train. One says to the other: "You, Isaac, you want to cheat me. By buying a ticket to Omsk, you want me to believe that you are going to Tomsk, while in fact I know that you are going to Omsk." When he came to dinner at my house, he would stick his head in the kitchen door and, seeing that everybody was having a good time, would ask peevishly, "Is there anything I cannot do?" Of course, he didn't mean to do or not to do anything; he only wanted to share in the fun, but not in the kitchen because to have men in the kitchen was against his principles. Some of his students had considerable difficulty understanding this inverted language, especially if they came from foreign countries and had their own funny form of English.

Heifetz was a patriot and a firm believer in democracy. On national election days he demanded that all his students who were American citizens go to the polls and vote. He even asked them to show proof of their voting in the form of voting stubs. He passed out fines and wouldn't listen for several weeks to the playing of those who neglected this duty. A similar punishment was due for those who neglected to attend concerts of well-known violinists playing in town. He wanted to make sure that his students had the widest possible range of exposure to all sorts of interpretations.

At the end of class sessions, Heifetz would watch everybody put their violins away and would make sure that they went through the prescribed cleaning and packing ritual. He was the last one to put away the Seraphin copy that he usually used in class. He had a large collection of fine bows. He used, in turn, his Kittel, a gift from Auer which was also his favorite bow, a Peccatte, a Tourte, or a Hill. (These are the names of the bow makers. Violins are named for the luthier, but among one luthier's output, individual instruments may also have names from other sources, including previous owners.) Heifetz never used fancy bows made for curiosity's sake, especially not the one with pictures carved inside in the frog, made by a jeweler. He did his packing slowly and lovingly, as one takes care of a baby; he cleaned his bow and violin meticulously and methodically in a ritual that never ceased to fascinate me. He never let a speck of dust or rosin stay on his violin or on his bow, and the surface of his rosin was worn evenly instead of having the usual groove.

Heifetz expected of his students total dedication to the master class. He strongly discouraged them from taking courses at the university for fear of interference. He forbade his regular, fulltime students to play in orchestras or in the studios while studying with him; he considered all these activities unproductive for their artistic development. For those who were in financial need, he established two foundations from which, without fanfare, he distributed funds to them. To the best of my knowledge the money in these foundations, one of which was called the Heifetz Fund, came out of his own pocket. Ordinarily he didn't let his students play as soloists in public concerts or even have auditions with conductors until he judged them ready, but sometimes he made exceptions. This rule, restricting his students from playing concerts, made it difficult for him to teach already-established violinists who wanted to go on with their career and work with him at the same time on an irregular basis.

Heifetz was the ultimate judge of a student's readiness to leave the class and enter public life as a concert artist. His permission to leave was the only authentication that someone was an original "Heifetz student," though many who where dismissed or who left the class without his permission claimed to have been one. He never gave diplomas or certificates and rarely even wrote letters of recommendation. Heifetz hated degrees and certificates and considered them unnecessary to succeed as an artist.

Jascha Heifetz was much faulted during his teaching career for not being able to produce stars of his own major stature. His detractors often accused him of being domineering, abrasive, and uncooperative for not helping his students to start careers as soloists. The answer to these accusations is not simple. To be sure, there was only one Jascha Heifetz in this century, and though other violinists may have approached him in stature, none achieved the total of his accomplishments. To blame him for not being able to duplicate himself is preposterous. I'm convinced that Heifetz had no intention of establishing a star factory, and he never claimed to have done so. His intentions, as I could see them, were pure and simple: he wanted to transmit the violin-playing tradition that he had learned from Leopold Auer because he believed in it. If he had wanted a star factory, he would have had to send his pupils to competitions all over the world, honing their skills just for that by drilling the same program over and over again until it sounded competition-perfect. Jascha Heifetz hated competitions and strictly forbade his pupils to enter them. He knew well that real excellence is intangible and rarely decisive in the awarding of first-place prizes. He was also aware that such decisions were often based on political considerations, whether geopolitical or local, or sometimes were simply the resolution of an inside fight or a compromise among members of the jury. To produce "stars" Heifetz would have had to coach instead of educate his students. He would have had to pull strings, hire promoters and publicity agents, do everything to keep the names of the star candidates in the public eye, and perhaps even let the public know who Jascha Heifetz's heir apparent would be. This procedure obviously didn't suit his personality, nor did he deem it necessary for launching an artist's career. He sincerely believed that the public would find those who are really good without much publicity, which he thought, perhaps mistakenly, was the case with his career. He didn't seem to realize that musicians in 1917, when he first appeared in America, needed just as much publicity as they needed in the 1970s and later, and that no sports heroes, writers, movie stars, politicians, and other public figures dependent on name-recognition could have been successful then or today without publicity. Heifetz also refused to join pressure groups or cater to them, groups that could make or break the career of an upstart artist. In fact, Heifetz was so out of touch with artistic interest groups that, as he told me, he was surprised when he gave some chamber music concerts in New York with Piatigorsky and other West Coast musicians during the 1960s and one of the "kingpin makers" sidled up to him to ask with a sneer, "Are you trying to muscle in on our territory?"

Unfortunately Heifetz's enormous talent and overpowering personality also made it very difficult for his students to find their own identities and develop their own distinct musical personalities. Many who realized this danger left his class before fully benefiting from it, while others stayed with him for years and later bitterly resented his influence and their own struggles to deal with it. Yet if someone stood up to him instead of cowering before him, he was willing to give even more, for he enjoyed nothing more than a good challenge, although there were few, if any, who could challenge him on musical grounds. Those who tried did so in such a defensive way that no good could come of it. Much of what Heifetz still could have given went with him to his grave. The greatest trouble is that great personalities are the death of epigones; well-known violinists are usually the product of a little-known master whose personality didn't hang threateningly over their heads and whose basic function was to open doors for them.

It was perhaps a pity that Heifetz didn't establish a violinist artist factory as was expected of him, but he never did the expected. In music and in his private life he was the master of the unexpected, and therein lay his doom and success.

5

Intermezzo

If you can force your heart and nerve and sinew
To serve your turn long after they are gone,
And so hold on when there is nothing in you
Except the Will which says to them: "Hold on!"

RUDYARD KIPLING

Jascha Heifetz limited the subjects one could discuss with him, but his own curiosity about people and places was insatiable. He had at one point smashed his television set with his bamboo cane in a fit of anger and thereafter settled for small talk with his guests as entertainment. If by accident everybody fell silent at the same time, he would usually call out, "It must be twenty minutes to the hour," and it usually was. Then he would demand, "Come on, somebody say something." However, having spent a major part of his life on center stage, he couldn't tolerate anyone's usurping his rightful place at the center of attention for too long. "Make it short—it's too long," he would say when somebody's yarn stretched beyond his endurance. For the stage always belonged to him, and prolonged encroachment on his rights invariably provoked a reaction from him: he feigned indifference, got up to adjust the fire, looked the other way to assure the storyteller that he was only mildly interested, or, with a foreign storyteller, corrected the speaker's accent or pronunciation.

When I had been at USC for about six months, I began to date my future husband, Michael, who was in a doctoral program in musicology at the university. When he first met Heifetz at his beach house and took off on an esoteric aspect of linguistics during the conversation, Heifetz told him that the traffic would be very heavy within a few minutes, and he should leave unless he wanted to spend a lot of time on the road. The "hint" was understood and no offense taken, which worked for the benefit of all three of us. If the raconteur was a woman, Heifetz rarely missed his chance to assure her with a favorite cliché, "Women talk too much." He was also apt to state that he suspected the storyteller of pulling his leg.

Yet during my fifteen years with him we had plenty of occasions to exchange stories from our lives. The best times for storytelling were the rainy nights when we were cooped up in his beach house in Malibu or the quiet summer afternoons in his yard under the beach umbrella. He liked to hear my stories when we were just the two of us; then he felt that he owned me through my stories and didn't have to share anything with anybody else. Thus the stories became our stories because he always reciprocated by telling me what happened on his side of the fence at similar stages of his life. He sometimes accused me of being a liar or of feeding him fish stories when he thought I was stretching the truth a bit. I don't blame him; life in mysterious Indonesia often sounds incredible to Western ears. In fact, rarely could I tell my stories in one piece without being interrupted with a "But when I was your age" or "When I played in that town." Then he would recount his stories in more detail than I could ever have drawn out of him by direct questioning. For Heifetz was a very private person and intimacy was not his way; if pressed for information he usually clammed up or shook off the question with a question of his own or with a cryptic one-liner, "It's for me to know and for you to find out."

Our lives held plenty of similarities as well as plenty of differences; he came from czarist Russia, fleeing the Communist revolution, and I from fermenting Indonesia, which during my childhood became independent from colonial Dutch rule. We both belonged to persecuted races: as a child he lived in a country where Jews were still confined to ghettos and had to ask for permission to stay within the city gates overnight, and I, as a member of the Chinese minority, had to fear for my own life and my family's during the time when Sukarno was ousted by Suharto and about a million Chinese citizens were slaughtered in Indonesia as Communist sympathizers.

Although Heifetz had spent some time concertizing in Indonesia, he didn't know much about its people or their culture and mentality; he stayed in Western-style hotels where service and people were not much different from those in other luxury hotels anywhere in the world. My Indonesian origin made him curious. The following story is a condensation of what I told him during our many years together and of what he told me in return.

INDONESIA IS A LARGE COUNTRY, but most of it is ocean. Its history, much different from history in the modern Western sense, centers around the island of Java. Many of Indonesia's large islands are sparsely inhabited, some smaller ones have no population at all, and some don't even have a name. Its history is shrouded in the ocean mist surrounding the islands, but anthropologists tell us that manlike apes roamed round the island of Java 500 thousand years ago and that their favorite dessert was the brains of their fellow apes. They ate themselves out of existence in a relatively short period of time, to be followed by pygmies who came perhaps from Africa when the Indonesian archipelago was still connected to other parts of the world. Some natives in the jungles of Sumatra and Borneo still show traces of their pygmy ancestry. The pygmies were pushed back in the jungles or eliminated as new races arrived on the islands, among them several tribes of Malay origin. Hindus came in the fourth century; later Arabs from the Middle East brought Islam with them, followed by Chinese from the mainland. The Portuguese, English, and Dutch were latecomers, all looking for a colony to exploit. The ardor of exploitation by the white man, however, was considerably mitigated by the terrible tropical heat and an even worse concentration of humidity that overwhelmed ambition and destroyed the health of the European conquerors.

My native town, Yogyakarta, is situated some 700 kilometers (450 miles) east of the capital, Jakarta, which was called Batavia until Indonesia's independence from Holland in 1949. Our neighborhood has two world-famous monuments, both built during the Hindu invasion: a huge Buddhist temple at Borobudur and a smaller monument at Prambanan. Both monuments are being restored through international efforts.

Most of the major islands were ruled by rajas, sultans, and sunans. The most powerful sultan in Indonesia resides in my native town: he is still a sort of political power in Indonesia, with several thousand subjects in his walled, one-kilometer-square territory within Yogyakarta's city limits. The sultan of Yogya, as we affectionately abbreviate Yogyakarta, is also the titular vice president of Indonesia.

More than one hundred native tribes occupy the islands of Indonesia, and they speak more than two hundred languages and dialects. Since its independence, the country's official religion has been Islam. The government claims that eighty percent of the population is Muslim, but all those whose religion is not acknowledged by the state are automatically counted as Muslim. Although most native tribes of the islands are animists, an officially ignored "religion," some have been nominally converted to Christianity. The majority of the Hindus and Buddhists occupy the islands of Bali and Lombok.

Although Indonesia appears in Indian sources as early as the sixth century B.C., its modern history began with the Dutch occupation early in the seventeenth century. The Dutch were expelled by a long revolutionary process brought about by General Sukarno, and the country's independence was universally recognized on 27 December 1949, three days before my birthday. (Indonesia's official date of independence is generally recognized as 17 August 1945.) To begin the unification of Indonesia, Sukarno imposed a version of the Malay language on the whole nation. Native languages persist, however, and the servants in my family's home in Yogya speak only Javanese, and even that in its lowest dialect. Refined, literary Javanese is spoken in the courts of the sultans and among the highly educated Javanese. Our famous shadow-puppet plays, the Wayang Kulit, used to be narrated in this refined Javanese, but parts of them now are told in modern Indonesian.

During his reign President Sukarno turned against his Western allies and began currying favor with the People's Republic of China. The Indonesian army intervened under the leadership of General Suharto, and Sukarno was deposed; at the same time the nation's Muslim majority seized the opportunity to get rid of the hated Chinese ruling class. In the fall of 1965 about a million Indonesian citizens of Chinese descent, branded as Communists or Communist sympathizers, were massacred by Muslim fanatics. I remember, as a fifteen-year-old, seeing hundred of bodies floating down the river in the center of our town, all of them Chinese. My family is fourth-generation Chinese, and I remember the terror we lived under during those days. Had a jealous neighbor or a disgruntled worker pointed a finger at us to settle an old grudge or to obtain our properties, we would have been massacred. We changed our name from the Chinese Lim to our present Indonesian name and tried to be as inconspicuous as possible.

As a child I spoke only Dutch (which ultimately became a forbidden language in independent Indonesia) because my mother's education was in that language and she preferred to speak it. I also learned street Javanese from the servants in our home before I learned Indonesian, as a means of communication with them. I learned Indonesian only in school, ironically, mostly from Dutch nuns and from my classmates.

My mentioning the word *Javanese* triggered a memory for Heifetz, that most of the people in Indonesian hotels were different from the Chinese he met in the concert halls. From his description I could safely guess that he was mostly exposed to people of Javanese origin who staffed the hotels where he stayed. The educated Javanese are highly refined and courteous, and their attitude toward life often borders on the mystical, while members of the lower classes are submissive, smooth, and subservient in their behavior. In comparison with the Javanese, the Chinese seem boisterous, loud, unrefined, and quite materialistic, though also ambitious and hard working. In the field of music, the Javanese have their traditional gamelan orchestra, consisting of several small and large instruments similar to the marimba or xylophone but made with heavy brass plates, as well as gongs, wooden flutes, a primitive two-stringed instrument, and singers. The gamelan orchestra plays unwritten, ancient melodies in simple harmonies mostly for the traditional dances, while the Chinese lost their musical tradition in Indonesia and are more inclined to cultivate and appreciate Western music. When I explained this to Heifetz, he immediately anointed me a Javanese, which is partially true; I have Javanese ancestors several generations back on my father's side. I must have other mysterious ancestors as well, because Japanese people mistake me for their own at first sight and are surprised when I don't speak their language.

Heifetz and I found that the common denominator in our childhoods was that neither of us had one. In retrospect we both felt that we had been exploited in our early years; he was the breadwinner for his family beginning at the age of seven; as the eldest child in a Chinese family, I had the responsibility of bringing up seven children who came after me as soon as I was old enough and could be trusted with them. Neither of us had a moment of escape from our family even in our teens. Heifetz was constantly supervised by his father or mother, including his practicing and going on concert tours, until he broke away from his family at the age of twenty-one. As a form of escape as a child, he collected and treasured bottle caps and corks, the only things that seemed really his own. Heifetz kept up his passion for collecting things to the end of his life; later he collected stamps with musical subjects; photographs, of which he had several huge albums; and gold coins, whose value amounted to hundreds of thousands of dollars. As a child I had only a single doll which I poured my affections over even in my late teens whenever I could steal a little time away from my duties and from practicing. Neither of us was ever told as a child that we may have been entitled to pursue our own happiness, the way we wanted to be happy. Both of us were told or were made to feel that we existed on earth with the sole purpose of making our parents happy. Strangely enough, we both found this a challenge rather than something to resist, while its consequences showed up later in our adult lives.

As for the differences in our childhoods, Heifetz, being very gifted, at least had adequate teachers from the beginning and began early to study the violin with a superb educator in the person of Auer. My teachers on the violin were amateurs in the beginning, and later when I found quite a good one, I could study with him only for one month of the year. As a prodigy Heifetz led a sheltered, hothouse life and grew up on the concert stage rather than among other children. I had my share of concertizing by the age of seven but never on that scale: I performed mostly to raise money for the missionaries for whom my father built churches and schools. On the other hand, I was lucky enough to go to school with other children. Heifetz never had that precious chance to mix with normal peers in this way; other children always looked up to him, and he was fawned upon by adults. If nothing else, this was enough to handicap him for life. He didn't speak much about his childhood, and when he did it was mostly in short fragments, apropos other events.

What I have pieced together is certainly not complete and not to be found in his official and unofficial biographies, but it is a reflection of what stayed in his mind as significant from his childhood, even in his old age.

I have mentioned that it was difficult to make Heifetz open up and talk about himself; suspicious by nature, he suspected ulterior motives, liked to sidestep direct questions, and often gave nonsensical answers to his interviewers. He opened up mostly unasked, and I had to grab the opportunity when it was the right time for him to be questioned. On one of these occasions I asked him about his birth date, mentioning that there was some doubt about whether he was born in 1899 or 1901. He gave a quizzical smile and an evasive answer, saying that if anybody knew, *he* should know when he was born, but he didn't deny or confirm either date. It would have been useless to point out to him that hardly anybody knows for sure when he was born; we have to believe hearsay evidence, supported by more or less reliable records. Official records at the time of his birth were not regulated as strictly as today by civil authorities, and births were mostly registered by the various churches. I don't know about records in the synagogues when he was born, but given the Jews' tenuous situation in Russia, I doubt that his records survived. Moreover, in the nineteenth century it was quite common to postdate prodigy birth dates for the purpose of commercial exploitation. He could have put the question to rest by showing his birth certificate, but he never did, and I doubt that he had one.

He told me that his father played the violin in the theaters and cafes of Vilna as well as at weddings and funerals and on other social occasions. His father also gave private lessons. Heifetz was proud of his father's reputation as a very methodical teacher, but I don't remember his ever saying that his father was concertmaster of the Vilna symphony orchestra, as has been suggested. And even if he was, the income from a small provincial orchestra probably could not support a family of five. In keeping with Jewish tradition of the time, his father apparently had only a religious education from attending *shul* or synagogue, as secular education then, as even now, was not considered essential among Orthodox Jews. How he learned Russian grammar and arithmetic, I can't imagine. As I heard from other sources, Heifetz's mother had a green grocery street-stall in Vilna to supplement the family income, but his father never participated in this business. According to stories, he preferred to supervise and give advice about how to run it.

Heifetz never mentioned going to any secular school, public or private, for a general education. He never spoke of classmates except for having made friends with a few little girls, learning some Polish from one who spoke only that language. He did talk a great deal, however, about his two sisters who were no match for his male chauvinism and who, in keeping with cultural tradition, were considered vastly inferior to a male child. Having had no schoolmates, friends or enemies, against whom to measure his strength, Jascha grew up without child role models, either in the positive or negative sense of the word. In the parental home Jascha always received special attention; he told me that he could do anything he wanted without interference from his parents as long as he practiced the violin to their satisfaction. He described at one time wanting a rocking horse very badly: his father tied its acquisition to his learning a few pieces on the violin by heart, which he did. Thus was Heifetz brought up in his own cocoon; out in the real world he would become insecure, often abrasive, and sometimes inconsiderate. He grew up in an ugly, competitive adult world rather than in a child's world of playfulness, games, and imagination. Among his most powerful childhood memories was his mother's constant admonishment, "Jaschinka, it was not good enough," when he wanted to play after practicing the violin. He mentioned this to me quite often and apparently could not prevent his mother's nagging from becoming his motto. Nothing was ever good enough. Although his father was given credit for discovering his son's gift and guiding him through the early stages of its development, Heifetz gave me the impression that it was his mother who pushed him to seek the limits of his talent in his quest for perfection. One may wonder if his mother indeed knew whether Jaschinka did or didn't need more practicing or just nagged because it was her nature. Heifetz learned this lesson from his mother so well that he developed the habit of dismissing all, including his own, less-than-perfect jobs with the same statement. He must have told himself "not good enough" millions of times in his life while practicing the violin. It was his immediate reaction and a permanent yardstick not only for the violin but for everything else he had ever done. In his later years, a certain amount of resentment was evident in his voice when he talked about it.

MANY MUSICIANS have a legend to explain how they started out on the long and hard road toward becoming a musical artist. These legends usually begin at the cradle. My mother was an amateur pianist, and often invited other amateur musicians to the house, mostly Dutch players, to play chamber music. According to the legend, when someone played out of tune or made a gross mistake, I tried to stand up in my cradle and cried as loudly as my lungs would let me. After I was able to walk, I gave other indications of my musical talent. My mother gave piano lessons to local children, and as soon as the lesson was over, I toddled over to the piano and picked out, at the correct pitch, some of the tunes I had just heard. As my mother's students played their pieces over and over again, I learned them by heart even before I could speak or write or read. I still play many of these pieces without ever having seen the printed score. I also learned by heart a large number of violin pieces from the Heifetz records that my mother played. This habit worked to my advantage because unwittingly I memorized both violin and piano parts, which eventually came in handy when I began to study these instruments; printed music was hard to obtain in Yogya because we had to import it from Holland. As soon as my mother discovered that I had perfect pitch, my fate was sealed; she decided that I had to become a violinist.

To become a violinist in Yogya, Indonesia, is easier said than done. There was only one violin teacher of some repute in my town, a Mr. Tan, who had had a few violin lessons from someone who claimed to have studied with Leopold Auer's teacher. Other than that, Mr. Tan had learned to play the violin from books. He was a determined man and not without talent, for he became the concertmaster of the local radio string orchestra and also a founder of the Academy of Music of Yogyakarta. At the age of six, I began to take lessons with him; it was fortunate that I spoke Dutch because that was the only language Mr. Tan could speak, along with some Chinese, which I never learned. He taught me how to get around the fingerboard, how to hold the violin and the bow, and other elementary steps toward becoming a violin virtuoso. Mr. Tan was a methodical person, and to support his authority he showed me pictures in his imported Dutch violin method books that were supposed to help me understand what he was talking about. I didn't pay much attention to the books, though, because my anxious mind was always occupied with the frightening prospect of absorbing and practicing the large quantity of musical material that he presented to me at every lesson.

I must have made rapid progress, because Mr. Tan soon ran out of things to teach me. Yet he did me quite a big favor in his bumbling way. For lack of anything else to teach, he made me play all my etudes and exercises in all the positions that my small left-hand fingers could reach and insisted on my always staying in the same position without shifting. Unfortunately he never taught me scales, which he considered a waste of time, nor could he play them himself. He knew little about fingerings, and for lack of guidance I had to figure out ways to finger my pieces. I also learned a great deal from listening to the Heifetz records, especially for shifting from one position into another, and I even experimented with his slides, in which the same finger moves or slides on the string from one part of the violin to another. I heard Heifetz records day and night: my mother put them on when the family awoke and put them on again when she came home, after which we went to bed accompanied by the sounds of still another Heifetz record. I was taken by the intensity of the Heifetz sound and never stopped trying to figure out how he did it. I was about seven when Mr. Tan did me another favor; he took me to the house of someone who had the film of the concert Heifetz gave at Claremont College. What impressed me the most was Heifetz's bowing technique, which I found quite different from Mr. Tan's. From then on my chief ambition was to imitate Heifetz as he played on that film, especially his majestic way of bowing, as best I could remember.

Not long after I saw the Heifetz film I received an invitation from the sunan of a neighboring town, Solo, to play the violin in the Kraton, as we called his palace in Indonesian, at a party for his birthday. Sunans rank below sultans, and this one had a somewhat smaller independent state than the sultan of Yogya's, but he had a reputation for cultural aspiration which he fulfilled with musical performances in both Western and Far Eastern tonalities. I heard that he had invited Western guests to this party, and perhaps he wanted to show off with an Indonesian prodigy. It was indeed strange that the sunan wanted to hear Western music at his birthday party; the usual fare at such occasions was the traditional gamelan music accompanying Javanese historic dances, followed by the Wayang, the shadow play, which would last all night.

At the party I played, among other pieces, Charles de Bériot's *Scène de ballet*, a technically quite difficult piece for a seven year old. My mother accompanied me at the piano, and I was told I did very well. This was my first time in the court of a potentate, and I can still recall the details. I was led by my mother through a grand, seemingly endless hallway filled with ornately carved and gilded teak furniture. Mirrors in golden frames glittered everywhere in a scene so beautiful to behold that I had difficulty keeping my feet moving. My mother dragged me along, and servants and courtiers accompanied us in their tight gold and silk outfits, but I noticed that they were barefoot, as was everyone who worked in the palace. We entered a huge hall, with women and children sitting by themselves on one side dressed in their fancy court costumes; male guests sat on the opposite side, as in a village church, but mostly in their street clothing. I thought some of them could have been the sunan's Western guests. Later I was told that all those women and children were the wives and the offspring of the sunan. As a Muslim ruler he could have as many wives as he wanted, but an ordinary Muslim male was entitled to only four wives. The Koran prescribed that all wives should have equal privileges; the theory was that with more than four wives an ordinary man would have difficulty providing equal opportunity. I don't remember what we ate at the party. There were mountains of food, but I was too busy admiring those marvelous people and their fantastic, ornate costumes.

A week after the birthday party a messenger came to our house from the sunan, bringing His Majesty's present for my performance. It was a full-size violin and bow in a case. I don't know what became of that violin but only that it wasn't a very good one. We attached neither sentimental nor snob value to such gifts, and my mother perhaps sold it or exchanged it when she bought a better one for me.

My mother ran my life with complete and unquestionable authority; she never asked whether I wanted to play a recital of her choosing, and I had to play even if I felt sick or didn't feel like playing at all. She bought my dresses; it never occurred to her to ask my participation in the choice or whether I liked them. She never let me get out of her or a supervisor's sight beyond shouting distance. I could never play with other children because I always had to practice or, later, supervise my seven younger brothers and sisters in their practicing. To say no to my parents was unthinkable, and they planted in my mind that God's sole purpose in creating me was that I should please them by fulfilling even their most secret wishes. I never got praise from them, only criticism that often was merely destructive, and my mother objected to everything I planned to

My mother photographed me playing the violin and preparing for my piano lesson at age ten in Indonesia. Behind me in the violin photo is a painting of a famous volcano, Merapi, which still erupts above the terraced rice fields from time to time.

do on my own. Things didn't change much as I grew older, and I was expected to be a good little girl even when I was already sixteen. I promised myself never to marry a person as tyrannical and critical as my parents were and not even to work for one. Heifetz never thought of himself as a tyrant, nor as a critical person. He always said that "constructive criticism is healthy."

My mother dragged me along to play concerts all over the island of Java, mostly for the benefit of the Dutch missionaries. By the time I was eight years old I had to take classical ballet to improve my posture, and at seventeen I even performed in a Javanese classical dance. For months I had to practice the positions for my fingers, toes, legs, and body in order to perform the sinuous motions that the dance required. My body must have had secret resources to survive all these activities, because I tended to be a sickly, anemic child, and I fainted in church on Sundays because of the fast required before receiving Communion. I always had a sore throat, I presume from the combination of heat, humidity, and the all-pervading dust, which never settled in our town except during the rainy season when it was replaced by knee-deep mud.

Our house was open on all sides to let air from the distant ocean percolate through it, but its openness also gave free reign to mosquitoes and innumerable bugs and insects which invaded and pestered us without relief. Lizards ran on the ceiling over our heads, sometimes falling on us or into our plates as we ate our meals. At night my father closed the doors and windows and fumigated the whole house with DDT to exterminate the day's accumulation of pests and to make sleep possible. I suspect that the DDT had something to do with my permanently sore throat, my fainting spells, and perhaps even my mother's death from leukemia at a relatively early age. In case of illness, the traditional medicine was the Javanese *kerik*, which our servants administered to us. It consisted of rubbing our backs just under the neck with a copper penny until the skin turned copper red. It was supposed to open up the pores of the skin and let the bad air escape from the body and the bad spirits with it. Our backs looked whip-welted after such a treatment, but this would never show because the nuns in school required that our clothes completely cover our bodies, including our arms, tropical heat notwithstanding.

Mr. Tan taught me for only five years. At the end he threw up his hands and said, "I can't teach you anything any more," but he found me a teacher some 450 miles away in Jakarta. His name was Adidharma, and he had studied the violin with Louis Persinger at the Juilliard School of Music in New York. At the time we became acquainted, he was the con-

Costumed as the hero Arjuna in a famous Javanese epic folk tale, I prepared to dance, accompanied by Javanese gamelan music. I was seventeen years old.

ductor of the Jakarta Symphony Orchestra. Adidharma was an excellent violinist, a good musician, and a patient pedagogue. Summer after summer, starting when I was eleven, my mother took me to Jakarta and left me for my month of summer vacation in my grandparents' home under the care of an unmarried uncle who still lived with them. I took lessons every other day from Adidharma. The only trouble was that my grandparents lived at one end of the town and Adidharma at the other; to get me there, my uncle drove me to my lessons. The trip took hours in the traffic, heat, and humidity. My uncle patiently waited for the three to four hours until my lesson was over; apparently he had plenty of time—the only thing most Indonesians have. I spent the rest of the day practicing. There was no air conditioning, and today I wonder what kept me going.

Adidharma made me learn the standard concerto repertory, some sonatas, and a number of small pieces. He didn't work much on small details and points of interpretation, but gave me a great deal of technical guidance and concentrated on style. Upon returning to Yogya I was supposed to practice for eleven months what I had learned in Jakarta in one month. In order to help me a bit, my mother bought or borrowed many of Heifetz's recordings and some other violinists' recordings of the pieces I was working on, but I always ended up listening only to Heifetz's. After a while, without ever seeing a live Heifetz performance, I was able to recognize the fingerings he used and figured out how he did his slides and how he shaped a phrase without crossing strings. I imitated everything I could, which was not necessarily good for me, but I could have done worse. When I turned sixteen, a Russian cellist, Nikolai Varvolomieff, came to town as a visiting professor, stayed for a while, and gave me some pointers in musical interpretation.

Without a teacher for eleven months of the year, I found that practicing the violin lost its challenge, and I soon turned to my other love, the piano. My first teacher on that instrument was my mother, but she quickly recognized that I needed something more than she was able to offer. I was practicing the piano every free minute I had, even while doing my homework. I would prop up my schoolbooks on the music stand and read them while my hands raced up and down the keyboard in scales and exercises. Eventually I could play whole pieces by heart while studying. I overheard my mother telling my siblings not to interrupt me when I was practicing either the piano or violin, my only activities that were protected in this way.

My mother saw how much I loved the piano, but she considered the piano unfair competition for her determination to make me a violinist.

Her solution was to let me take lessons from professional teachers only when I promised her I would not allow myself the luxury of piano playing before I had practiced the violin at least two hours every day. There were excellent piano teachers in Yogya, and some taught at the Academy of Music as exchange teachers from Australia, England, Holland, Germany, and even from the U.S.A. All my piano teachers were foreigners and from them I acquired a solid, basic technique. The unexpected benefit of my piano playing was that I was now able to accompany my violin pieces; I recorded the accompaniment, then turned up the volume and played the violin to it.

One may ask why there were so few professional violinists in Indonesia. Heifetz himself supplied the answer when he told me of an adventure he had while on tour in my country. He played several recitals in Jakarta, and just before the last one, the Strad which he used at that time came apart. The glues used in more temperate climates couldn't stand up to the heat and humidity of the tropics. While his violin was being put together, he played the concert on a borrowed violin. Nobody seemed to notice that he was not playing his Strad, but after the concert a Chinese gentleman came to his dressing room and wished to see his famous Strad. Heifetz always liked to play games, so he closed the door, showed the gentleman his borrowed violin, and told him what had happened, under the condition that he wouldn't tell anyone that he hadn't played the Strad that night. The Chinese gentleman, however, didn't let it go at that. He asked Heifetz why he played the Mozart sonata with an Andante movement taken from a different sonata. Heifetz couldn't stop laughing when he told me this story because, he said, he did this trick all over the world and was never called on it anywhere else. "It had to be in the jungles of Indonesia that I was caught," he said. He explained to the gentleman that he simply didn't like the original Andante and substituted another that he liked better. As for his violin coming apart, I could only confirm what he said because my violin also came apart several times and had to be glued together with a special glue that was supposed to withstand the climate. Pianos, however, do not fall apart that easily, though they need to be tuned more often in the tropics than in temperate zones. To counter such hazards as termites, my mother always stood the legs of our pianos in bowls of water and injected pesticide into every hole and opening she could find. True, we still had lots of bugs to eat the felt off the hammers and the damper, and the action often got sticky from the humidity, but constant use kept the bugs away and the action in tolerable operation.

My mother tried to keep ahead of piano tuners and repairmen by learning piano tuning and maintenance from Dutch books. Eventually she bought some used pianos, mostly from the nuns or priests who needed money, trained some natives in piano repair, and made extra money by selling reconditioned pianos. With work progressing on several pianos at the same time, our large living room as well as other rooms in the house often looked rather like a piano sales and maintenance workshop. I also became interested in the craft and learned some basics in tuning and maintenance.

THUS WE COMPARED OUR STORIES, but my parents' unfortunate efforts to control my life were perhaps no match for the struggles Heifetz endured in childhood. His problems were magnified by his much larger talent and his early international fame. His parents' work soon brought the much-desired result, and Jascha was already a famous prodigy at the age of six, first in the town of Vilna, then in the whole province. I once talked to an elderly gentleman, a contemporary of Heifetz, who lived in Vilna when Heifetz was a child. He vividly described boy Heifetz striding through town in a long, flowing cape, his violin in one hand and his father's hand in the other. Street urchins stood aside, pointing at him, their mouths agape. News travels fast in little towns, and even the street urchins knew who Jascha was. One time Leopold Auer, Imperial Concertmaster of the St. Petersburg Symphony Orchestra and teacher of a class of violin prodigies, came to town from St. Petersburg to visit friends. He let himself be persuaded to listen to Jascha's playing, although he was loath to listen to another prodigy. Auer was so taken by the boy's music making that he immediately invited the child and his family to move to St. Petersburg and offered Jascha enrollment in his class.

A few months later father and son boarded the train to St. Petersburg in search of their fortune. It is beyond imagination what this move meant to the child. St. Petersburg was considered the Venice of the North, built on the banks of the Neva River. Its canals draining the surrounding marshes served as waterways, while its palaces, squares, and beautiful public buildings rose at the czar's command from the wetlands at the shores of the Neva River. I saw the city only through Heifetz's eyes, aided by a large painting in his house in Beverly Hills depicting the Neva River and some of the famous palaces he so often described. Whenever we looked at this painting, I could feel emotions swelling up in his heart and memories crowding his mind as he related to me in great detail the names of the buildings and the directions where the streets and broad avenues led. He also showed me the approximate place where the Imperial School of Music used to be.

Upon their arrival in St. Petersburg, father and son faced the obstacle of registering in the Imperial School of Music. They reported to Auer's office, but the old master seemed to have forgotten his promise and either had no time to take care of the newcomers who had failed to warn him of their arrival, or perhaps he didn't even want to see them. In his book, *Violin Playing As I Teach It,* Auer explains that knowing the difficult life that would follow, he was leery of accepting more prodigies at the time that father Heifetz and son showed up in his office. Perhaps he also realized the problems he was going to have with the two Jews from Vilna because of the political climate and the rigid city regulations designed to prevent the influx of strangers, especially Jews, to the capital city of all Russians. It took some persistent pleading to have an older Auer student come out and give Jascha an audition. At any rate Auer at that time already had a class full of young geniuses and was understandably reluctant to take on one more. Jascha had to study for a while with an assistant, but all that Heifetz mentioned about this event was that admission was difficult and that he couldn't even study with Auer for one semester. Among his strongest memories from these moments was that he felt great anxiety possessing his father while they went through the process of being accepted in Auer's school.

Here we must remember that at the time Heifetz was a student in the Imperial City, Jews were permitted to live officially only in the ghetto, perhaps just officially, for I have my doubts that Leopold Auer, a Hungarian Jew and the Imperial Concertmaster, ever had to live in the ghetto. The first challenge Auer had with the newcomers was that, according to city regulations, nonresident Jews were supposed to be out of town before sunset when the city gates were closed. Apparently Alexander Glazunov, the head of the conservatory, stepped in and intervened with the mayor of the city, presumably after having heard about Jascha's playing, so that for the moment father and son were permitted to stay inside the gates overnight.

A further issue was Jascha's age: he was too young for admission to the conservatory. According to the story that Heifetz told me, the solution suggested by Auer was to enroll only his father at the conservatory, while actually Jascha was attending the classes. Since he wasn't enrolled in the school, Jascha had no legal status and therefore no right to stay in the city. Apparently only his father, the registered student, was granted residency, and his son officially wasn't even there. Heifetz often talked about his fright when city controllers came to his father's apartment in St. Petersburg to check the number of residents living there. Whenever they heard a knock at the door, his father sent Jascha to hide somewhere in the apartment, fearing that his son would be thrown out of the city as an illegal resident.

Little Jascha was even more frightened when his father had to go back to Vilna to wind up his business there and to make arrangements to move his family to St. Petersburg. Incredible as it may sound, Heifetz told me that he was left alone in the apartment for days, and not only once; even as an old man he still remembered the fear he had there without his father. This story also suggests that he could have already been nine rather than the official seven years of age when he first moved to St. Petersburg, since leaving a seven-year-old child alone in an apartment is even more unimaginable. Eventually the rest of the family, mother and two daughters, also moved to St. Petersburg. I suspect that for a while they must have survived on the proceeds of what they had sold back home, but they also received some support from their friends in Vilna who had faith in Jascha's talent and future. When I once asked him how they made a living in such a strange and anti-Semitic place as St. Petersburg, Heifetz replied, "I took care of my whole family since I was seven years of age, and I am proud of it."

Heifetz indeed took very good care of his family, but at the price of his childhood. He suffered from the effects, knowingly or unknowingly, for the rest of his life. So painful was the price he paid that as a teacher he didn't like even to hear of child prodigies. He didn't mean that there is something wrong with them; he knew from his own experience that parents would be responsible for ruining the life of a precocious child as his parents had ruined his. He rarely accepted prodigies in his class because, as he said, "I would have to deal with the child's parents." During the time I was with him, there was only one audition with a child whose parents considered their son a prodigy. They were Russians, and their secret desire was that their boy should take private lessons with Heifetz. After the audition Heifetz told me that the boy had potential and with proper guidance could develop into a good violinist and become a sensitive musician. Despite his misgivings against prodigies, Heifetz accepted the child into his class. A few days later a letter arrived, written by the boy's father. Heifetz loved to examine every detail of what he read, especially when it was handwritten, so he carefully considered the format of the envelope, the handwriting, and everything else about its appearance before he even opened it. However, as soon as he started reading it, he told me that there was something very wrong with these people: his name was misspelled on the envelope and in the letter. "For a Russian," he said, "the least [the father] should know is how to spell my name." I knew already that the "prodigy" was a lost cause. In the letter the father requested private lessons with Heifetz, which of course he didn't grant. The boy never showed up for the master class. We can only wonder whether Heifetz would have granted private lessons had his name been spelled correctly.

After the Heifetz family moved to St. Petersburg, Jascha seems to have been his parents' sole occupation, for he never mentioned that his father or mother did anything other than supervise his practicing and take him to school. Jascha apparently took very good care of the financial aspects of their life, because he told me that he had two nannies, one French, one German, who even accompanied the family to a summer resort abroad where Auer was spending his vacation. Auer not only served as Jascha's violin master but also introduced the Heifetz family to the ways of the world, in which they were totally inexperienced. In this artificial atmosphere Jascha became a petulant, pampered, headstrong child, spoiled by success and by the power he had over his parents in his role as breadwinner. Jascha was lucky, though, to find in Auer not only a role model to emulate at least in matters of art and proper social behavior, but also a man who modeled the discipline of which the young artist was so much in need. Auer was a man of the world who could teach him to navigate the maze of backstage intrigues. Auer was the role model for whom he looked in vain in the naive and often boisterous father whom he loved and respected but found difficult to admire. Obviously Jascha's parents' didn't know how to handle him, and their permissiveness caused a tremendous feeling of insecurity in Heifetz as an adult. He couldn't accept contradiction, neither to his will nor to his ideas or comments, and it was hard for him to tolerate a contrary opinion without feeling that the whole world around him was falling apart. If I happened to disagree with him in any matter, he interpreted it as a personal rejection. I often had difficulty convincing him that one could love him despite a difference of opinion.

Heifetz never spoke to me of his fellow students in the Auer class though I have seen several pictures showing him in the company of his classmates. He always spoke about Professor Auer with great reverence, not so much of the artist but rather of the highly respected teacher and mentor to whom he attributed his artistic development. From the way he spoke of Auer, I felt that he was closer to him than to his parents, and

Auer's influence must have been a welcome change from the carping "not good enough" of Heifetz's mother. Having spent his formative years with Auer meant a great deal more to Heifetz than just learning the art of playing the violin. He also acquired from his master what he liked to call the "get up," meaning all the attributes needed by a concertizing artist, from stage presence to the collecting of fees. Although he never said so, I'm quite sure that most of Heifetz's lectures on extramusical subjects in his own master classes were in one way or another influenced by Leopold Auer.

I HAD NO SUCH GUIDING LIGHT in my early years as Heifetz had. Not only was I expected to be an example and disciplinarian to my brothers and sisters, but I also incurred the blame and sometimes even physical punishment if they got into mischief. This wasn't exceptional in a Chinese family where the eldest child carries the most respect among children and with it most of the responsibility in running family life.

My family wasn't rich, but by Indonesian standards we were comfortable. My father came from a large, very poor family. His parents were, I think, pagans of the Chinese-ancestry-worshipping variety. My father was picked up by the Dutch Jesuit missionaries as a talented lad and a promising convert. They educated him free of charge from high school to college, and when he graduated as a civil engineer from the Jesuit College of Jakarta, he got his first job from the missionaries. In gratitude for his education he promised himself never to work for anyone else but the missionaries. He worked on a one-percent commission, and when he retired at the age of seventy, he reaped the harvest of the just: he had nine children, a large, unmarketable house, and not a penny to his name.

My mother came from a "good" family from the island of Sumatra, which in Indonesian parlance only meant that her father had a roof over his store and a little money to send his daughter to a missionary boarding school in Jakarta. I learned from the nuns who had taught my mother that she met my father at a church affair, and when they were married they had literally nothing. When I was born, we lived in a vacant room in hospital in Yogya run by the nuns of the Boromeus Order. When the second child was born we moved to a vacant classroom in a Catholic high school in our town. Eventually my father was able to acquire a run-down house with his one-percent commissions. He remodeled it and built a high brick fence around it with barbed wire on top to keep thieves and friendly borrowers out of the building materiel that he had to store for his projects. A pack of semi-wild dogs guarded our property; I was mortally afraid of them and rarely ventured into our backyard other than to chase down a chicken for our dinner. It also was my lot as the oldest child to kill the chicken, for none of my brothers could stomach it, and somebody had to do the job if we wanted to eat. I would order one of my brothers to hold the chicken while I cut its head off. He would turn his head away, sometimes even throwing up after the operation.

My mother was a born organizer and kept my father's building materiel in manageable order. She knew exactly how many nails and sacks of cement were needed for a particular phase of a job and doled them out with precision every day. One of my chores was to help her at the crack of dawn counting out these small items and putting them into different sacks. Surplus materiel had a tendency to disappear at the end of the day, and the loss also came out of the one-percent commission. My mother was a simple person; she bought herself one or two cheap dresses once a year and was happy with them. Yet she also had three servants and a driver, all needed because beside our own large family and the inevitable unannounced guests at meal times, she had to feed the army of my father's workers as part of their meager pay. My father hired them for about twenty-five cents a day, but feeding them and letting them sleep in a shed during the week was also part of the deal. My mother gave the workers an occasional present to keep them happy. The workers' social security for old age depended on the number of children they had sired; accordingly, they worked at it quite industriously when they went home for the weekend.

Though we were Catholics, went to Catholic schools, attended Mass every Sunday, and received the priest and nuns at our home almost weekly, all this religious influence couldn't eradicate from our minds the ancient Chinese-Javanese traditions and superstitions. Being a Catholic only meant that we belonged to a certain group whose religious beliefs were somewhat different from those of other Christians and quite different from the Muslims and from the superstitions of the pagan village people. We went through the observances our religion required and in return expected jobs from the missionaries. The nuns taught us to go to Mass on Sundays, observe Fridays as fast days, and diligently warned us that having sex outside of marriage is a mortal sin. We had a solid foundation in the power of prayers, but I don't think any of us gleaned more than these few tenets from our religious classes. I don't remember the basic Bible stories; perhaps they were never taught to us, or perhaps I have forgotten them, possibly because they were alien to our cultural concepts.

Beliefs in the "real" spirit world were handed down to us by our native servants, workers, relatives, and friends, and we were indoctrinated even by people on the street and by shopkeepers. Beliefs in monsters and spirits both good and bad coexisted as peacefully in our minds as monsters and devils lived side by side with saints, bishops, popes, and the Virgin with her Child in the carvings on the walls of medieval Christian cathedrals. Our life was permeated with black and white magic—black for negative, evil causes; white for the good, the positive—and full of spirits and taboos as old as the people of the Indonesian islands. This common belief in the spirit world held together the people of the islands regardless of their nominal religions or of their tribal divisions, more than has any political system past or present.

The measure of Western education one had received from the missionaries offered no protection against the power of magic either. My father eventually bought a larger, rundown house and rebuilt it for his large family from the savings that took him about eighteen years to accumulate. Soon after the house was finished, a series of accidents happened at a certain door. Every time a female member of the household passed over that threshold, she would stumble and have to hold onto the door to keep herself upright. My sister had sprained an ankle over that spot and my aunt broke a hip, but when one Javanese servant broke a leg there, all our servants panicked. They demanded that my father let them call a dukun for consultation. Dukuns are sort of magicians, some practicing white, others black magic, and you call for one service or the other according to your needs. Since we had no harmful intentions against anybody, my father reluctantly permitted the servant to call for a dukun who practiced white magic.

The dukun, a small, wizened, dark man with a few whiskers hanging from his chin for a beard, examined the ominous spot and declared without hesitation in a high-pitched, singing voice that something evil was buried under the threshold of that door, and it should be dug up immediately. My father had just installed beautiful glazed tiles there and was reluctant to break them, but eventually it became evident that he was no match for all the women in the house. When the tiles were broken up and a shallow hole dug at the spot pointed out by the dukun, sure enough, two clay figurines of women were found exactly where the women stumbled. The dukun had his explanation ready: some time ago there had been a Chinese cemetery where our house stood now, and someone had buried these clay statuettes there with evil intentions toward someone unknown to us. This unknown person also attached a strong curse to the figurines. Because we rebuilt and fixed that rundown house there and the figurines could no longer find the original object of the curse, they came to haunt us as innocent substitutes. To get rid of the curse, we had to bury the figurines in the present Chinese cemetery accompanied by the proper ceremonies. The dukun just happened to know how to perform such ceremonies and was willing to do so for a small fee, of course, but with guarantees as to its efficacy. My father had no choice but to pay up. We owed it to the dukun that the charm worked. During the burial ceremony for these figurines they shed tears, and from then on, the spirits left us alone. There were no more accidents over that spot.

When I told Heifetz this story, he suspected that the dukun made money twice on those figurines; once from us, the second time when he sold them to souvenir-hunting tourists. Then he laughed and said, "How did I get mixed up with this jungle girl?" Upon reflecting on my story, a few minutes later he suspected that I invented the whole thing to amuse him.

The power of superstition took on a more serious aspect when my mother became ill with leukemia. Since her treatment with Western medicine proved hopeless, my father was again pressured by relatives and friends to resort to traditional medicine and had to call for a medicine dukun. The medicine dukun was tall, fat, and a bit pompous, as befitted a man of authority and prosperity. First he walked around the house, inside and outside, appraising its position and its openings in relation to the four corners of the earth. After a thorough survey he berated my father, screaming at him at the top of his lungs that the layout of the house was altogether wrong because all windows and doors were facing in the wrong directions. The house was built with utter disregard for the principles of Feng Shui, he said, and in its present state permitted evil spirits to enter it but gave them no openings through which to leave the house, even in the unlikely event they wished to do so. Further, the directions from which the good spirits could enter were all blocked by bare walls without openings, and we gave them no opportunity to come in through properly placed windows and doors. As a matter of fact, the dukun screamed even louder, the house was built with such crass ignorance of tradition and proper building principles that every single door and window had to be walled up and new ones cut in the appropriate places. The dukun then marked the places on the walls where the new openings should be cut.

My father, having been educated in a Jesuit school, was totally ignorant of the principles of Feng Shui, and I learned only recently what these principles mean. Feng Shui refers to the science of wind and water, and since the Chinese believe these two forces have a basic influence on human life, Feng Shui came to signify a certain mystical power that influences man's relation to man, man's relation to Nature, and man's relation to the forces of Heaven and Earth. If this is all very confusing, one must note that even real Feng Shui experts find it difficult. Much study of the surroundings is required before the expert can establish the energy lines of Nature, Heaven, and Earth in relation to the movements of the stars and the planets over a certain spot and recommend the proper positioning not only of a house and its openings but of its furniture as well. I don't know how much real Feng Shui our dukun knew, but he certainly was nimble at translating his knowledge into the more commonly understood concepts of superstition.

An engineer and building contractor, my father was a proud and critical man who never tolerated criticism and rarely praised anyone, but this time he knew that if he didn't concede defeat, my mother's eventual death would be upon his soul and head. Didn't the dukun make it evident to all relatives, neighbors, and friends that my father was a wayward Chinese who had forgotten the correct traditions? My father swallowed his pride and had the whole house redone according to the dukun's specifications. To our great sadness, my mother died anyway in January of 1974, but my father knew that he could not be blamed for it.

The missionaries wisely closed their eyes to such backsliding and perhaps weren't even in complete disagreement with it all, for doesn't exorcism exist in the church, too? Who really knows how the dukun's prescriptions compare with incense and holy water? At any rate, the missionaries couldn't do much about dukuns and their black and white magic even if they wanted to.

When I was about eighteen, I fell madly in love with the boy next door. However, there was no chance of private meetings between the two of us. I would go to the five-o'clock Mass in the morning, mainly because the church was the only place my parents would let me go alone. When my mother found out that the boy was also attending the same Mass and suspected that we stole a few glances at each other, she cut off my visits to the church. The boy tried to visit me in our home, but my parents managed to turn tropical heat into wintry frost as soon as he appeared. My brothers openly made him the butt of their jokes, and nothing cools off a man's ardor faster than being made ridiculous.

It was around that time that through a missionary nun I received a violin scholarship offer from a women's college in Buffalo. I had received several scholarship offers before from various schools in Holland, England, and Germany, all of them through my piano teachers, but my parents had turned them down because they considered me too young. This last one, however, seemed to be a godsend, mainly because of their objection to my apparent choice of a future husband. However, I couldn't get an exit permit from the Indonesian government, and no citizen could leave the country without one. Perhaps the fact that I was the only active and well-known violinist in Indonesia made the bureaucrats unwilling to let me go. I was considered a national asset which should not be allowed to leave the country.

While I was waiting for my exit permit, my grandfather became ill and needed twenty-four-hour care. When I was sixteen my paternal grandparents had come to live with us because my grandmother had been left paralyzed by a stroke. Now I took it upon myself to take care of my grandfather during his last days, a terrible job for a teenager without nursing experience. It lasted for about six months. My grandfather was helpless, and I had to feed, clean, change, and bathe him in his bed. I made my task bearable by convincing myself that if I endured this hardship, as a reward I would get my exit permit. The day before he died, he suddenly regained consciousness, sat up without help in his bed, and asked me for the date in Javanese. When I told him the date according to the Western calendar, he became irritated and asked for it by the Javanese lunar calendar. When I told him, he sank back on his pillow and said that the next day he would die. He requested strong coffee, which he was forbidden to have. That evening grandfather became unconscious and was taken to the hospital.

The next day I happened to be at home for a few hours to do my homework when I smelled a strong scent of incense coming from under my bed. My father came in a few minutes later, and just by looking at his face I could tell that grandfather was dead. My father, too, smelled the incense in my room, and that scared him a bit. As soon as the servants heard about the smell they made us call a dukun again, this one versed in matters of the hereafter. He declared that my grandfather's spirit was still lingering in my room because I was the last one to take care of him; he wouldn't let go of me unless we performed the proper ceremonies to put his spirit to rest. Then he prescribed the proper rituals: the night of the first full moon following my grandfather's death, my father had to go around the house accompanied by a female member of the household, both totally naked, burn incense in every room, and put some rice and water in the corners to support my grandfather in his journey through

With Governor Ali Sadikin of Jakarta after my concert with the Jakarta Symphony Orchestra in 1969 just before I left Indonesia.

the spirit world. My father had no choice again but to agree. My mother was still alive at that time, but she refused to participate in the ceremony. A Javanese servant was elected to fill her place, but to make allowances for Western hangups and Christian decency, she followed my father a room behind as they performed the prescribed ceremony. I have to admit the magic worked again and the incense smell disappeared. In 1969, soon after my grandfather's death, I was invited to Jakarta to play the Henryk Wieniawski Violin Concerto in D minor with the Jakarta Symphony Orchestra in the presence of the governor of the city, Ali Sadikin. After the concert he handed me an envelope with a one-hundred-dollar bill in it. This was the first real money I had ever made with music. My concerts before were usually rewarded with gifts of silver trays, batik material, dresses, and other forgettable memorabilia. I stopped to speculate whether my grandfather's spirit or other, more earthly powers were at work, but the fact is that the next day I received my exit permit from the government of Indonesia.

6

Preludium and Fugue

If you can dream—and not make dreams your master;
If you can think—and not make thoughts your aim

RUDYARD KIPLING

*H*eifetz described his own struggle for independence from his parents as a quiet one that grew in intensity over many years. Before he reached the legal age of twenty-one, he lived under the constant supervision of either his father or mother and sometimes both, during concert tours and at home as well. I gathered from what he told me that his parents were simple, unsophisticated people who never quite overcame their provincial roots. They held onto their son, looking to him as their sole source of income and financial security. His father, an inveterate meddler, coached Jascha ceaselessly, continuing to tell him how to play the violin even when he had already become a world-famous artist. To his credit Heifetz tolerated this meddling, which wasn't easy for him; his father would be telling him what to do even in his dressing room just before he went onstage. He tried not to become impatient with his father, uttering a mere "Yes, father" even in nervous moments as he prepared for an appearance. He knew that vicariously the old man had more stage fright than he did.

His mother was more business-minded than his father. She held the purse strings tightly and made sure that her son received proper compensation from his managers. She even skillfully broke up Heifetz's first, hastily agreed-upon American contract when she discovered the difference between the value of money and living standards in St. Petersburg and in New York. She also had the brains to seek advice when she felt that her son's financial affairs went over her head.

Heifetz had little to do with money while his mother managed their finances, and he even had to ask for cash for his personal needs. His mother never got used to the way money was made and spent in artistic circles and often became upset when she felt that her son was wasting hard-earned money. To illustrate, Heifetz once told me his famous London caviar story. He and his mother were staying in a suite in a London hotel during his concerts there, and he would invite friends and new acquaintances to their suite after concerts for a drink and refreshments. On one such occasion they had an icebox stocked with vodka and a jar full of caviar with a ridiculously low price tag on it. Heifetz encouraged his guests to eat as much as they wanted, saying that he never in his life had eaten such good caviar at such a low price. When the day of reckoning came in the form of the hotel bill, there was an enormous charge for the caviar, and his mother was furious. She protested, and the caviar jar was brought down from their suite; the concierge carefully measured the missing amount and then pointed at the price. The ridiculous price was not for the whole jar, it was "p.p." as two small letters in the corner of the tag indicated. The concierge further explained that "p.p." stood for "per portion," the size of which was entirely up to the hotel to determine. Heifetz learned his lesson. The incident only confirmed what he already knew: that everything that sounds too good to be true should be approached with caution. Half a century later he still laughed at his mother's astonishment and aggravation over wasting so much money on people whom she considered completely useless strangers.

Heifetz, as he matured, increasingly felt the strain of his parents' vigilance. They conveniently didn't realize when the time arrived that their son was a little boy no more. His father still oversaw his practicing and incessantly advised him on how to play the violin. Heifetz could take only so much of this and eventually put his foot down, telling his father that he had decided to practice alone. Heifetz told me that his father was very hurt; the old man must have thought of himself as indispensable to his son's success. Though his parents should have seen the incident as the first sign of an impending break, they refused even to think of it. Tension between son and parents built up for some time, and once Heifetz told me with emotion quivering in his voice that he could hardly wait for the day of his independence at the age of twenty-one. He had great respect for tradition, law, and order, and didn't want to break away from his parents sooner than was generally considered proper, although he could have done so earlier without any difficulty. On his twenty-first birthday he surprised his parents by announcing that from that day on he would take care of himself and his finances and that he already had an apartment ready to move into. The fact that Heifetz prepared his move in great secrecy, acquiring an apartment with the help of a few of his friends but without his parents' getting wind of it, must have hurt them even more. There were tears, recriminations, scenes, and accusations, but none of these could make him change his mind about his independence. His mother was even more hurt when Heifetz respectfully told her that if she wanted to visit him, she should call first. The break didn't mean that Heifetz had abandoned his family; he supported all of them as long as they needed it and visited them regularly.

ONE EVENING after Heifetz had told me his story, he began to wonder aloud about my love life and wanted to know the continuation of my story. Looking at me sideways and feigning as little interest as possible, he asked, "But how did your love affair turn out?" He remembered the boy next door and how we met only in the church, Renaissance style.

"Not much happened worth talking about," I said lightly. Then I told him that once I sneaked out of the house for a motorcycle ride. Holding the boy tightly from behind was as close as I ever got to him. For a while I considered eloping with him, but that surely would have been the death of me. I heard later that he became a Bible-toting, religious maniac, reading the Bible to people on the street and even to the customers in his trucking business. He surely would have forced me to do the same, perhaps even to drive his trucks, all unimaginable. Once, after he heard that I had played a concert in Buffalo, he wrote me a letter telling me to ask for his permission if I had plans to give a concert again.

Heifetz laughed, not quite believing what I had just said. "He must have felt pretty sure of himself. But how did you get to Buffalo?"

I continued my story. The break from my family began with less drama than Heifetz's had, but it took a longer and more circuitous route. By accident or perhaps by design, my maternal grandparents planned to go to Holland at exactly the same time that I was supposed to leave for Buffalo, and I was supposed to accompany them. My grandmother had to have a cataract operation, and she picked Holland as the best place to have it done. One of her sons, my mother's brother, married to a Dutch woman, lived in Holland, and his place in Amsterdam was the goal of our journey. These grandparents had become quite prosperous by loan sharking and by doing some other business the nature of which I was not told. As I understood, Grandpa was even in trouble with the law a few times and escaped jail only by paying heavy bribes. They moved from Sumatra to Jakarta and acquired a huge house, and as often happens in the Far East, most of their children and their families moved in with them, all living under the same roof. There was nothing more natural in my parents' opinion than for me to travel with my grandparents as far as Holland and take off from there alone for the U.S.A.

While I was waiting for my exit permit, my father had his own ideas about how to prepare me for the culture shock of living in America. Every evening he gave me a thimbleful of Scotch whiskey, alternating with Bols, the Dutch gin. Watching cowboy movies on television apparently convinced him that in the Wild West whiskey flows even from the faucets, and he didn't want me to get drunk early in the morning while brushing my teeth. I came to hate Scotch—I thought it smelled rather like crushed bedbugs.

Two days before our departure my father and mother took me to Jakarta. We stayed at my grandparents' house where a flock of relatives and well-wishers milled around all day long, worrying about the safety of flying our national airline, the Garuda, and about my future lonely life in America without my supportive relatives. My father gave me a notebook full of addresses, telephone numbers, and names of various relatives, friends, and classmates of his, all of whom I was supposed to ask for guidance immediately upon my arrival in America. Even more relatives came the next day to see us off at the airport; I couldn't help wondering if anybody had anything else to do but meddle in other people's business. The well-wishers pressed us with gifts at the last minute; one gave me a rattan wastebasket that I couldn't pack anywhere, but he anxiously accompanied me all the way to the gate to make sure that I wouldn't throw it away. I didn't have the heart to chuck it and after thirty years I still have it.

For most Indonesians the excitement of travel brings out the survival instinct, and they get hungry as soon as they enter the airplane. We were hardly in our seats when my grandmother carefully unfolded a large package that she had carried on. She slowly unpacked her favorite delicacy, raw duck eggs cured for a hundred days in heavily salted clay. She also opened up rice containers and little jars containing strong Indonesian condiments. The condiments were quite pungent, but their smell seemed the smell of roses in comparison to the shock waves the hundred-day-old eggs emitted. The flight attendants didn't even blink, but some travelers, with noses reared on other kinds of food smells, did. However, the noisy protests calmed down as soon as the airplane motors started up, and the circulating air somewhat improved the situation.

We interrupted our journey for a few days in Singapore, where my grandparents had a number of relatives to visit. It was the end of June, which is among the hottest, most humid times of the year in Southeast Asia. We received more useless gifts from our relatives, then flew on to

Bangkok where we went through the same program. Our next stop was Rome. These grandparents were Catholics, and this city was the object of their dreams. I think this was the first time that my grandmother traveled outside of our home town, and she was quite frightened of what she observed. Her more experienced friends must have warned her about thievery in Europe, because she appointed me the guardian of our mountain of luggage. Whenever we were at an open place waiting for a taxi, bus, or train, she made me count the pieces every few minutes. I had to count them quite loudly so that she would be sure that I was on the job. She was also conscious of those handsome Italian men looking at me in a strange, bold way that perhaps scared her more than the prospect of losing her property. She was sharp enough to notice that I curiously returned their looks, which is considered a serious breach of our Indonesian etiquette. In my country men may look at women any way they want to, but only loose women return their looks by making eye contact. The proper way for a woman to talk to a man, whether she knows him or not and even if he is a relative, is to turn her head slightly sideways and talk into the air at about a thirty-five-degree angle below the man's eyes. I could not help noticing how Italian women looked back at these men, and I found their game rather intriguing.

When in Rome and unable to look and behave like Romans, the next best thing is to take tours. We checked into an inexpensive hotel and the next day were corralled into one of those ubiquitous bus tours that pick up their victims in hotel lobbies and show them the wonders of the Eternal City at an exorbitant price in the shortest possible time. Our bus driver did his best to do just that, but he didn't count on my grandmother who had to go to the bathroom every half-hour. The driver put up with us for a while but eventually he left us behind somewhere near the catacombs. We were a long way from our hotel, but grandmother wouldn't take a taxi. Taxi drivers, she was warned back home, are notorious robbers, and in Rome taxi rides should never even be considered. We walked all the way back to our hotel asking for directions by showing our hotel card. I remember nothing of Rome, not a distant sight of St. Peter's, not a bridge over the Tiber, not an ancient Roman monument, not a fountain nor a modern shop. Instead of looking for famous churches and antiquities, my grandmother made me fix my eyes on the sign of the next restaurant in the distance where she might find relief. Though we were booked for one more day in our hotel, the next day we didn't dare even to leave our room. For grandmother, life had always meant panic, only more so in a strange country. We guarded our luggage all day in our hotel room, and I obediently counted each piece every time she returned from the bathroom. The third day we left for Amsterdam.

For me Amsterdam is famous for two things: the narrowest and steepest staircases in the world, attached to the smallest rooms and apartments, and freedom, the place where, for the first time in my life, I willfully and deliberately disobeyed my grandmother and thoroughly enjoyed it. My uncle's apartment must have been among Amsterdam's smallest; he also had a flock of six children who slept in the basement stacked up to the ceiling. I was squeezed in with them. My grandparents occupied the largest room all by themselves, about half the total area of the apartment. Seeing the family's poverty and their struggle with daily life, I was totally embarrassed by our imposition on them. One of my cousins confided in me that their father was angry with us because he had three extra mouths to feed. Apparently my grandparents didn't help with the expenses for the extra food they had to buy. I offered to help them with the chores around the apartment, but grandmother didn't let me do even that; I had to sit by her all day long, all the time, to assure her that I wasn't getting into mischief.

After we had settled into my uncle's apartment, I told my grandmother that I wanted to visit a former piano teacher of mine, a Javanese man who had emigrated to Holland with a Dutch wife. Before he left Indonesia, he told me to look him up if I ever visited Holland. Even the thought of my visiting a man at his home by myself upset my grandmother, even though he was married. By the rigorous Chinese etiquette of her generation, no unmarried girl should ever meet a man, married or unmarried, without a chaperon, not even if the man was engaged.

At eighteen I was uncorrupted by any kind of formal or informal sex education. The word *sex* and anything connected with it was taboo; it was never mentioned in school, in the church, or in our home. Priests never preached about it, nuns never acknowledged its existence, parents and relatives avoided the subject like the plague; my only source of information about it was the catechism with its vague allusions to sins against the Sixth Commandment. And neither I nor my classmates understood what the catechism's carefully formulated words meant, but we never dared to ask for enlightenment. The traditional place for sex education was on the street. I suppose my brothers and sisters got their information there, but they never shared it with me and my mother's refusal to let me out alone cut me off from that source. Nobody ever explained to me the basic biological facts of life, including menstruation. When I first menstruated, I thought I had cancer and went to confession to a Dutch priest to make peace with my Maker before I died. I naively told the priest everything that was happening to me; I suppose he knew the facts of life from books only and must have been terribly embarrassed to hear my candid explanations. The best he could do was to advise me to talk to my mother about it. That, however, I couldn't do; we were never that close. Instead I asked one of our Javanese servants and she explained to me what to do, but she didn't know biology either. Eventually I figured out how babies were made; I watched our dogs in heat and observed how puppies came along in due time.

If I couldn't talk to my mother in confidence, woman to woman, daughter to mother, I could expect even less understanding from my grandmother. When she forbade me to visit my piano teacher, quoting old, meaningless Chinese rules, all the pent-up feelings of my young adulthood broke loose against parental authority and I went to see my teacher anyway. This was the first time that I had gone by myself on public transportation, but my rebellious feelings overcame any fear of getting lost. It didn't matter that the visit was a flop. He hardly remembered me, and we had nothing to say to one another. I played a few pieces on the piano for him, and when his Dutch wife began to fidget I realized the visit was over. But just knowing that for the first time in my life I had dared to disobey, willfully and deliberately, made me feel good about myself.

(Here Heifetz couldn't help himself from making a remark: "Good for you; I know how it feels. I wish I had had the courage to break away from my parents at the age you did.")

When I returned from my visit, my grandmother gave me hell for disobeying her orders. She called me names and promised me the future of a streetwalker, but her ravings only strengthened my decision to take an even more drastic step toward independence. I had a Dutch "uncle" named Leon in Holland, tucked away somewhere in the southern part of the country. He was actually a distant cousin by marriage—his wife was my mother's second cousin. The address list my father gave me before I left Yogya told me that they lived in the town of Ede near the German border. The only money I had was the one-hundred-dollar bill the governor of Jakarta had given me shortly before my departure. In fact, that was the only money I had for my journey and for my years of study in the United States; my father had had to scrape together two thousand dollars which, to satisfy the U.S. Immigration Service, I was supposed to deposit in a bank at the place of my studies to insure that I could return home without public assistance. The two thousand dollars plus my extra hundred I carried with me in cash all the time, as my father would not have trusted any bank in Indonesia to take that hard-earned money and give him a piece of paper in exchange. My hundred dollars seemed to me a lot of money at that time, especially when I translated it into our Indonesian rupiahs; one could live in my country for several months on it.

In preparation for my trip to Ede, I cautiously changed ten dollars into Dutch money, packed a small suitcase with the absolute necessities, and was ready to throw myself at the mercy of my Dutch uncle and his wife. I was literally shaking in my boots early the next morning when I sneaked out of the apartment in search of my freedom. This was only the second time I had ever traveled alone, something I had never done in Indonesia, and I knew very little about how to go about it. I walked for a while in the streets and when I saw a man who looked trustworthy, I asked him how to get to Ede. I still knew enough Dutch from my childhood, and that helped. The kind Dutchman explained to me how to get to the railroad station and what train to take. I took a bus, and after some frenetic inquiries at a ticket window, I got on a train. Two hours later I arrived in Ede. There a new surprise awaited me: Ede had no railroad station. The train skirted around the town, and I was able to get off several miles away. Another round of anxious inquiries followed until a railroad officer showed me the road to Ede.

My uncle was a pharmacist's aide and had worked in Indonesia in the Dutch colonial organization. There he married his Indonesian wife, my mother's second cousin. Originally he had his eye on my mother, but the feelings weren't mutual. During World War II before he came to Indonesia, he had joined the Dutch resistance and for that the Gestapo had beaten his head with a rifle stock. He suffered terrible brain damage, which despite somewhat successful surgery ultimately forced him to retire. He and his wife welcomed me into their home with open arms. When they saw my lightweight clothing from Indonesia and heard that the rest of my wardrobe left in Amsterdam also consisted of tropical garments, my uncle told me what kind of weather I would be facing in the northern parts of America. He kindly bought some heavy winter clothing for me, which was the first time I had ever seen a warm overcoat. I stayed with them until the day before my scheduled departure for Buffalo a month later.

My uncle took me by car back to Amsterdam when the time came. My grandparents were still there, but my grandmother didn't want to see me. She held her grudge against me for the rest of her life, and she never received me even years later during my infrequent visits back to Jakarta. Later I learned that during my absence from Amsterdam I had received several letters, but I never found out what was in them; she took them all and probably destroyed them.

My grandmother's character has always been a puzzle to me. When my mother, her daughter, was dying of leukemia and had to be sent to Jakarta, she stayed in grandmother's house for a few months to receive radiation treatment in a nearby hospital as an ambulatory patient. After my mother had passed away, grandmother sent a hefty bill to my father for her daughter's lodging, food, transportation, and whatever else she could think of. My father had to borrow money because she wanted her money immediately. Grandmother died some fifteen years after I left for America, never forgiving me.

At the end of my story Heifetz looked at me with sympathy and uttered another gem of his wisdom: "I have never been much for family; friends you can choose, but you're stuck with family."

He pricked up his ears when he heard that my American life started in Buffalo. He had played there once or twice, he said, but at that time none of the local colleges had a decent music department. He tried to be sarcastic when he asked, "What did you do to those missionaries that they punished you by sending you to Buffalo, of all places, to study music?"

For him the last place anyone would ever want to study music was Buffalo. Apparently Heifetz's memories of Buffalo weren't too pleasant. He must have played there on a slushy winter or early spring day, with the wind blowing the smoke from the open furnaces of the Bethlehem Steel plant located on the shores of Lake Erie. The plant had since been closed, but that didn't change his memories. In fact, I liked it there, perhaps because in Buffalo I went through what I like to call my American childhood. I felt that I started my life over again in this city, and I became a new person at the age of eighteen. To answer his question, I explained to Heifetz that an American nun in Yogya, who was taken by my violin playing, belonged to the Franciscan order that had a women's college in Buffalo, New York, and it was through her efforts that I received a scholarship to that school. Her name was Sister Bridget. Until her generous offer I had not been aware that she had been following my musical career since I was a little girl.

By the time I arrived in Buffalo I had only ninety dollars in my pocket for my own use, left from my adventure in Holland. Sister Bridget also arranged for an Irish family to take me in until a more permanent situation was available. There were already six children in that family, and I suppose that a seventh didn't make much difference. My culture shock in this new country didn't come from whiskey pouring out of the faucets, as my father had presumed, but rather from the laissez-faire way of life in my new family, which was in sharp contrast to ours in Indonesia. I was amazed that the food was never locked away, and that there was plenty of it. To my eyes plenty of it was wasted, too, but nobody seemed to care. The children were fearless; all had bold opinions of their own and freely expressed them to their parents. The parents, so it seemed to me, were scared of their children and anxious for their approval, rather than trying to discipline them. In Indonesia we were brought up from an early age with a great deal of anxiety over our future; these children didn't show the least concern over their own future, and neither did they seem concerned about their parents' opinion of how they should prepare for it. To my surprise, the word *no* had never been uttered in the presence of the family's youngest children, seven-year-old twins, and in case of emergency the older ones spelled it out among themselves. I heard some talk that the offensive word could cause irreparable damage to their psyche, which utterly baffled me. All in all, they seemed a wild bunch in comparison to my own family. Yet there was something there I had never experienced in my home life and upbringing: an emotional bond among children and parents, a demonstrative love and affection for one another. They generously shared their family feelings with me, and I quickly felt myself enveloped in hitherto unknown emotions. My parents never gave this kind of love to their children nor expected it from them. Love for them was something like obedience and respect for the elders, and they didn't seem to care how we children felt about one another.

My new family in Buffalo lived in the same block as the Catholic church, and I soon learned that another Indonesian girl lived in its rectory in exchange for helping the cook and other employees of the church. When I told Heifetz that the girl turned out to be the older sister of the boyfriend whom I left behind in Indonesia, he said that this time I was going too far in making up stories, and for a while he didn't want to listen any more. Yet it was true. I hardly knew this girl, since she was brought up in boarding schools, and when she was home during the summers, I was in Jakarta studying violin. Something good came from our meeting, though; she introduced me to the church organist who needed a substitute for the Sunday afternoon Masses. I gave myself a crash course on the organ, and the next Sunday I was earning my very first and very small stipend in the United States.

I sorely needed every penny I could lay my hands on. As soon as college began, I had to buy lots of fat books with mysterious titles and with their even more mysterious contents. My ninety dollars were gone before

I knew it, and I had to borrow money from my new family to make ends meet. My heart broke when I found out after the first semester that most of these books, which we had hardly cracked open, were useless in the second semester because new and even more expensive ones had to be bought to satisfy another set of teachers. Neither did I know that the school derived a hefty profit from selling those doorstop-size books; they seemed to be written for weight, size, and price rather than for content. The word *racket* wasn't part of my vocabulary yet. When I tried to figure out what the books were supposed to be for from the course descriptions in the college catalog, my classmates laughed and told me that those course descriptions were lifted from the catalogs of Harvard, Yale, and other Ivy League colleges to impress the students, their parents, and the heads of the departments, and had little, if anything, to do with what was being taught in the classes. I had no idea what "Ivy League college" meant, I had never even seen ivy in my life, and when I was shown some, I failed to make the connection. The Indonesian language doesn't leave much room for creative imagination.

I was pleasantly surprised that I was allowed to take elective courses in the school. I took everything offered in math and science. In these courses at least I understood the mathematical formulas and didn't have to fight so much with the language, for language was a great problem. The English I had learned in Indonesia was useless, and this college didn't offer English for foreigners, as I was the only one among its two thousand students. To compound my problems, in Indonesia I opted for science courses in high school and consequently lacked any background in history, social studies, and the humanities. My only college experience in Indonesia was a two-month crash course in English. I still have nightmares about the course I had to take in Psychology of Education. I was overwhelmed by its pseudo-scientific vocabulary, and its concepts were totally beyond my comprehension. After a brief struggle to understand the course, I gave up and used my photographic memory to fix the images of the pages in my mind; when the time for exams came, I tried to match up the questions with the senseless texts I had memorized. I passed the course with a C. One passage from the book still clings to my mind, and I would challenge anyone to explain to me in plain English what the "phenomena resulting from the assimilation of the unconscious" means. To my pragmatic mind it is still absolutely puzzling how one assimilates something of which one is unconscious.

My knowledge of history was nil. Indonesia, as an independent country that was only a few years old, seemed to have no history in the textbook sense beyond its struggles for independence. The ancient history that I knew was static, an insignificant and endless enumeration of which sultan or rajah ruled which territory in what era. What's worse, its study never held any relevance or connection to the great historical epochs of the West. We learned in high school every detail of the Sukarno revolution, but everything beyond the shores of the Indonesian islands that could have been relevant to the revolution remained in the dense fog of the ocean surrounding us. During my studies in college I discovered that even the very nature of the Indonesian language discourages understanding of the concepts of history. Our language has neither past nor future tense; we always speak in the present tense, and if we need to indicate that we are speaking of the past, a vague "yesterday," "some time ago," or "already" is added as a prefix to the present tense. Then the listener knows that what we talk about has no importance, as it has no immediate relevance to the present. For the future tense, we use a prefix indicating "tomorrow" or "soon," and again we pay no attention to it because it is not yet here. This manner of speaking affects both our way of life and our attitude in a way that Westerners describe as primitive. We consider history, social studies, and politics as subjects for the amusement of the idle rich; the vast majority of the country has to worry about putting rice on the table on a daily basis and about how badly the roof over their heads will leak during the long rainy season.

We have no philosophers in the Western sense and no abstract vocabulary to practice that discipline. Our wise men give us pragmatic advice about our daily life and explain our relationship to the spirit world in easily understood terms. No one felt as powerless before such lack of abstract thinking as the Christian missionaries when they tried to translate the ancient Latin texts of the Mass into some sort of equivalent in Indonesian. As long as we heard the Mass in Latin, it perfectly fulfilled our yearning for the mysterious, and we readily identified it in our minds with the powers of white magic. When the words were translated into Indonesian, they lost their mystery without telling us what they meant. At any rate, only a fool would try to explain how white magic works; it either does what it is supposed to do or not—understanding adds nothing to its efficacy. In fact, our language so much lacks precision that we can't even differentiate between *coming* and *going* without getting into lengthy explanations, which we consider hardly worth the trouble. The only tangible result of the missionaries' efforts to translate the Mass into Indonesian was that it became twice as long.

To ease my financial strain in Buffalo, I entered and won a few local violin and piano competitions with prize money attached to them. In addition, during my second semester in college, my violin teacher got me a job with the Buffalo Philharmonic as a substitute violinist. In a few weeks I became a regular member of the orchestra, which freed me from financial worries. Once I was even able to go back to Indonesia for Christmas vacation and learned that nothing had changed. It was nice to be welcomed back among family and enjoy the admiration and respect an oldest child commands, yet I had tasted freedom and had no desire to return.

7

Passagework

If you can keep your head when all about you
Are losing their and blaming it on you

RUDYARD KIPLING

Jascha Heifetz didn't seem to be as proud of his artistic achievements as of the fact that he was a difficult person. The ultimate paradox was that this person who could not live without company eventually did everything in his power to get rid of people. In his time he accumulated many friends, admirers, and casual acquaintances, and he liked to talk about the lavish parties of his salad days in his large New York apartment. He loved to have fun and often pulled innocuous practical jokes. For Christmas one year, some time after I had married and had a baby, he gave my little daughter, Ada, a small box. When she opened it, something funny jumped out; neither of us had ever seen a jack-in-the-box before.

Yet it was in his nature to suspect that his friends were not looking for the company of Jascha Heifetz, the person, but were using him for name-dropping, trying to bask in the sun of Jascha Heifetz, the world-famous violinist. As he became older and his "friends" diminished in number in proportion to the waning of his fame, he only saw his suspicions confirmed. He liked to test people for the sincerity of their friendship. A major component of these tests was an unconditional surrender to his whims; he expected all his friends to be at his beck and call when he needed them. Heifetz accepted no excuses, and "offenders" were rarely invited again to his presence. He pulled no punches if he wanted to get a point across and offended quite a few of his guests by telling them off; rarely, if ever, would he listen to explanations if he was convinced he was right. Though he was a gracious host, he was also a master at making people feel uncomfortable in his presence if he was in a bad mood or felt crossed. Eventually most of his friends chose to admire him from a distance. I had the feeling that somehow he had great difficulty seeing things from anyone else's point of view.

I had the good sense never to ask him about his love life, and from his short and bitter references to women I gathered that this was a wise move. Nor did he volunteer information other than a few cryptic asides. He told me quite often that he should never have gotten married; he found nearly everything wrong with his own children and with himself as a father, and he poured out any remaining familial sentiments on his students. They were his ideal children who couldn't talk back to him as his own children would, children whom he could dismiss or accept at will without the emotional ties and obligations of a blood relationship. For example, he had often made promises to his own children which he couldn't keep, and although he always had had professional reasons, he felt he needed to avoid even the possibility of not keeping a promise in his later years. His solution was to say no to all sorts of requests. He felt he could change his mind later, but at least this way would not break his promises. Thus he attempted to bring up this family of musicians in the ideal way as he perceived it, but the results were not much better than those of the many failed experiments of other idealistic educators in history.

Since many of his students were from abroad, some from the Far East, to provide them with a sort of family feeling he invited them home several times during the school year, to his house in Beverly Hills or at the beach. I suspect he learned this from Auer, who spent his summers in the company of some of his students at foreign resorts, which at times apparently included the whole Heifetz family.

Heifetz had a summer home in Malibu where most of these communal gatherings took place. The first such event of the school year was on Thanksgiving Day, another one on Easter Sunday, and a more exclusive party for a smaller number of his students on New Year's Eve. To this party he would have only those who were needed to play chamber music with him in the presence of invited guests.

All these parties were run on rigorously kept schedules. On Thanksgiving all students were invited for the day, which included a turkey dinner in the late afternoon. Since it was usually quite cold at the beach in November, he appointed someone to be his "fireman" whose duty was to take care of the fire in the fireplace. All sorts of tools necessary or unnecessary for this job, including a fireman's hat, hung over the fireplace, and all tools had their appointed places. If someone moved them an inch to the left or to the right, he put them back in their proper place and reminded the fireman and everybody else within earshot of their proper

The Thanksgiving party at the beach with his students in 1982. Left to right: (standing) San Do Xia, Ayke Agus, Yuki Mori; (seated) Maarit Kirvessalo, Elliott Markow, Heifetz, Sherry Kloss.

position. He had no qualms about doing this with other guests, too; it was his way of keeping everything and everybody under his control. The day was spent with games of table tennis, various musical and parlor games, good drinks and food, and brisk walks on the sandy beach. Heifetz was very fond of the ocean; he couldn't get enough of its immensity and loved to gaze over its endless horizon.

The main attraction of the Easter Sunday ritual was the Mexican piñata game. His assistant was commissioned to buy its main ingredients on Alvarado Street in Los Angeles. The piñata, a tough bag made of sheets of newspaper glued together and filled with all sorts of candies, was made to resemble a lamb in keeping with the spirit of Easter. The piñata was suspended from the rafters of the teahouse at the beach, then one by one the blindfolded players, after being turned around several times by the host himself, were let loose to try to hit the bag with a baseball bat. We all stood around laughing as the player was batting the air sometimes near to and sometimes quite far from the piñata. If someone succeeded and hit it, the piñata fell apart, its contents crashing to the ground and subsequently distributed among the players. Heifetz had great fun watching it, and sometimes he took his turn with the bat. Once he commissioned me to find candies for the piñata, but they had to be an international mixture of candies. It was quite an experience to track down the various kinds of candies various nationalities enjoy, starting with Austria and ending with Zambia, though I don't think I found all of them. When I finished with my candy-hunting safari, Heifetz wanted to know everything that had happened on the hunt.

The beginning of my closer acquaintance with Heifetz was connected with my first Easter Sunday at the beach in the spring of 1972. Toward the end of the afternoon when all the students were told to leave, his assistant told me to feign leaving with the rest of them but then just to drive around the block and come back because Heifetz wanted me to stay for supper. I'm still not sure if this little deception was his idea or if it was suggested to him.

I followed the game plan, and with that afternoon commenced my fifteen years of bittersweet association with Jascha Heifetz through hell and high water, from musical exaltation to mundane daily care, a relationship in which sometimes I was the whipping post and at other times the spiritual counselor of a superannuated, insecure, and immature child who often threw away what he wanted and wanted badly what he rejected. Through all these tribulations music was the spiritual bond that kept us together and made it possible for me to put up with the paradox he represented. Even during the days when he hated me and thought of me as a poison of which he could not rid himself, even when he made me the object of eternal, purposeless suspicions that totally obsessed him in his dark days, our bond of music triumphed over the near insanity that would cloud his mind for weeks. For in Heifetz's mind the rational often was in a mortal combat with the irrational, while he viewed both these antagonistic forces with suspicion.

Heifetz was an astute observer of human nature and had good eyes for someone or something that could be useful for him. Years later he told me what made him make his first move to absorb me into his inner circle: "I noticed that you never asked me or anyone else what needed to be done; you just did it without asking or making a fuss about it." It didn't occur to me to tell him that I was born, by the Chinese zodiac, under the sign of the cow, which is supposed to make me susceptible to exploitation. I'm sure he would have been delighted to know about it, for soon after that first dinner at the beach, Heifetz quickly made further moves to make good on my exploitable nature. First he asked me to come to his house on a Wednesday evening to discuss some "very important" matter. He neglected to tell me that Wednesday also happened to be his cook's day off. The very important matter turned out to be next to nothing, but he invited me for dinner provided that I would prepare it. For me to accept the invitation took a certain amount of courage because my mother had kept me out of the kitchen, and all I knew about cooking was based on observing our cook as she prepared the Indonesian and Javanese specialties which took her hours to create. At the time Heifetz asked me to cook our dinner, my specialty was fried rice, and I let him know it. He didn't relish the thought of fried rice, so he came with me to the kitchen and gave me general instructions for cooking stew, which was his favorite dish. He supervised to make sure I did things as instructed, and then he declared that "making a good stew is the first step toward becoming a good cook." However, even during my first attempt at cooking he wouldn't let the job take me over completely; every once in a while he would stick his head in the kitchen to demand my presence in the living room for a drink with him. Heifetz had very low tolerance for competition, and damn the cooking.

For the next few Wednesdays he used the same "important discussion" trick to get me to his house, but eventually he just told me that he needed help on Wednesdays and that I should come automatically unless otherwise instructed. I presume he considered all this part of my job as the class pianist. To my own surprise I began to enjoy domesticity, perhaps because he let me do what I wanted as long as I didn't get too absorbed in it. Perhaps it also helped that I had a chance to get back at my mother, who always insisted that I was born to do things considerably more important, like practicing the violin, than wasting my time in the kitchen. The irony of the situation began to dawn on me that now it was her violinist idol who taught me how to cook instead of my learning from her, excellent cook though she was. Heifetz's cooking course consisted mostly of giving me general information about the ingredients of a certain dish and how it should taste, but eventually he told me only his recollections of a taste, and I was supposed to whip up the food that matched it. Later he told me that he didn't mind my adventurous cooking and even enjoyed the concoctions that I somehow managed to adjust to my

Indonesian palate. Besides my becoming a willing apprentice in the kitchen, Heifetz discovered other sides of my personality that particularly pleased him: I never argued with him and always listened to what he had to say without interrupting him. I never "knew better" when he stated an opinion, spoke very little, and above all, I never refused to drink with him, of course in my much smaller capacity. To a Russian this counted perhaps more than all my other assets lumped together. Soon he expected me to cook some of his favorite Russian dishes, sometimes sharing his mother's recipes. I took a crash course from cookbooks, and he introduced me to his Russian friends whom I could ask for advice if I got into a jam. He was never disappointed, for I always produced something that resembled what he had in mind.

Heifetz wanted not only a cook but also a companion to help him pass the loneliness of an evening. He always asked me to stay after dinner; we played card games, of which gin rummy was a favorite, or other old-fashioned, nearly extinct parlor games, but music was also part of the after-dinner activities. I either accompanied him or we played music for four hands, sitting together at the piano that he was very fond of. He also loved to improvise, and at times not until the crack of dawn would he stop playing for me as his private audience. Sometimes he asked me to play something for him on the piano, and he pointed out to me that the sound of an accompaniment should differ from that of a soloist. To demonstrate, he would sit down at the piano and show me what he meant. I was surprised that he was able to make his point at the keyboard, even though he felt that he was out of practice. In turn, he sometimes asked my suggestions for fingerings at the piano, which on occasion he grudgingly accepted before suggesting how I might get around problems caused by my small hands. He also liked to pull tricks on me and once asked me to close my eyes while he played the Chopin black-key etude in G-flat major, Op. 10, No. 5. It sounded strange, and when I peeked I saw that he was playing it with an orange. Soon I looked forward to our meetings because he always had a surprise in store for me.

At that time I was still studying for two degrees at USC, my bachelor's and master's in Music Performance, and I found that he never made cracks about my scholarly ambitions, neither in class nor outside of it. Besides playing in the class and rehearsing with his students, I also had to be present at the auditions, which gave me better insight into how he handled new candidates. First they usually came to my apartment for a rehearsal and asked anxious questions about the procedure and how to behave in his presence. Amazingly enough, often they didn't have the piano parts of the pieces they were supposed to rehearse with me and were surprised that I had all the music they selected to play at the audition. Only a few knew scales, and some didn't know the main requirement, the third movement of the Mendelssohn concerto, at all. Contrary to his previous custom, Heifetz asked me to stay with him during the auditions, from the beginning to the end, even during his private interview with the candidates. Although his routine was mostly the same as during my audition, during these interviews I came to know what a psychologist he was and how he handled a variety of candidates of different personalities.

Lack of talent in a candidate didn't bother him as much as fakery and insincerity. Heifetz intensely disliked sloppiness and made short shrift of those he found wanting in this department. However, he could be very polite with candidates whom he judged without a necessary measure of talent; he always went through the motions of interviewing them even after an unsatisfactory performance. He asked these candidates about their hobbies or other talents and their professional interests besides music, and then usually advised them to play music as a hobby only and to pursue their other interests in which they may have had greater talent. He advised others, for whom his expectations were not so high, to enter his class as auditors, and he made them understand that they were not the kind of students he was looking for. Some others who were talented but past the age of twenty-five, he accepted only as auditors. He was convinced that beyond the age of twenty-five one was not capable of absorbing and retaining anything technically new. Auditors in general were permitted to play once in a semester for him, and he gave them a lesson if they deserved it, just as he did to his regular students. Auditors also participated once in a while in the chamber music sessions.

He had another category of auditors as well whom he called observers. Most were on the mature side and held teaching positions somewhere in the Los Angeles area. These observers could play once in a while in the chamber music sessions but not during regular class hours. If the candidate showed promise on his or her instrument at the audition, Heifetz carefully reread the curriculum vitae, noted if the photograph was out of date, and sometimes asked silly questions such as "When was this taken, twenty-five years ago?" Next he asked the main question, "What did you come here for?" or "What do you think I can do for you?" The clichéd question should have received a clichéd answer, yet some applicants gave astonishing replies: "I have always heard of Jascha Heifetz as the greatest violinist; I came to see what he looked like and perhaps to hear him play some day," or "I just wanted to meet you." I even heard a candidate say "I would like to have private lessons with you, Mr. Heifetz," even before he knew whether he was accepted. Heifetz didn't downgrade candidates for such silly statements, yet he knew that something wasn't quite right with them. He was inclined to pass a quick judgment on a candidate just from the neatness or untidiness of the application in front of him, and claimed to foresee from it whether the prospective student could put up with the rigors of his master class or whether bothering with him or her would be just a waste of his time. He also very carefully watched how the candidate handled his instrument and how clean and well maintained it was; a dirty and unkempt instrument was almost a sure portent of rejection.

In due time after the interviews he would privately ask my opinion of the candidates and even what I thought of his handling of the auditions. First he gave me his assessment of each candidate and the reason why he accepted or rejected any of them, and when I pleaded for someone who was rejected, he would cry "Appeaser!" "Munich!" and "Chamberlain!," none of which meant anything to me until he explained the events preceding the Second World War. Apparently the Munich Pact had gotten quite badly under his skin because he always used these figures of speech when he wanted me to take a hard stand on an issue or against a public person whom he considered weak.

When an interview was over, Heifetz would shake hands with the candidate and wish him the best for whatever he was going to do. He rarely announced the results immediately except for outright rejections, but it was a good omen if he advised someone to stick around a day or two. He always entrusted his assistant with letting the candidates know the outcome and with taking care of the "gruesome details" if financial assistance or help with lodging were needed. A number of kind-hearted people, usually admirers of his, were willing to put up a future student for a while until more permanent arrangements could be made. Heifetz automatically expected these details to be taken care of and never wanted to hear about difficulties or failures. After the new student was settled and had spent a few weeks in the class, Heifetz usually asked his assistant to drive him to the student's living quarters for a surprise visit. When he came to my apartment for the first time, he went through everything but my mail, including the closets and the space under the sink.

He must have liked the way I kept house because the Wednesday visits to his house eventually blossomed into a closer friendship. He began to take up more and more of my time, and I became a more or less permanent fixture in his household. On weekends he would ask me to drive him out to his beach house at Malibu. He was very fond of his beach house, and the weekend stay there in all seasons was a ritual that tolerated no exceptions, not even life-threatening situations. At one time his obsession with Malibu almost came to a tragic end.

It happened during one of those lengthy Pacific storms that come with unusually high tides around the winter solstice and usually last several days. This particular storm destroyed several houses on the beach; huge waves crashed across the beach and even across the Pacific Highway at several points. In the middle of the week, the usual warnings were announced over the radio and television to residents of the beach area and to curiosity seekers to stay away from Malibu and the highway leading to it. Eventually the highway collapsed at several places, while the storm loosened up huge boulders which rolled down the adjacent hillsides to make the road impassable.

I asked Heifetz Friday night what his plans were for the weekend. He seemed to be surprised that I would even ask and said that nothing had changed: we would go as usual. When I told him what the reports said, he made light of it and was sure that we could get to Malibu through the mountain roads above the ocean. I had never used these roads, and I doubted that he knew much about them either. However, to press the issue would have been useless, and I came in Saturday morning ready for the adventure.

It was raining hard when we left his house in Beverly Hills, but it became worse as we approached the beach. The rain, driven by the Pacific gale, came down in solid sheets, so that I could hardly see the barricades closing off the road to Pacific Highway. Heifetz pointed out a street leading to the mountain road, but even there I had to drive around a "Danger" sign. He looked like a naughty kid who was having great fun knowing that he was doing something that he was not supposed to do. He instructed me to ignore all danger-signs wherever they occurred and continue driving on that road. I faithfully kept on driving, slowly creeping up the hill and driving around rocks that half blocked the road; we were lucky to escape one or two that came down just before or behind our car. Once we were temporarily stuck in a pile of accumulated mud; I backed up the car and was lucky enough to get out of it. Later we saw cars ditched on both sides of the road, with people standing in the rain and looking for help in vain. They all must have had the same adventurous spirit as Heifetz had but considerably less luck. Here and there the road was flooded knee-high, and as I swished through I felt my nerves begin to unravel. It suddenly occurred to me that I was alone with Jascha Heifetz in a quite stupid situation; what would the news say if we had an accident? The rain didn't let up for a second, the wipers could hardly cope with it, and I couldn't tell which side of the road we were on. My throat was dry from fear, and I looked at Heifetz, but he showed no sign of panic and motioned to me to drive on. He had always been a great backseat driver, usually telling me what to do and how to drive; this time he didn't say a word, only kept his eyes on the road and signaled with his hand if a rock suddenly showed up in the middle of the road.

I had no idea where we were, and I felt lost in space and time; we seemed to be fighting the road and storm for an eternity. Suddenly another barricade loomed up in front of us: "Danger. No passing. Road closed to all traffic." I noticed that the road widened a bit in front of the sign, and there was just enough room to turn around. I pointed at the barricade and pleaded with him to turn back; there was no point in putting our lives in more danger. He looked at me and with a child's immensely trusting simplicity said in all seriousness without the slightest doubt in his voice, "You can do it." I must have been over the edge because his confidence in me restored my nerves. My mind told me that I should have gotten out of that car, left him there, and started walking back on the road, but I also knew that he would have tried to drive the car himself and God only knows what would have happened if he had. I got out and removed the barrier, and as I got back in the car, soaking wet, Heifetz looked at me with appreciation and calmly said, "Let's go."

I drove on but soon felt a bump under the car; we were stuck in the middle of the road. I went out to investigate. A small rock was wedged under the front bumper, but I was able to get off of it. I told Heifetz to keep a closer watch on the road; when other rocks appeared on the road, he had to get out and direct me around them. Without this precaution we could have ended up either in the ditch on the mountainside or rolling down the hillside into the raging Pacific. The rain never let up, and at some places we had to ford heavy streams pouring out of the side of the mountain. If the car had stalled, I'm sure we would have been washed down the hillside.

All through the ordeal Heifetz was strangely quiet. He hardly said anything except to give directions or to warn me of upcoming danger. At first he enjoyed the ride as we took off from the house, but after seeing what we had gotten into, he put on his impassive face, as when he played the violin onstage, and let things happen without trying to interfere. Obviously he was determined to go through with it as obstinately as when he was conquering an awkward passage on the violin. It seemed an anti-climax when we arrived at a narrow, paved road leading into another one, all clear of rocks and mudslides. Eventually we came out at the Pacific Highway several miles beyond Malibu and had to turn around to get to his house.

The trip lasted from ten in the morning till three in the afternoon. The usual driving time was about forty-five minutes. We found his house unaffected by the storm when we quickly checked it after unpacking the car. Heifetz fixed drinks for both of us in his usual unhurried fashion. We clinked our glasses and he said, "Here is to you and to me, and bravo to you." I answered by quoting one of his favorite sayings, "And here is to 'not doing things by the book.'" He gave me a hug, smiled, and for a change didn't challenge my toast. He brought some wood in from the doghouse that was used for storing it, and we sat for a long time in front of the crackling fire not saying a word.

His property in Malibu stretched from the street to the beach, about a hundred yards from the water line. It was long and narrow, and his house sat close to the street, away from the water. The two-story building consisted of a collection of rather oddly arranged rooms and useless spaces. For example, the kitchen was on the second floor, so that hot meals had to be brought down the stairway to be served. He often said it wasn't the kind of house he really wanted, but it was a bargain that he couldn't resist. He bought it from an old lady who let him have it for a song just because he was Jascha Heifetz. This lady had been housebound for years and was only using the upper quarters of the house, from where she had complete control of all entrances and doors by means of various electric buttons and contraptions. Heifetz personally ripped out these gadgets except for a couple of buzzers. He liked gadgets only if he had them installed to his own specifications.

From the street side his property was enclosed by a white wooden fence about seven feet high. His house was easy to identify. While all the houses on the street had five-digit house numbers, his had a large number 2 painted in blue, his favorite color, on the fence right next to the entrance. His official story was that the street's addresses used to have one- or two-digit numbers, and when he bought the house it had a number 2 on it. But somebody in City Hall, always a mortal enemy of his, decided to change them into these impossible numbers which he claimed he couldn't remember. His mind was reserved for more important things than five-digit house numbers, and he decided to keep the old one. The probable truth of the matter was that he considered two his lucky number for some cabalistic reason. He also had that number painted on his mailbox, and the post office had no choice but bow to his petulance and deliver his mail to number 2. It was a matter of principle, and Heifetz insisted that anyone sending him a piece of mail to Malibu should use his privately official number. While trying to make you believe his story, he would conveniently forget that his house number in Beverly Hills consisted of four numbers, but he didn't meddle with that one and remembered it well.

Heifetz was superstitious about charms. He taught me how to nail a horseshoe on the wall properly with its open end up so that good luck doesn't drain out, he carried St. Christopher medals in his car as protection against accidents, and the auspiciousness of his birthday was even insured by a Mormon charm which he apparently received in Salt Lake City after a performance there on 14 February 1935. It's a gold charm with the date of the concert engraved on one side and on the other side "Heifetz Mormon Good Luck Piece, February 2, 1901." Heifetz provided me and even my husband with an ample number of St. Christopher medals showing his eclectic taste when it came to protection. Not to leave his Jewish heritage out, he had several mezuzahs nailed on his doors, and he gave me one, too, with instructions for nailing it up in the proper place and angle. The next time he came around, he made sure that I hadn't made a mistake.

He had a horseshoe properly arranged on the fence in Malibu, which had two gates, a large, two-winged one for the cars and a small one for foot traffic. At the smaller gate the visitor was confronted with a short piece of chain-link hanging down at about eye level, which upon skillful manipulation released an inside latch. With luck a small crack appeared between the door and the fence, and the visitor was free to push the sometimes sticky gate to a full opening. If the chain was broken or if after a heavy rain the latch decided not to cooperate, the pertinacious visitor had the choice of either going through a neighbor's lot to enter Heifetz's place from the beach side or of climbing over the fence. If his luck held and the neighbors let him through their property, he had an easier entry through a lower and less pesky gate from the beach side. If no visitor was expected, the gate was usually bolted from the inside. Sometimes Heifetz forgot about an invited visitor, who would have to use one or another of the above methods if he wanted to keep his appointment. The visitor met his challenge if he couldn't get through a neighbor's property; shouting at the top of his lungs was of no use because the roar of the crashing Pacific waves made such a primitive form of communication impossible. Trying to telephone from the supermarket would have been similarly useless; Heifetz had a one-way telephone hidden in his bedroom, whereby he could communicate with the outside world but not the world with him. His beach telephone could only transmit; it did not receive messages. Only his secretary and a select few, including me, knew about the existence of this telephone reserved for emergencies, and he strictly forbade us to tell anybody about it. Thus the adamant visitor's last way to enter was by climbing over the fence, which some did. Heifetz had even prepared for such emergencies, for he had a large wooden bin built for the two tall garbage cans at the inside of the fence, on top of which an athletic visitor could easily land and gain access to the inside of Heifetz-land.

For first-time visitors Heifetz left nothing to chance; once inside the fence, one way or another, one could not get lost. He had a large arrow painted on the left side of the wall pointing toward the front of the house. In exactly the middle of the narrow passage between his house and the high fence, another gate blocked the entrance toward the promised land with another chain contraption, but that was easy to circumvent; one could reach over the top of that gate and undo it if it was stuck. Had a novice visitor complained about the trials of reaching Heifetz's beach fortress, he would get only an indifferent shrug from him accompanied by a laconic statement, "But my friend, you are here, aren't you?"

Conscientious visitors were also told how to get in touch with Heifetz if the impossible occurred and a cancellation of the visit became necessary; they were to call a certain liquor store in the area, order a bottle of Heifetz's preferred vodka, put it on their own charge account, and have the bottle delivered to his house with the appropriate message. The delivery boy knew his ways about the maze of beach houses without climbing a fence to deliver it.

Most of his lot was covered with brick and cement, but a few round spots were left open for vegetation consisting of flowers and some trees. Heifetz trained and cut the trees with the same passion as he attempted to regulate his students. He would have a certain shape and mold in mind and would spend hours pruning and cutting the trees when the mood struck him. At the beach-end of the lot there was a gazebo which he called his teahouse. It contained his ping-pong table and a built-in couch covered with colorful pillows. The ping-pong table was quite old and worn; it had a number of dead spots where the ball wouldn't bounce any more, but he staunchly refused to put up the new table which his friends gave him for a birthday. "They don't make them any more as they used to," he would say as he suspiciously viewed the new table in its box. As for the dead spots, he maintained that the spots were bad on both sides, thus making the odds even. He liked to play, singles or doubles, almost every day; therefore guests with ping-pong playing ability were somewhat preferred. Heifetz always had a number of Asian students in his master class, almost all of them excellent ping-pong players. After an unusually good set he was fond of telling his students that once, in his New York apartment where he also had a ping-pong table, he beat some sort of champion, the nature of the person's championship, however, never being made clear. When the champion asked for a return match, Heifetz wisely refused the challenge. He wanted to live with the memory, he said, that he once beat a champion. He was quite a good player in a careful manner and a good loser; he never made his students feel that he had to win; in fact, he became incensed if he noticed that someone was trying to lose against him.

Staying at the beach had its own ritual. He rarely got up before ten in the morning, came around about eleven, had breakfast, and made all sorts of superfluous noises and commotion under the pretense of being busy. Guests were warned not to come before one in the afternoon, by which time he had usually recuperated from his night's rest. Guests were let loose for an hour or two to take a walk on the beach, sometimes with, sometimes without him, but eventually all were expected to sit down under the beach umbrella and have lunch at three, after which the bar was open. Heifetz loved to hold court and make small talk, and expected everybody to have a drink, even if it was just a glass of water. At these times, unless he didn't feel well or something upset him, he could be quite charming and a good storyteller, but the conversation was kept strictly on his terms. This meant that the topics of religion, politics, and anything smacking of philosophy, as well as family matters, were strongly discouraged in his presence. If someone dared to bring up any of these subjects, he quite bluntly cut off the discussion or made fun of the offender's "learnedness." The only way science could be discussed in his presence was by mentioning its failures; it always made his day when he heard that somewhere a computer broke down and people in the bank had to wait in long lines because of it. Computers he regarded as abominable substitutes for human brains and services. His opinion was that the world had become much worse for "the two Cs: Compete and Compute." Politics were also excluded from the possible topics of discussion, basically because people usually lose their common sense on this subject and are inclined to become bent all out of shape over all kinds of things

Heifetz loved being near the water. On a fishing trip in 1979 he was in a pensive mood, relishing a moment of serenity. I was a captive audience for his imitation of a fish breathing through its mouth. Photo by Norman Tremaine

that didn't make sense to him. Religion, like politics, was rather a matter of faith than a subject for a sensible discussion.

Heifetz mentioned to me several times that as a child he had to study Hebrew to please his grandfather who was a rabbi. Apparently the only school Heifetz had ever attended was the *shul* or synagogue. He had some knowledge of the Hebrew alphabet, and at one time, he said, he could read Hebrew script. As far as I know, he didn't join religious organizations, but he believed in the value of the Jewish tradition. He had a fatalistic view of life and God's role in it and didn't believe in the rigid, dogmatic attitude with which most religions approach the idea of deity. In his last years he usually spent Christmas Eve in my home, and once the conversation turned to Christ's birthplace and the Bethlehem legend. When he heard during the conversation that modern religious scholars maintained that Christ was born in Nazareth, not in Bethlehem, Heifetz got all shook up: "You mean, there was no manger, no angels, shepherds, beasts, and Three Kings?" he asked in amazement, though trying to sound sort of cynical about it.

He fell silent after a "learned" answer and then cracked a joke that now even this was taken away from him. By the end it was an unpleasant and unnecessary incident, and it just further confirmed his opinion that religion should never be discussed in company.

Heifetz was very proud of his American citizenship and appreciated the constitution that protected all American citizens equally. He told stories about how, before he became a citizen, he had to report to American consulates all over the world during his concert tours, a State Department requirement for "second-class citizens" abroad. He recalled how officials at the consulates were embarrassed to subject him to this humiliating reporting routine, but he brushed their apologies aside and told them to do their duty. It must have hurt him to be called "second-class citizen," and he was happy to hear that the obnoxious term had been abolished.

On national holidays he was among the few in Malibu who always raised the flag in the morning, and he took it down himself at sunset. He rigorously required all guests to be present at the ceremony and to display the proper respect toward the flag while it was lowered. Heifetz made it his business to know about flags and their proper handling when he still had his sailboat, the *Serenade*. If his students were present at the beach, he never missed the opportunity to teach them how to fold the flag properly and how to store it in its box. He had a tall flagpole and when the gilded sphere on its top showed signs of wear, he went to the expense of having it regilded. Finding a company that would accept the

In his eighties, at the beach in a favorite hat. Photo by Ayke Agus

job of gold plating it as Heifetz wished, instead of just adding gold leaf, was difficult. In this case as in others when I had something special to be done for him, I discovered that I had to find the person in a company who remembered him as the famous violinist; it was easier to make someone go the extra inch or even extra mile if he knew that it was for a man whose name, in his time, was synonymous with perfection.

Heifetz loved to watch the sunset and the full moon. He kept track of the days when the full moon would appear and made sure he was at the beach when it happened. Those nights he sent me around to the neighbors asking them to turn off their outdoor lights so that he could watch the spectacle of the moonlight playing over the waves of the ocean without the interference of artificial lights. To the neighbors' credit, they usually complied. He spent hours in his teahouse on such nights watching the silvery moonlight dancing over the waves. I think these were the only moments when he felt content, much more so than in the limelight of the stage at the summit of his success. The lonely man, looking for company of his liking, found it in the setting sun and the rising moon.

8

Development

If you can wait and not be tired by waiting,
Or, being lied about, don't deal in lies,
Or, being hated, don't give way to hating,
And yet don't look too good, nor talk too wise

RUDYARD KIPLING

*I*n his own way Heifetz did appreciate the value of publicity. Although he liked to say that anybody good will be found by the public, in the bottom of his heart he knew that the public is fickle and easily forgets even those who are good or had once been so. He was also aware that without the publicity machinery going, even he was forgotten by the general public. He never discussed his own contribution to the art of violin playing, never compared himself to others, and never discussed others' weak points in comparison with his own strengths. But although he implied that such behavior would be a big bother, in ensemble performances he would give the impression that his way of doing things was the best. Often he was right, and although his attitude was invariably interpreted as a high-handed slighting of others' opinions, Heifetz couldn't have cared less. Similarly, he felt bothered by the adulation of his public, and stories to that effect were incessantly circulated to cut him down. One such story, quoted even after he stopped playing in public, told of a young man who came to him after a concert with tears in his eyes, saying that he was so moved by Heifetz's playing that he was at a loss for words. "That's your problem," Heifetz coldly shut him up. Such stories, and the very behavior that they described, brought about his isolation from nearly everybody. Though he liked to look at popularity as only a nuisance, I suspect that he secretly missed being recognized on the street and consoled himself that both old and new generations were much too quick to forget the values of the past. It didn't help that by nature he was secretive, and his gruff behavior often was nothing but a desire to play hide-and-seek games. In his last years, however, he had to be satisfied with hiding only from me since his public and fellow musicians were not usable for that any more. His games sometimes resulted in less-than-amusing consequences.

I often took him downtown in Beverly Hills for errands, the nature of which he always kept secret from me even though often they were nothing more serious than going to his tailor or to his bank. I usually had to drop him off at a certain corner and wait for him there or at some other designated place. He rarely told me when to expect his return, and I never asked. Once he played this usual game during the rainy winter season, and it took a bad turn. I couldn't park where he got off, and while I cruised around looking for a parking place I forgot where the drop-off was; all the stores in the area happened to have the same kind of awnings and display windows, and I couldn't identify the one at which I had let him out. As it happened, I waited for him at the wrong spot for an hour. Meanwhile it started to pour, and I began to worry that I was waiting at the wrong place and he was waiting for me somewhere else. I drove around and found him waiting for me in the rain at the curbside a few blocks away. Heifetz was furious. As I took him home, he made me roll the window down on my side of the car just to make me have the experience of being as cold and wet as he was on account of my stupidity. I didn't even try to explain to him what had happened; it was my fault, regardless of the fact that he let me know neither when nor where I should have picked him up.

Heifetz even traveled under his assumed name and had his airplane tickets made out to "Jim Hoyl." That there could have been some real confusion in case of an accident didn't bother him at all. Once we were flying somewhere together, and the president of the University of Southern California happened to be sitting behind us. President John Hubbard, recognizing Heifetz, respectfully leaned forward from behind with a greeting, "Mr. Heifetz, how are you?" But Mr. Heifetz didn't budge and didn't return the greeting, for at that moment he was Jim Hoyl, and he even had his airplane ticket to prove it. President Hubbard repeated the greeting, this time a little louder, but the result was the same. Eventually he turned to me and asked, "Isn't this Mr. Heifetz?"

But I, the well-trained companion, also an instructor at Mr. Hubbard's institution, smiled only and said nothing. The president, looking puzzled, sank back in his chair, probably doubting his own or our sanity. After a while Heifetz turned to me and whispered in my ear, "Who is this man?" When I told him that this was his boss at USC whom he had met several times, Heifetz kept a straight face and kept quiet. A few minutes later he got up, went to the lavatory, and on his way back stopped at the president's seat to say hello to him. They exchanged a few polite words, and Heifetz considered the affair closed. I was dying of embarrassment, but he thought nothing of it. Luckily, Mr. Hubbard was good-natured, didn't take offense, and perhaps wrote off the incident as part of Heifetz's personal or artistic peculiarity.

Jim Hoyl, strangely enough, always expected treatment due to Jascha Heifetz. If a flight attendant recognized him on the plane, he would retreat behind his dark glasses and declare that his name was Jim Hoyl. Yet he always expected the airline's hospitality service to give him the royal treatment, which included waiting for him with an electric car at the gate. He expected me to arrange for that but forbade me to reveal the real identity of Jim Hoyl. He got angry with me when I couldn't accomplish this mission without revealing to the airline who Jim Hoyl really was. He got even madder when the service waited for him at the gate with a wheelchair instead of an electric car. Of course, he wouldn't sit in it—he wanted his electric car ride.

The pseudonym went together with the dark glasses, which he wore even in the movies, the hat pulled down in the front and a scarf up to his mouth, to avoid the intruding public, even when the younger generation no longer knew his name and few from the older set cared to recognize him. Sometimes I noticed older people on the streets whispering behind him and identifying Heifetz to one another; other times he was greeted by an older gentleman with a civil "Excuse me, aren't you Mr. Heifetz?" Once in a while he accepted such a greeting and chatted a few seconds with his admirers, but usually his response was "No, you are mistaken."

Heifetz had a low tolerance for children, but he considered Halloween a legitimate children's day, an occasion when adults should make some concessions to their offspring. If we were at the beach on that day, he would open the large front gate, set up a table in the center of the courtyard, fill it up with bags of candies, put a pumpkin in the center with a candle burning in it, and seat himself behind the table waiting for the children to appear. Unfortunately there were very few and some years no children at all in Malibu during Halloween. When he got bored with the game and with the scarcity of customers, he would put a sign on the candies: "Come and help yourselves; we waited for you long enough," and retire to his house, leaving the gates open for them.

In his last years he guarded his privacy from all intruders even more jealously. One day some members of the string section of the Vienna Philharmonic came to his house in Beverly Hills, hoping to talk to him or

Heifetz donned wig and hat for a Halloween party in my home, shown with
my sister Laili. Photo by Ayke Agus

at least to take a look at the living legend of all string players. Unfortunately they had not made an appointment with him. Heifetz never received unexpected visitors, including his mother after he left home.
Since I was away when the members of the orchestra came, I learned
what happened from him. Someone rang the bell, and he answered the
call because, I presume, he was curious to see what a whole gang of people was doing in his front yard. The person at the door introduced him-

self, identified the orchestra to which his group belonged, and asked him if they could meet Mr. Jascha Heifetz. I think Heifetz would have met them if he had been prepared for the visit, but when he saw a group of strangers, his first reaction was to say no. He told them that he was Mr. Heifetz's brother and Jascha was unfortunately out of town. Sorry, folks. I hope the group knew that he had no brother and didn't buy his story. Anyway they could rest assured that they had seen Jascha Heifetz.

His compulsion to protect his privacy sometimes went to silly lengths. Once an ex-student called him, one whom he had not seen for a year or so. Heifetz must have recognized his voice but apparently didn't feel like talking to anyone that day and answered the student in a high-pitched voice: "Mr. Heifetz is out of town; this is the housekeeper. Any messages?" Of course, the former student knew who answered the telephone but could not call him on it. Why Heifetz picked up the phone if he didn't feel like talking to anyone is a good question, but he thrived on self-contradiction. Other times he played even sillier games over the telephone: he would make all kinds of noises as if he were speaking some Asian language until the other party would hang up in despair. Such nonsense didn't enhance his popularity with anybody, but he didn't care.

I must say, though, that his refusal to meet strangers had a legitimate foundation. He knew well that during recent decades a number of celebrities had come to a sorry end at the hands of deranged strangers. Among others, the Kennedys and various celebrities in the entertainment world were murdered, and President Reagan and other politicians barely escaped with their lives. Heifetz often showed me letters he had received with weird, sometimes life-threatening messages from apparently deranged persons. He was aware that meeting a total stranger always carried a certain amount of risk for celebrities. Since some of these letters attempted to blackmail him, he saved them for a while in a special file in case he needed them as evidence, but eventually he destroyed them all.

I felt his misgivings confirmed when a woman came to the house one day; the housekeeper, who was new and naive and didn't even know who her employer really was, let the stranger in. Perhaps the housekeeper could not be blamed because the woman introduced herself as Mr. Heifetz's long-lost cousin. The "cousin" got herself seated in the living room, and the housekeeper brought the message to me that Heifetz's cousin was waiting for him. I was working in the guestroom and came out to see for myself who the woman was. Again she insisted that she was Heifetz's cousin. I asked the housekeeper to keep an eye on her and reported the story to Heifetz, who gave me hell for letting such a thing happen and told me to get rid of the visitor immediately. I had a difficult time explaining to the wild-looking woman that Heifetz was out of town, and she must come back at a more opportune moment to meet her cousin. She felt quite at home by that time and questioned my right to ask her to leave; after all, she was a close relative and I was nobody. She put her dirty sneakers up on the elegantly upholstered sofa and refused to go. She left only after I threatened her with a call to the police; perhaps she wasn't that crazy after all. After she was gone, Heifetz gave me the job to get rid of the housekeeper, too.

Another day another strange-looking woman showed up at the door, wanting to buy up Mr. Heifetz's music books. I told her the usual answer that Mr. Heifetz was out of town. She had a camper and camped out in front of the house for days. She disappeared for a while but two months later turned up again with the same camper and still wanted Heifetz's books. I called the police, but they couldn't do anything because parking wasn't restricted in that particular street. Strangely enough, she wasn't in her camper all the time, although there was no public transportation within miles, and going in any direction involved descending and climbing steep hills. That made me think that she wasn't alone and was perhaps "casing the joint." The police, however, noticed that she had housekeeping equipment in her van, and that was the hook they needed because housekeeping on the streets was forbidden. Yet they were reluctant to move in on her until Heifetz's lawyer called the chief of the precinct to cite numerous cases in which celebrities were killed by crazy fans. Meanwhile she kept ringing the doorbell, knocking on the door, and kicking the fence, and I had to make sure that the doors to his house were locked all the time. Under pressure from the lawyer, the police put her under closer surveillance and caught her cooking something in her van. They made her leave, but a month later she returned to check whether the books were up for sale. This time, however, threatening her with the police worked and she left for good.

Despite his fear of intruders' violating his privacy, Heifetz wasn't paranoid about security and had no security equipment of any kind in his house. His front gate at Beverly Hills was generally open, though he kept a red light on at the side entrance gate leading to his studio as if to indicate that the house had a security system connected to the police station. This studio was built in the middle of his property, connected to his house by a breezeway. To my horror I discovered only later, when he had become ill, that the door of the studio was improperly installed; the pins and screws holding the hinges in place were installed on the outside instead of being put toward the inside of the frame. The pins, and with them the door, could have been easily removed even by an amateur thief. Heifetz also kept a considerable supply of cash in the office for daily expenses, locked in a flimsy drawer of his desk. His violins, including his priceless Guarnerius, as he called it, were kept in an unlocked cupboard.

Opening his violin cases is a story in itself. For years he always wanted me to stay with him when he opened and closed his violin case. Heifetz had special locks made for his violin cases, all of which were opened by a single solid-gold key. He never told me to watch what he was doing when he opened a case nor gave me any hint about why he expected me to stand by for these occasions. He even gave me a copy of the key, apparently for emergencies, although he never had me use it in his presence. When the day came that Heifetz needed to be hospitalized, I immediately removed the double case containing his Guarnerius and Tononi violins from the unlocked studio and took it to his lawyer for safekeeping. After Heifetz passed away, the case had to be opened to verify the violins' existence. It was taken back to his studio, but strangely enough, nobody, including Heifetz's violin repairman, the lawyer, and the executrix of Heifetz's will, was able to open the case. The key was a simple one with no apparent trick to it, yet it didn't work no matter what the experts tried. Finally in despair I asked them to give me the key. I didn't know, in the sense of "knowing" something, how to do it either, but I had a picture in my mind that suddenly came into focus. The trick was to push in the key and give it a jolt, apparently to unlock a hidden spring. By the way, and perhaps significantly, the key Heifetz had given me had a little horseshoe on it for good luck. (In his will Heifetz donated his Guarnerius to the de Young Museum in San Francisco. He particularly liked this museum and considered it one of the world's most outstanding. He also specified in his will that "worthy performers" should use his Guarnerius for concerts in the museum.)

His nonchalant attitude toward safety got him in trouble only once that I know of. His house in Beverly Hills was robbed, and I was present when it happened. We were about to play cards after dinner, and he sent me to his bedroom to fetch something for him. I immediately noticed that a pillow was out of place, a highly unusual breach of neatness for him, and that the pillowcase was missing. There were other signs, too, that the room's usual order had been disturbed: the glass door was wide open instead of being only cracked ajar as he liked to keep it for fresh air. I also noticed that the screen door, which was inside the glass door, had a hole in it and was also open. I ran back to the living room and reported to him what I had just seen. Heifetz didn't get excited but calmly came to his bedroom and took note that several gold watches were missing, as well as a jewelry case containing precious cuff links and several other pieces of jewelry. The obvious conclusion was that someone, coming through the side door into the small courtyard, found easy access to his bedroom through the open glass door. The intruder cut through the screen, which was locked by a latch, and opened it from the inside. Most of the missing things were presents he had received on his tours. One of the gold wristwatches was a unique piece worth tens of thousands of dollars. I was shaken and in tears when I called the police. They came and took fingerprints and asked for an inventory of what was missing; he never heard from the police again. I was shaken up for days afterward as if my own things had been stolen. When Heifetz couldn't stand my talking about the robbery any longer, he took my hands and said, "Darling," (he always called me darling when he was upset or angry with me) "what's the matter? Don't be upset—these were only material things that we can be without. The robbers could have come inside the house and robbed us of our lives. Thank God, you and I are OK. So, let's be grateful just for that." He didn't even carry insurance for all those valuable articles.

Heifetz received a motley collection of letters and packages every day. Some writers were asking for photos or recordings of his; others sent him Heifetz recordings to autograph, and he received records and tapes from violinists known or unknown to him, some asking for his opinion, most likely looking for his endorsement. If a self-addressed, stamped envelope was enclosed, he usually sent the requested photos and returned the records autographed, but to my knowledge Heifetz never endorsed anyone's recordings. "It could be held against me" was his standard formula to justify his refusal to put something in writing. In fact, he often advised me not to write down anything that later might get me into trouble. If there was no request to return a recording, he mirthfully destroyed it, just as a child would. He cut up the records and pulled out the tapes from the cassettes, then threw the whole mess in the wastebasket. He didn't even have a cassette player, and I had to bring mine in the rare event that he wanted to listen to a cassette. He listened to and kept only the records of his former students and close friends, but he never told anyone what he thought of them. We listened together to some of these records, and sometimes he got quite annoyed if a former student failed to come up to his expectations. Heifetz could not repeat often enough that both live performances and recordings should stir some emotion in the heart of the listeners. If a recording of a former student failed to evoke emotions in him, Heifetz often felt that he had failed as a teacher. "What have I done wrong?" he asked himself after listening to such a record. I could only soothe him, for there was no answer to the question.

Although he routinely gave away his signed publicity photos, he never gave me a single picture of himself with his signature on it. Giving someone close a signed photograph was a bad omen according to his set of superstitions, because it may have meant that a friendship would be cut short or that one would lose someone sooner than expected, or it might even signify an outright dismissal. Heifetz was extremely superstitious in this way, as he was with numbers, and not only for his street address. He considered the thirteen letters in his name a good omen as well. That the number two was lucky he determined through a complicated computation. He was born, his speculations went, on the second day of the second month of the year 1901, a number which also accrued to two by a peculiar way: $1 + 9 = 10$; by ignoring the zeros he added the remaining 01 of 1901, thus arriving at $1 + 1$, which, presto, came out again at the desired number two.

Number two also signified to him the eternal relationship of the male and the female, the constant tension between good and evil, the fight between the strong and the weak. He liked to enlighten me on the subject of the male-female relationship and explained countless times that human life essentially is based on a continuous tension, which he viewed as a kind of game, between man and woman. As for his role in this tension, he was a confirmed male chauvinist, deeply convinced of male superiority; his opinions on the subject were full of bigoted clichés and antiquated principles about women's role in married life and society. He seemed to have had bad experiences with women, yet surrounded himself with them all his life. One can only wonder how much his principles contributed to his bad experiences. Most of the time he was quite gullible and easily influenced by his friends' opinions, men or women, but he never failed to blame them if things didn't turn out the way he had expected. Whenever we talked about the male-female relationship and about the problems women caused for men, his often-repeated opinion was that "A woman can make or break a man; it's always up to the woman to make their relationship work." In his mind, the man was never to blame if the relationship turned sour, yet he felt comfortable only in female company. Heifetz, it seems, wasn't quite at ease in the company of all those other superior men. Based on his own experience, Heifetz tried to discourage his students from getting married, especially to another musician, until they got settled; what he meant by being "settled" he never explained. The slightest reference to his own two failed marriages always brought on the seething remark, "But I was busy making a living and was on tours all the time; I should never have gotten married in the first place [let alone] have children." This was his way of exonerating himself from all responsibility in family life and in rearing his three children. I must concede, he was right to a certain point. But in both his marriages Heifetz went for glamour and social status rather than for the woman who, according to his principles, was supposed to keep the home fires burning while he was on tour.

There was also a lighter side to his male chauvinism. He invented facetious words to help separate the sexes; for example, in the Heifetz language, a female hero was a "shero," and a hysterectomy became "herterectomy." "What does the poor guy have to do with her hysterectomy?" he would grumble. "He has enough trouble as it is already." When a female guest once called him a male chauvinist pig, Heifetz furiously paced up and down in the room. I saw the wheels turning in his mind as he searched for a cutting answer. Finally he found the right one, and he stopped in the middle of the room to declare, "Well, as our female chauvinist sow friend said—" and took over the conversation on an unrelated matter but made sure that the words "female chauvinist sow" played a major role in it.

As for getting married, perhaps he was right; artists of his stature do not have it easy when they attempt to settle down to ordinary housekeeping ways of life. He found this out too late and bitterly blamed his female partners for everything. In defense of his wives, Heifetz was proud of the fact that he was difficult and liked to call himself "im-possible—two words." This meant that he did everything in his power to make himself unacceptable, sometimes even repulsive, and considered it a test of love to accept him as he was, the whole twisted package with the never-ceasing challenges. Perhaps with his precocious childhood as the indisputable, and possibly petulant and feared, breadwinner for his family, he developed this twisted view of himself—that the more impossible he behaved, the more control he had over everyone, and accepting him was the ultimate proof of loving him. But woe to those who tried it.

To protect himself from the world and also from his own caprice, Heifetz built a protective wall of precepts and principles around himself, and he relied on these as ironclad guarantors of his own survival. Some of these principles went from the ridiculous to the plain ornery. He allowed only one woman in the kitchen because two women in the same place make only trouble, not dinner. A male person wasn't allowed in the kitchen because the kitchen is the woman's place where she should stay and work, leaving it only when she was needed elsewhere. He was absolutely sure, and made it known to everyone, that if he had two women in his employment on the same job, there would be trouble, and to prove his point, he would stir things up to make trouble develop. He never paid money back unless the borrower asked for it, because the borrower should look after his own interest. Heifetz wasn't stingy or a bad debtor—he always paid up when asked—it was only a matter of principle. For years the housekeeper received the same monthly allowance for household expenses; I had to put forth considerable effort and powers of persuasion to make him understand that times and prices had changed. The housekeeper had to be in the kitchen on a certain, inflexible schedule, regardless of whether she had anything to do there. To check on her, Heifetz got up early in the morning to watch her coming down at the prescribed time, even if he was sick and knew he would not be getting up the whole day. Checks written for utilities or taxes often bore a notation from him, "Under protest," for he believed that there was no reason for raising prices for anything. He forced issues if it served his set of principles; if anyone's music in his master class had gotten dog eared or torn at the edges, ready to fall apart, or even if it was overly marked, Heifetz would hold it up in his hand, look at the owner for a while, then with a trace of smile tear it up, throw it in the waste basket, and say benevolently, "Now you have no choice but to buy a new copy." However, Heifetz was willing to pay for the torn-up music from his own pocket or from the class treasury if the student protested that he didn't have the money to buy a new copy. The list of his principles was endless, and I suspect he invented some of them as he went along to suit certain situations.

Except for the expensive caviar and lox that he loved, his taste in food reflected the simple Russian-Jewish cooking that he was brought up with. He certainly had had his share of fancy dishes on tour, having been exposed to innumerable receptions and banquets. Sometimes he spoke of the famous restaurants he frequented all over the world. He must have been quite adventurous with tasting unusual food in strange places because he told me that a few times he became ill from eating food that his stomach wasn't used to. As a virtuoso he knew what it took to become good at a trade; Heifetz spoke with admiration of a certain captain of the waiters at Maxim's in Paris who could peel an orange with a fork and spoon, never touching the fruit with his hands nor spilling a drop of its juice. As Heifetz became older, his taste returned to that of his childhood, and he detested sophisticated sauces and gravies, of which he said he had enough in his traveling days. He once fired a gourmet housekeeper for cooking too well, mainly for serving too many kinds of fancy sauces. A good stew was what he could always eat, and he liked seafood, especially lobster and crabs, and fish, usually of the deep-sea kind, but otherwise he was a meat-and-potato man. He had a mania for certain Russian dishes, such as herring salad, chicken cutlets, and soups, and he taught me how to make them. These dishes must have been his mother's specialties, because eating them always brought to the surface countless childhood memories. However, Heifetz didn't have much practical sense in the kitchen; once, trying to make his own breakfast, he put a two-gallon kettle, filled to the top, on his electric stove to make one cup of tea. He then bitterly complained that something was wrong with the stove because a cupful of hot water was taking forever to make, and he made me call the service to check the stove out. Strangely enough, explaining to him how to boil just one cup of water didn't seem to make a dent in his head.

To continue with more of his principles, Heifetz had faith in everything old and distrusted everything new, to the point that it sometimes became exasperating. He stubbornly maintained that his old telephone books were better than the new ones and didn't let me throw out his ten-year-old copies. I had resort to subterfuge and take the old books to my house to throw them out because I knew he would look for them in the garbage and bring them back if I put them in his own trash. After he couldn't find the old books he was quite content to use the new ones and didn't press the issue. Nothing new was ever good, and that went for other books too. Once in my house he discovered a 1971 edition of *Baker's Biographical Dictionary of Musicians*. He took it home with him and returned it a week later saying that his, the previous edition from 1958, was better because it was thirteen years older.

Nothing could be moved in his house, and his housekeepers were forbidden to dust certain shelves because he was afraid that they might move objects that had been in the same place for more than forty years. Once he rented an unfamiliar place for vacation, moved everything in the place to suit his convenience, then memorized carefully the position of every single object and insisted that they stay there for the duration of his vacation. I also had to memorize all the original positions so that I could put everything back before we left. He was always mildly upset when he came to my house for dinner and found familiar furniture moved to a different place since his last visit. He thought I had an unstable character because I liked to move my furniture every other month. He prided himself on being a good home decorator and was disappointed when in my home I didn't follow his advice. I learned from him that a home should be a place where one feels comfortable and not a museum stuffed with precious furniture and art objects to which one has to give a wide berth in fear of touching or breaking them. Chairs should be placed in pairs with a lamp in between or on both sides for the purpose of intimate conversation or for reading together. He also practiced what he preached and read to me or made me read to him on such a pair of chairs.

In spite of his rigidity, when he wanted to change or get rid of something or somebody, it had to be done without the slightest delay. He was a life-long subscriber to *The New Yorker*, but when Andrew Porter replaced Malcolm Sargent as its music critic, he wanted to cancel his subscription immediately because the magazine wasn't the same any more. I had to call the magazine to do that without delay. When next week he still got a copy, he became all upset and made me call New York again to ask them to discontinue sending copies at once. Someone there patiently explained to me that even cancelation takes time; they didn't quite understand what Mr. Heifetz was upset about.

Heifetz even attempted to subjugate City Hall to his principles. When the taxes on his properties were increased, he refused to pay them because to his mind the increases were not justified. In fact, he was against any kind of property taxes if the property was acquired with honest work; he considered taxing such properties to be against the principles laid down in the constitution. Despite his principles, City Hall put a lien on his property that even figured in the settlement of his estate. He supported all sorts of civic action groups fighting City Hall, including Proposition 13, which advocated lowering property taxes.

Though Heifetz abhorred taxation, he expected services and order from City Hall down to the minutest details. One day he noticed that the street sign on the corner of his block had disappeared, perhaps broken off by a passing truck. He wanted the sign restored as soon as possible and gave me two days to get results. First he made me call a neighbor across the street; since the sign was on this neighbor's side of the street, Heifetz expected him to do something about it. The neighbor assured me that such things take time and that eventually something would happen regardless of our interference. This was, of course, not good enough for Heifetz. He told me to take up the street sign cause quickly and without using his name. I refused to accept the latter condition. I had to make a round of calls at City Hall to find out what department was responsible for taking care of the street signs. It turned out to be the Department of Water and Power because, I presume, they get around the most often to read the water and electric meters.

By that time I had wised up and asked the first person who answered the telephone in the Department of Water and Power, "Do you like classical music?" At the affirmative answer I continued my query toward a street sign with "Do you know who Jascha Heifetz is?"

No, the lady had not the faintest idea, but I continued to follow the scent: "Could you connect me with someone sixtyish who likes classical music?"

To the astounded question as to why I would want to talk to anyone sixtyish who likes classical music, I replied that it was a matter of utmost urgency that I talk to someone of that qualification since my life depended on resolving the replacement of a street sign within two days. The crazy logic must have sounded convincing, or she thought that I was out of my mind, but she connected me with an elderly gentleman who lived up to the description. Yes, he knew Jascha Heifetz, even had some of his records and liked the way he played the violin. When I told him what Mr. Heifetz wanted, he patiently explained to me that to do such a thing would take time since the department responsible for signs had other priorities, some of which were more urgent, like putting up stop signs at corners where the appropriate number of people were killed (which seemed to be an absolute requirement for erecting a new stop sign), and since those stop signs were mass manufactured and distributed, they had no time to bother with single street signs until they ran out of their urgent assignments. However, since it was Mr. Heifetz, the symbol of perfection, he promised to see that an exception would be made.

The sign indeed appeared within a reasonable time, but as soon as Heifetz laid eyes on it, he noticed that the color of the sign was turquoise blue, unlike the rest of the signs that were marine blue. I was scared to death that he would commission me to have the sign taken down and replaced with a marine blue one. "But isn't it a pretty color, all brand new and shining, while the others are already faded?" I pleaded with him in desperation.

"Yes, but it is a turquoise color and sticks out like a sore thumb from the rest of the signs."

"I'm quite sure there is a reason for that," I said, trying to disguise my shaky voice. "I heard from someone that they are going to replace all the signs in the future with turquoise blue ones." He looked at me suspiciously but let me get away with the lie. And who knows? Perhaps he even believed it.

Heifetz was a very proud person, but perhaps it was part of his reluctance to use his name that made him shun honors, especially if he felt they were not genuine or came too late. He was proud of his French Legion of Honor distinction and occasionally wore his medal on the lapel of his jacket, especially on French holidays. He was selected for the American Presidential Medal of Honor but refused to accept it because receiving it involved a great public show, and besides, as he said, "It was too late." He would not have objected to having his image on an American postage stamp, as he was an ardent stamp collector, but only if the stamp represented a musical subject. Some noise was made about creating a Heifetz stamp, but nothing came of it.

Superstitious as Heifetz was, I would not be surprised if he followed the advice he received from George Bernard Shaw. Heifetz liked to talk about his meetings with Shaw and with Jean Sibelius. He sought appointments with each of them and was very happy that Shaw came to his concert in Great Britain in 1920 after their visit. Shaw wrote him the famous letter in which he earnestly admonished Heifetz, "If you provoke a jealous God by playing with such superhuman perfection, you will die young. I earnestly advise you to play something badly every night before going to bed instead of saying your prayers. No mortal should presume to play faultlessly."

Much later Heifetz visited Sibelius when he concertized in Finland because he loved the Sibelius violin concerto and wanted to gather impressions for its authentic performance. He described to me in great detail how the visit went. Sibelius lived out in the country, and Heifetz was overwhelmed by the austerity of the landscape and the bone-chilling cold that he experienced there. The air was humid, and shifting fog hung over the lakes and the woods as he approached Sibelius's simple country house. He decided right there, even before talking to Sibelius, that his interpretation of the violin concerto should somehow reflect this first impression. Heifetz often spent hours with a student to explain what this concerto was all about and how certain passages should be interpreted. I don't know if Sibelius gave him performance advice for his concerto, and if he did, to what extent Heifetz followed it; this Heifetz did not say.

Heifetz had a very few favorite records, some of which he kept at hand all the time at the beach, others at his home in Beverly Hills. As far as I know, he never listened to his own recordings but kept a collection of them in his studio. When I persuaded him to listen to the radio at times when one of his records was played, he usually shook his head and muttered, "Too fast," when the fast movements were played. I think he would have changed some of his interpretations had he persisted performing in his late years.

Heifetz was a private person and didn't like to promote himself or anything else, either in public or in private. Once, late in his life, he received an offer, I think it was from a brewing company, with a fee of several hundred thousand dollars attached to it, to play a few notes on his Guarnerius on television and to say only as much as "Now here is our sponsor." He staunchly refused the offer and told me that he had more self-respect than to make a laughing stock of himself. In passing he once mentioned that he made only one television appearance during his career and that it was so bad that he was still embarrassed about it. This was his appearance in 1970 with the French National Orchestra in Paris for American broadcast; he played the *Scottish Fantasy* by Max Bruch, along with other works. That the proposed commercial also would have promoted the sale of his own recordings apparently didn't occur to him, or he didn't care.

9

Musica Disciplina

If you can meet with Triumph and Disaster
And treat those two imposters just the same

RUDYARD KIPLING

L eopold Auer, Heifetz's revered master, was a Jewish immigrant who
came to Russia from the backwaters of nineteenth-century Hungary.
His family was poor, and as a young man he struggled mightily for his
education and career as a violinist. As a penniless student he lived on wit
and charity until he gained recognition. How long Heifetz studied with
him is not clear. He never told me, and from the conflicting dates I have
seen, it could have been anywhere from two to five years. According to
the much-respected Hungarian music dictionary *Zenei Lexikon* edited by
Denes Bartha (Budapest, 1965), Auer lived near Dresden from 1911 to
1914, thus beginning at the time when Jascha was only ten years old. Yet
in *Baker's Biographical Dictionary of Musicians* Nicolas Slonimsky tells us
that Heifetz began his studies with Auer in 1910. In any case, although
Auer was the first man to assume a towering presence in Jascha's eyes, he
quickly recognized that his mentor was not the greatest violinist in the
world. At the time that Heifetz was in Auer's class, the master's solo performances consisted mostly of playing the rare solo parts in orchestral
works, a privilege of the Imperial Concertmaster of the St. Petersburg
Symphony Orchestra. Whenever Heifetz and I listened to a Tchaikovsky
ballet recording, he was quick to point out that Auer played the solo parts
in a certain characteristic and inimitable way, differently from all other
concertmasters. He also remembered that Auer's playing was acknowledged by applause which always started from the imperial box and only
thereafter was picked up by the entire audience. Heifetz never mentioned having heard Auer play an entire solo concert, as apparently he
didn't concertize at that time. Auer, though, was not an insignificant performer; Tchaikovsky originally dedicated his violin concerto to him, with-
drawing the dedication, however, after Auer suggested changes in the

score. Heifetz always spoke of Auer with a certain humility even in his late years, with the pupil's respect toward his master, a rare phenomenon among famous artists. He seemed to be admitting that Auer had made him what he was, both as an artist and as a man of the world as well.

Only Heifetz knew what in his artistic development he really owed to Auer's teaching, but technique probably was the least of it. He often mentioned that Auer left teaching of the mechanics of violin playing to his assistants. In fact, Auer didn't change the way Jascha held his instrument because the child accomplished everything in a way that seemed natural for him.

Leopold Auer's book of 1921, *Violin Playing As I Teach It,* was displayed in a prominent place in the library of Heifetz's studio. I don't know how often he read it, but it certainly didn't look very worn. Heifetz showed me the book and asked me to read it carefully and to take my time in doing so. I remember looking at him very surprised because, as a matter of principle, he always put a strict time limit on everything I had to do, which included reading books. I don't remember Heifetz's ever referring to the Auer book in his class, nor during our conversations, but quoting authorities wasn't among his idiosyncrasies. After his death, I read the book again and could see that Heifetz's teaching method clearly reflected the precepts that Auer had laid down in his slender essay. Auer's warning toward the end of the introduction must have made the deepest impression on Heifetz because it was implicit in the way he handled his own students: "The majority of those who wish to become musicians, in spite of the fact that they may possess unusual gifts, have no idea of the difficulties they will have to surmount, the moral tortures they will be called upon to endure, the disillusions they will experience, before they win recognition."

That difficulties did not cease even after recognition is gained Heifetz had found out the hard way. As he acknowledged in a public statement, he had had a serious crisis in 1921 after W. J. Henderson, music critic for the *New York Sun,* criticized him for a certain lack of depth that had begun to creep into his playing, and also for his tendency for superficial brilliance. Henderson warned Heifetz that he owed it to his talent and to his audience to forsake the easy road to success, and to immerse himself more in the depths of his music. The changed attitude which Henderson criticized was attributed by Heifetz himself to his newly found wealth and to his discovery that there is more to life than just practicing the violin. The more he pursued this discovery, the more superficial his music making had become.

Heifetz had to confront both the artistic and the personal aspects of the crisis. First, he had to deal with the merits of a criticism he had never encountered before at this level of seriousness and iconoclastic audacity. His usual reviews up to that time were raving praise and mindless admiration. Having been brought up as a pampered child and adulated, spoiled youth, he took Henderson's review much harder than more hardened artists might have done; in fact, the review thoroughly crushed him.

Heifetz, like Hercules, faced a crossroads in his life. According to the legend, Hercules was given a chance to choose between Pleasure and Virtue, the former promising all carnal delights but with it the life of an ordinary mortal, and the latter only hard work but immortality beckoning at the end of the road. Heifetz knew well that a considerable number of talented artists had chosen the road of Pleasure and fallen by the wayside, yet his decision to take the road toward immortality didn't come without a struggle that shook him to the depths of his soul. Reminiscing over this incident, he told me that he considered committing suicide upon reading the review. Although his life had not been easy, his upbringing had not prepared him to face the inevitable ups and downs; he seemed not to know that continuous success without setbacks exists only in movies and cheap novels. As he talked to me about this period of his life, he took from his pocket a carefully folded sheet of paper, opened it up, and read to me the poem "If" by Rudyard Kipling. This poem must have fallen into his hands at the right moment; it became his oracle, his creed, and a protective talisman for the rest of his life. He always carried a copy of it, like a shield, wherever he went; he told me that he used that piece of paper so much that he had had to replace it several times. He also wrote a commentary on this poem, entitled "Words to Live By." He begins with a quotation from the poem:

> If you can meet with Triumph and Disaster
> And treat those two imposters just the same

In the commentary that follows, Heifetz says that this was a popular poem when he made his debut in this country. He learned it by heart and had carried a copy of it with him ever since. It had special meaning for him because an artist "must steer a mean course between triumph and disaster and learn to live with both." Of the two, triumph is the greater test because many emerge as heroes under suffering but then succumb to success. He met triumph early and did not have to face disaster until he was quite grown up. The first serious criticism he had to face, when he was about twenty years old, was a terrible shock. For one's artistic balance, the "heady wine of continuous praise" is even more challenging. Yet triumph and disaster are two faces of the same coin, the currency of the world of art.

The Jascha Heifetz success story that followed the crisis at the crossroads is quite well known; his name became synonymous with perfection, in both the artistic and technical sense of the word. Heifetz told me many times that he felt grateful to Henderson for reminding him what he owed to his talent and to his public. In fact he wrote Henderson a letter in gratitude for the review that had brought him to his senses.

Heifetz's seeing disaster in such a comparatively mild review, to the point of considering suicide, may seem an exaggerated reaction, but we can somewhat understand this hypersensitivity if we take into consideration the pressure he was exposed to as a prodigy. Apparently it didn't help much that his master, Leopold Auer, knew well about these dangers and summed them up in his book on violin playing.

In his introduction Auer berates parents who lightheartedly decide that their child should have a musical career and who even select the violin as the instrument by which the child and, not least, his parents should achieve fame and wealth. Driven by the fame of the great violinists of the nineteenth century, the parents don't even pause to consider that their misguided ambition could sacrifice the child's whole future, not to mention mental and physical health. They seek out famous teachers of successful prodigies and obstinately persist, in spite of the child's evident lack of sufficient talent, in their pursuit of a phantom that can only lead to the ruin of the child. Auer tried to persuade many determined parents to find another profession for their young "virtuosos," some other vocation where their child could "stand a better chance of being useful to his fellow-beings, and at the same time gain a more assured means of support for himself."

A typical result of pushing the child into this "prodigy disease," as Heifetz jokingly described his own prodigy past, was the ruin of the child's nerves. The unnatural expectations were almost certain to put the child on edge, even if his nerves had been stable enough to begin with, the very nerves on which a performer's career stands or falls. As Auer points out in his book, there exists no remedy to cure an artist's stage fright. The presence or absence of bad nerves is a matter of sheer luck and coincidence, like being born under a benevolent star or an ill omen or, as we Chinese like to think, in the year of a favorable or an unfavorable sign. While a pianist may be able to disguise a certain amount of nervousness by banging out a few loud chords on the keyboard at the outset of his performance, there is no such camouflage for the trembling bow that will give the violinist away.

Heifetz's superb control over his nerves gave rise to the accusation that he lacked temperament and that therefore his playing was cold. The best rebuttal for this argument comes from those who knew his performances only from recordings: they find the charge of coldness absolutely ridiculous. As Heifetz told me several times, before his performances he was nervous, perhaps a little less than others but he was nervous nonetheless, because every appearance onstage brought with it eventualities over which he had no control. Memory lapse, a broken or suddenly loose string, a mistake by the pianist, a page falling off the stand, a conductor's or an orchestra's incompetence: all were circumstances over which he had no control. And Heifetz wanted control, not only over these circumstances but also, above all, over his audiences; he wanted his performances to be exciting, not just beautiful, and he watched his audience for the slightest sign that their attention had been lost. If he noticed that his listeners were not sitting at the edge of their seats, he did something about it. This something was not premeditated, so that his accompanist also had to sit at the edge of his or her seat waiting for it to happen. This sort of attitude toward performance indeed requires superb control over one's nerves and does not leave much room for self-absorption, which many performers seem to let themselves drift into. He was willing and able to change preset patterns, practiced phrases and even fingerings, as soon as he noticed that he was losing his audience. For Jascha Heifetz "taking chances" on the stage was a way of life, as if he were a gambler except with a more predictable outcome. Perhaps this high expectation of excitement was the reason that he was loath to over-rehearse with his pianist or fellow chamber music players. Heifetz expected, both of himself and of his collaborators, to create something spontaneous in every performance. Though he practiced every detail to perfection, his performance wasn't a string of details, as many virtuosos would have it; the details were only the polished components that he freely used in a new creation every time he stepped on the stage. He hated precalculated performances in his master class, even by established artists. Hearing such performances he would invariably remark, "This does not tell me anything."

Auer, and Heifetz as well, maintained that besides strong nerves, one must have the proper mental attitude toward being successful. He who wants the end must also want the means leading to it. A certain mental toughness is an absolute necessity to persevere through endless hours of practicing. However, Heifetz often warned against mindless, uncritical practicing that may lead to bad habits rather than to fruitful results. There is also a point beyond which mental and physical fatigue makes practicing a waste of time. Interestingly enough, Heifetz was against recording one's own practicing and then using the recording to make corrections. He would rather have the student listen with critical ears to his own playing as he practiced and correct his mistakes immediately, for that's the only way to simulate performance conditions. Listening to recorded practicing could destroy spontaneity, as would too many markings in the score, and result in visual rather than aural knowledge of a piece which may easily lead to disaster. Even after a flawless performance Heifetz would often baffle a student by saying "Not ready" when the student thought he did his best and there was nothing more he could do. Heifetz was a master in detecting when music was becoming mechanical from overpracticing without becoming the performer's own.

Sometime in his early years Heifetz stated that he practiced, on the average, only three hours a day, but then he immediately added that mental preparation for each work took him a great deal more time. Memorizing a piece even before touching the instrument helps to prevent mental block, which may happen to any performer no matter how many hours he had practiced. However, under pressure the one not cut out to be a performer can forget practically everything he had learned. Even famous performers were not immune to bad nerves and mental block. According to Auer, Joachim was a nervous wreck on the stage, and Anton Rubinstein's most beautiful performances were not onstage but in friendly company where he felt more comfortable. Auer admired some of his students, including Heifetz, for having much less tendency toward stage fright than he and many of his famous contemporaries had.

Mental block can happen even to performers with excellent musical memory. Heifetz had an exceptionally accurate and lasting musical memory; he kept in evidence a very large repertory and remembered most of it without the slightest hesitation even late in his life. He usually played from memory and told me that he hadn't touched some of the pieces for several decades; yet he remembered not only the notes but even the performance markings and the fingerings, both his own and the ones printed in the score. He also knew quite well the piano parts and their performance markings. He admitted to me that he had had a memory lapse only once during his career, a veritable record, considering the enormous number of concerts he played.

Heifetz seems to have had longer than average thumbs. He anchored his left thumb at the neck of the violin and could range from there into positions that most violinists find difficult if not impossible to reach without moving their thumbs. He had superb, instant reflexes that allowed him to transfer musical ideas from his brain to his fingers without the slightest hesitation. Heifetz's playing belied his age: even in his eighties his left hand maintained a safe grip and his steady right hand guided the bow without the slightest trembling.

Heifetz was full of energy, not of the bursting kind but rather of the slow, grinding type that kept him going even when he had to use a stick for walking. He was a heavy, two-pack-a-day smoker when he was concertizing but later gave up smoking entirely when he learned how harmful it was. Characteristically he wanted to make sure that giving up smoking was entirely his own decision, not one imposed upon him by someone else, not even by a notion of what was for his own good. To prove this to himself, for years he carried a few cigarettes and a lighter in his pocket, just in case he wanted to change his mind. He never did.

Drinking is not particular to any nationality, but Russians seem to do an outstanding job of it. Heifetz was no exception. Alcohol, the ruin of so many people living under constant pressure, didn't seem to affect him to any noticeable degree, and in company he always knew when to stop. When I knew him, he usually drank bourbon, but at the table he always wanted a set of vodka glasses, just in case he would decide at the last minute to have vodka. He appreciated people who "could take it" without harmful effects, which one day gave him quite a surprise in my house.

I happened to have a guest, a Dutch nun, staying with me. She had been my mother's teacher in Indonesia and later the principal of the school where I studied. She was a survivor of a Japanese concentration camp in the Philippines where she was stationed as a nun during the Japanese occupation. She and other survivors of the camp had had an anniversary reunion of their liberation, and after their meeting, which was held in San Francisco, she was allowed to stay in my house for a week. Heifetz's experience with nuns was quite limited, and he was curious about her especially after I told him about her background. She was a rather large, no-nonsense woman who didn't even wear a habit outside her convent, unusual for those days, and looked just like any other strong person coming from a country where delicate women seem to be the exception. She sat next to Heifetz at the dinner table. He looked at her with suspicion for a while and then decided to test her stamina. As usual Heifetz had brought with him a bottle of his favorite vodka to be served at the dinner. One toast followed another, and as the nun kept up with Heifetz's "bottoms up" requests, his eyes grew larger and larger until he asked her what her real name had been before she entered her religious order. She was called Agnes as a layperson, she said. Heifetz told her to stop using her phony religious name, called her Agnes, and gave her permission to call him Jim. "I had never seen a woman who could keep up with me drinking vodka without falling under the table," he told me later.

WHAT MAKES A GREAT PERFORMER? I would say that among the rarest talents in a musician is the ability to achieve a rhythmical coherence that fits the nature of the music performed. Quite a few performers and conductors can keep a steady tempo and rhythm, but few have the daring flexibility—the sense of freedom—to counterbalance the monotony that inevitably ensues. Heifetz had an ironclad sense of rhythm and could keep a steady tempo going forever, yet he endowed it with tiny, hardly noticeable changes within the measures, and even throughout whole phrases, to give the music a "lift," especially if the same rhythmical pattern continued for a long time. Such subtleties cannot be put into notation or dressed up in hard and fast rules; they are buried in the depths even of uninspiring scores for the performer to recognize and bring to life. "I feel nothing," Heifetz would say after a stiff, mannered performance, even one that was technically perfect, if it followed the printed score exactly. Nothing is more deadly than a "straight" reading of Chopin, Schumann, Brahms, Schubert, or any music whose effect depends on *not* being metronomic. Only when the performer could rise above technical problems, to think and feel the music without showing the seams of technical preparation, would Heifetz grant him the distinction that he or she was ready.

Auer in his book on violin playing attributes great importance to nuances in interpretation. Using nuances means employing a host of different shades of dynamics, accents, tempo, rhythm, and color, varying the performance of repetitions, phrase endings, and cadences, playing with or without vibrato, changing the bowing technique, making the music move or holding it back; it also means paying attention to hundreds of details that may be lost on the general audience and perceived only by other violinists. Yet the global effect of nuances is not lost at all; a music lover might say of the performance, "It was beautiful and different from all other interpretations I have ever heard, but I don't exactly know what made it so different or how the musician did it." Nuances are rather on the craft side of music making, and a good master could teach any talented and perceptive student how to use them. What cannot be taught is to make musical sense of the details and to render the nuances freely and with taste in an inspired way without becoming mannered and mechanical. The way Joachim, Auer's master, taught nuances was to demonstrate a phrase and say with a benevolent smile, "That is the way you must play it." Heifetz would characterize such approach as "Going by the book," which he detested and considered a source of stiff mannerism.

Heifetz was one of those gifted musicians who could look at a score and recognize a number of possible interpretations even before he played the piece. Composers are notoriously not the best interpreters of their own music; it takes a good performer to see beyond the composer's interpretative markings. Good examples are the Korngold, Goldmark, Conus, Vieuxtemps, and Spohr concertos and even the Strauss sonata; into these pieces Heifetz breathed the kind of life other performers attempted in vain. Being able to dazzle certainly helped, but he added to the interpretation of these pieces something that perhaps even their composers didn't see in them.

AUER SPEAKS of the heavy price musicians pay for their success, and part of the bargain is usually an incomplete if not disastrous family life. Children resent an absentee father or mother and may even take out their resentment on their parents and society. A musician's life does not follow a safe schedule in which children can look forward to seeing their parents when they need them. Even studio and orchestra players often work late at night, which can play havoc during the growing-up years. Unfortunately Heifetz was difficult by nature, and his hypersensitivity was at odds with the constant reconciliation and understanding that family life is all about. Thus the Heifetz household was not immune to strain, and he had his share of family troubles which accompanied him to the end of his life. I witnessed plenty of them, but his family matters are outside the scope of this narrative. I can say, however, that I did no better at maintaining my own balance between my devotion to Heifetz and my personal life.

The problem was that Heifetz's expectations were not limited to music. They affected all other facets of his life and therefore of mine. Even though he did not believe that perfection was possible, he was always trying to achieve it. He often said, "There is always room for improvement." In any given situation he could always find fault—naturally so, or there wouldn't be room for improvement. Although this aspect of his personality didn't bother me, it wasn't always easy to manage. I convinced myself that it was natural for a man of his stature to be so demanding.

He was concerned about every aspect of my life or of anybody else's with whom he was associated. He had to be involved in my daily activities to the point of meddling. Between his master classes and my own courses at USC, I had scarcely any spare time, but I often had to cancel even the rare date with friends. I would be ready to go out with someone when the telephone would ring. Heifetz expected me at his house right now because he needed help doing something very important. Or he would have me cancel an upcoming appointment because he had something more important for me to do. I had no choice but to reply "Yes, Mr. Heifetz" at all times, which did not go over very well with my friends.

An exception was Michael, whom I married in 1976. He understood my admiration for Heifetz and appreciated the influence Heifetz had on my musical life, and he was willing to put up with the demands and limitations Heifetz would put on our ordinary daily life. Life was not simple with Heifetz around: when our daughter, Ada, was born in 1979, I had the feeling that he was jealous of her, like two babes jealous for their mother's attention. When I asked his permission for the first time to bring Ada along to work when she was an infant, he turned me down: "It is not a good time right now; perhaps another time." The right time never seemed to arrive. When Ada was five months old and a little more manageable, I gathered my nerves and simply brought her with me to his house. To my surprise, Heifetz didn't refuse to let us in, but he succeeded in frightening Ada with a stern voice intended to impress upon her who was the boss in his house. To Heifetz's recital of the rules of the house, of which his talking to her mostly consisted, she responded only by crying. This elicited his favorite educational statement that "Children should be seen and not heard." Ada eventually became accustomed to his voice and even let him hold her for a while, but his words of wisdom never really worked with her, as I presume it didn't with his own children either. Over the years I observed him trying to make a headstrong child conform to his principles. When worse came to worst, he could frighten her into temporary submission but never to permanent obedience.

Fortunately Michael's work allowed him a more peaceful existence to balance my busy one during the eight years that I was with Heifetz after Ada was born, and a loving, elderly woman neighbor, whom Ada called Grandma, also helped. Ada knew her dad was the homebody, and that he enjoyed taking care of her. She recalls many nights when Michael tucked her into bed and she wondered when I would come home from work. I made sure that we did things together, just the two of us, but clearly she also wondered whether she or my job was more important, so perhaps it is fortunate that to a considerable extent, my working and home life were not separate.

Heifetz made himself part of our family life. He invited himself for dinner once or twice a week. When he was in a wine-drinking mood, he would bring the one he liked. He always brought an unopened bottle of vodka, which he either took back with him after consuming part of it or left with us. He did this on the rare excursions to other places, too. I think he didn't trust anybody to give him the right kind of unadulterated drink. He not only invited himself for dinner, but he also dictated what time and sometimes let me know what he wanted to eat. He insisted that the appetizers should be served in the living room along with the drinks while socializing.

Heifetz liked to believe that he was a born interior decorator. He often told me that he had a natural gift for that. After a few visits to our home he decided how the furniture should be arranged and where the pictures should be hung. It all came under the "there is always room for improvement" principle. The changes had to take place immediately. At first Michael was bewildered by the requests of this bold and cantankerous guest, but he had enough sense of humor eventually to laugh at the circus Heifetz created in our household.

From a very young age Ada was aware of this unusual guest whom she was allowed to call Uncle Jascha. Heifetz liked to call her Adatchka, using the Russian diminutive or term of endearment for Ada, just as his mother called him Jaschinka. I always dressed her nicely when we knew of his arrival and also asked any guests to be dressed semiformally; he would not abide trousers on female guests. Heifetz liked to know in advance who the other guests would be. To his credit he never asked me to cancel anyone, but when I took him home (he always had to be picked up and brought home), he discussed the guest list and told me whom he would not mind seeing again and whom to leave out. I usually warned the would-be guests not to ask questions concerning music. Yet some first-timers would forget my warning and bombard him with questions about his performances, his records, and which musicians he liked and which not, all of which he tolerated for a while in stony silence. Heifetz would just stare back at the unfortunate guest, hoping to get across the message, "Stop asking." When more importune questions came reformulated and rephrased, Heifetz usually gave his stock answer, "If these shop-talk questions continue, I will have to send you a bill." This usually resulted in a little nervous laughter but was enough to stop the questions. Heifetz liked to meet new people. Depending on the person's personality and that

Heifetz listening to Ada accompanying me in the Bach-Gounod *Ave Maria* in my home during the Christmas season, 1985. She did not really wish to play for him but complied with his authoritative-sounding request. Photo by Michael Palotai

certain empathy, he enjoyed making small talk provided that nobody brought up subjects concerning politics, music, and religion. He was always courteous enough to let the other person finish what he had to say and he even listened carefully enough to comprehend the gist of it.

Later, when Ada grew up a little, I took her more often to the Heifetz house, sometimes in Beverly Hills, more often to the beach at Malibu. At Easter Heifetz liked to organize the traditional egg hunting. For this, Ada was allowed to bring a friend along, just one, because "three makes a crowd." Heifetz was almost as excited doing this as the children were. He did most of the egg hiding himself and cheered them on during the hunt. He also taught them a race in which the kids had to push an egg in the grass with their noses until they reached his finish line. Ada seemed to understand that Uncle Jascha was just another big kid who was trying to make up for something that he had missed somewhere along the line.

Managers are an essential part of an artist's life, but apparently they found him difficult to manage, and he felt the same about them. "Managers! Who needs them, but who can do without them?" he would sigh when he recalled his troubles with managers. He never discussed whose doings caused the troubles, but even if he was to blame, I'm quite sure he would have managed to find the managers at fault. He used to complain that he "was the worst-managed violinist of the century." He was aware that the job the managers did for him was indispensable, but it was his nature to rebel against the harness they put on him, and he felt that his managers ran his life by setting up a tough schedule for him in which he didn't have much say. His time was taken up not only by rehearsals and concerts but also by publicity appearances that his managers deemed necessary for a maximum amount of exposure, all aiming at sold-out concerts. No wonder he often felt used; the management had to make money on him, as he knew well, and therefore squeezed him as much as they could. "Money, money, money," he would sigh, remembering the rat race but conveniently forgetting that through skillful management and publicity he became the highest-paid violinist of his times.

On his side of the bargain, as far as I know, he canceled concerts only once in his mature years, when he had suffered a nervous breakdown in England because he felt that his life was threatened. As it turned out, this feeling was the result of nerves overwrought by a crowded schedule. Heifetz felt responsible both to his contracts and toward his audiences. He told me that once he played in the tropics while he had such a tremendous fever from an infection that he hardly knew where he was. During the performance he felt the auditorium swaying around him and his eyes were unfocused, yet he had such self-control and such an ingrained routine that he was able to go through with it, and nobody noticed anything unusual in his playing. "I had a contract to perform, and I did it, regardless of how I felt," he said.

His accompanists were always carefully selected, and he never complained to me about any of them, although he did object to a habit of one of his early accompanists, a Hungarian who couldn't stand fresh air. Whatever season they traveled together, the pianist always closed the windows in the rail compartments, even in stifling summer heat. He was mortally afraid of being in a draft. He didn't last long. Heifetz liked fresh air and spent as much time outdoors as he could. In his house, even in the freezing winter, he always had a door or window open a crack for fresh air. As a result he had tremendous gas bills, which he found outrageous and tried to get out of paying. On tours, he told me, he spent the major part of his free days walking around in cities to get acquainted with the people and their habits. Even late in his life he could vividly describe most of the places he had been and talk about people as if he had just met them the day before.

As all artists do, Heifetz had his share of camp followers, self-appointed promoters, and publicity-, autograph-, and photo-seekers. During his public life he had hurt more than one newspaper reporter with his abrupt and abrasive remarks, especially when he was grilled on unfamiliar subjects or about his private life. As I have mentioned, he generally hated to be questioned, let alone aggressively pursued, as some reporters are wont to interpret their jobs; he learned the art of evasiveness and parried questions with questions of his own, and sometimes he gave silly answers just to get out of a tight corner. He knew how to step on sensitive toes; some reporters carried grudges against him forever and used every occasion to knock him down even when he wasn't concertizing any more.

Heifetz loved chamber music, and teaching it became an essential part of his master class. At the time I joined the class, we played chamber music at least once a month but sometimes more often. Many of his students had never played chamber music, as even now many famous artists shun playing or teaching it. Being a form between solo and orchestral playing, chamber music often requires extraordinary virtuosity of its instrumentalists without allowing them to shine as soloists. For some chamber musicians a solo career has not been possible; for others, chamber music is a first choice. Heifetz often said, "Chamber music is as life should be, a matter of give and take," and chamber music players must develop an ability to listen to one another or the group falls apart and never makes it as a viable ensemble.

The chamber music literature is vast and beautiful, enough to last several lifetimes. Heifetz knew quite a bit of it and used chamber music to make his students help one another. The members of a chamber music group have to be sensitive to each other's playing and must adjust the level and style of their playing to one another. Without this sympathetic response there is no acceptable ensemble playing. Weaker players automatically draw upon the others' strength just by playing with them. Even in technical matters, group playing inspires those with a lesser technique to exceed themselves, and sometimes they surprise themselves by playing passages they couldn't accomplish alone.

Chamber music is exactly what its name says: music played in smaller rooms, in intimate settings such as in a home or smaller recital space rather than in a concert hall. Chamber music's intimate nature calls for smaller rooms with just a few listeners or with no listeners at all, for the playing may be only for the pleasure of its players. There are amateur chamber music "junkies" who are addicted to playing it almost every day in one group or another, while others go to music camps during their vacations to play practically nonstop from early morning to late in the evening. Some groups like to play their pieces without interruption, regardless of whether the outcome is good, bad, or indifferent; others go over difficult parts several times and rehearse dynamics and other fine details until they are able to enjoy a polished performance for their own pleasure.

In preparation for his chamber music sessions, Heifetz always told us a few days ahead of time what works we were going to play, but no one knew who was going to play what part. We all had to be ready with all parts, including those for the viola. His assistant was commissioned to secure a cellist, usually a student from Gregor Piatigorsky's cello master class that ran concurrently at USC with the Heifetz master class. At the beginning of the session Heifetz assigned us the parts for the first movement; then we changed chairs for each following movement. Usually Heifetz took a hand in one or two movements, playing either the first or the second violin part and obviously enjoying making music with his students. It was his habit to give instructions even while playing in the group; without saying a word, just by the sheer power of his playing, he could communicate to us how the music should be played. He made us breathe with the music and opened our minds to its hidden treasures; instead of being tied to the notes alone, he gave us the sense of the pulse and flow of the music and led us to its climax. Heifetz had the perfect internal clock which signaled the appropriate length for the fermatas, dictated the speed of the accelerandos and ritardandos, and measured the crescendos and diminuendos; he knew how to vary tension with relaxation and how to let a phrase play itself out without rushing into the next phrase like a fool before the previous one was fully absorbed. He knew when to slow down, even if nothing was indicated in print but the music asked for it, and urged us to drive on forward when he felt that this was called for; he made us conscious of subtle preparations for definite attacks, and led us with elegance and style to the repose of a cadence. He had perfect control of his bow and seemed to be able to produce an endless line, even when he changed from up-bow to down-bow or vice-versa. Somehow he managed to give the impression of this continuous line even when he lifted the bow off the string, a phenomenon only professionals really appreciated. His audience was engulfed in this stream and never realized the technical aspects that made Jascha Heifetz so different from everybody else. But after all, this is what makes a great performer.

Chamber music playing was also a time of good camaraderie when we could joke about ourselves or the mannerisms of our classmates without hurting one another. It was the time to humbly accept mistakes pointed out by a fellow student, and we were all cut down to a common size for the sake of the ensemble. Heifetz stopped us only when improvement was in order but let the music go on when he knew we understood him just from a meaningful glance. Playing chamber music was a time to come out of self-involvement and watch for another player's thirty-second notes while playing a whole note, and Heifetz made us count every one of those thirty-seconds before moving on to the next note. He never let us get away with sloppy playing of duplets against triplets, and he knew how to keep three or four young "virtuosos" together, making sure that no one ran away with the show.

The last few performances Heifetz gave in public were in chamber music concerts at the USC Hancock auditorium when he played a few movements in his students' recitals. These took place soon after his final concert of October 1972 in the Dorothy Chandler Pavilion. Relatively few people knew about these appearances in advance, but the word always got around and the auditorium would be packed every time he played. Once in these recitals he played the Piatigorsky arrangement of Igor Stravinsky's *Suite italienne* No. 1, the first *Pulcinella* suite, with Piatigorsky playing the cello part; at the same concert he played his last public solo appearance, a Villa Lobos song on the violin, accompanied by an ensemble of cellos. Even at these concerts, his punctuality was almost comical. One time he stuck his head out from behind the stage door exactly at the scheduled hour and announced, "Now we'll give you three minutes to settle down and then we'll start." Any money these concerts made always went into the music scholarship fund.

I often played chamber music with Heifetz in the class, as well as in his house and in other people's homes. Once, in Piatigorsky's home, we played the Brahms C minor Piano Trio. The main theme is a broad, long, romantic melody, which Piatigorsky played with such feeling and expression that it was ready to fall apart. I followed his way of playing but from the corner of my eye watched Heifetz fidgeting in his place, almost ready to jump in and correct Piatigorsky's tempo and straighten out his wallowing in romanticism. He held his horses and said nothing. When Heifetz took the same theme, I had to follow his version of it, which was quite different from the Piatigorsky interpretation, as if he was telling the cellist how to do it. At first I expected trouble when the two of them came together, fearing that each would assert his own interpretation of romanticism and attempt to dominate, but soon I felt the music overtake their individuality, and they resolved their differences without snarling at each other or saying a word about who was right or who was wrong. After they had shown each other how it should have been done, they let the music speak in perfect collaboration.

Heifetz did plan another public appearance at the Sitka, Alaska, Festival of 1974, organized by his students. The festival went on for several years, and after Piatigorsky made his appearance there, Heifetz decided to appear as well, as a tribute to his students. He asked me to be his pianist, and we began to plan a program when disaster struck. He suffered a subcutaneous hemorrhage in his right shoulder when the muscles and tendons separated from the shoulder bone, as I understood what happened. He had had trouble with his shoulder for years but dismissed it as a "professional hazard" and kept on playing. Now, though, at seventy-three, he couldn't ignore it any longer, and his doctor recommended immediate surgery by a specialist in Philadelphia. Heifetz may not have felt up to the journey and argued that someone in Los Angeles should be able to do a good job. The operation was only a partial success, and he never recovered complete, uninhibited use of his right arm. Heifetz blamed himself for this injury, thinking that it could have been prevented if he had stopped playing at the age of fifty as his father had once advised him. Although he did lighten his schedule around that age, he felt that he should have followed his father's advice.

The first time he played after the operation with other people present was during a New Year's Eve party in the home of his violin repairman, Benny Koodlach. To help him raise his arm to the height he was used to, a contraption was made consisting of a stainless steel arm rising from a pedestal at an angle, set with a spring to make it flexible. The end of the arm, which was padded, was supposed to help him by holding his arm up at the elbow. Heifetz tried it for a few seconds, then disdainfully pushed it aside and played without it. I remember the occasion very well because the pianist, Brooks Smith, who was supposed to play in the Antonín Dvořák Piano Quintet (Op. 81, B. 155, in A major) didn't show up, and I had to read it without preparation. Heifetz played one movement of the quintet, and I could hardly keep my eyes on the music while watching him struggle with his bow. Since he couldn't lift his arm properly, he compromised by holding his violin lower and turning it sideways to meet the angle at which he could move his arm. He was embarrassed at his inability to do things right and even felt he had to excuse himself after he finished his movement, saying, "This is not the way to play the violin." After he played he was completely exhausted and didn't even make his usual comments on the other players' movements. With iron will Heifetz overcame this impairment and found a way to practice the violin to the end of his days in spite of all that pain, though he was never again able to hold up his violin "properly."

In the first few years I knew him, for the New Year's Eve parties, he usually rented a house or an apartment in the desert, a two-hour drive east of Los Angeles, but later he tired of the hassle of traveling and held the parties at his beach house and, for the very last ones, in his Beverly Hills home. The music always started at seven in the evening, and guests were told not to come before six. He always came down sharply dressed and expected his guests, too, to dress up for the occasion. While Heifetz was still teaching, some of his students were invited to participate in the chamber music and to stay for the evening, and they were allowed to bring a date. If we played in the desert, he put his guests up in a hotel for one night and paid the expenses. Usually the evening started with a Haydn quartet in honor of the father of the form, after which we played various opuses of the genre, one usually with piano. He stopped the music about ten, and eating, drinking, and conversation filled out the time until midnight. A few minutes before midnight someone was entrusted with finding on his ancient radio from the 1920s the station that carried the New Year's Eve ceremony from Times Square in New York. Champagne was passed around and at the moment that the arrival

Heifetz played chamber music with student San Do Xia before midnight at his New Year's Eve party at the beach, 1981. Photo by Ayke Agus

And then he danced with friend Tamara Chapro beneath the streamers after midnight on New Year's day. Photo by Norman Tremaine

I accompanied Heifetz and his students in chamber music at the New Year's Eve party at the beach, 1983. Photo by Michael Palotai

of the New Year was announced, we would all clink our glasses. He made a point of going around and wishing happy New Year to every one of his guests. After midnight, he would put on some of his favorite recordings of light music, and there was dancing until the wee hours of the morning. He was an inveterate night-man and always the last one to get tired and leave the scene. New Year's Eve parties were sort of an article of faith with Heifetz, a kind of superstition, that the New Year couldn't be auspicious without celebrating its coming in.

The very last New Year's Eve party of his life, 31 December 1986, was an exception to the rule. At nearly eighty-six he wasn't teaching any more; the years had taken their toll on his physical appearance and his demeanor, and he leaned on his bamboo cane when he walked. He didn't even mingle with his guests and didn't give his orders about what to do next as he usually did, but left it to me to direct the evening. Heifetz sat alone in his favorite, hard-back loveseat next to the piano all evening, passively watching people milling around and hardly saying a word to anyone. Going through with this last party must have taken tremendous effort, and he couldn't bring himself to mingle with the people around him whom he hardly knew. Since he had no more students, he invited some professional musician friends of his to play chamber music. They were sternly warned not to rehearse ahead of time, which would spoil the spontaneity of music making. But they did. Heifetz immediately knew that the players had rehearsed their pieces in spite of his warning; apparently they had the mistaken idea that nothing less than perfect could please him. After they finished the first number, Heifetz stood up from his chair, red in the face and obviously very angry, banged hard with his bamboo cane on the top of his favorite piano, and shouted as loud as he could: "I told you not to rehearse; this is not a concert, this is a chamber music evening."

It was embarrassing, but he didn't care; it was his house, and as he often said, I do in my house as I want. I went over to soothe him, and he told me to find other music in his library and have the group play some unrehearsed pieces. This they did, less perfectly, which made him happier. Order, according to Heifetz, was restored, and he saw to it that the tradition—his tradition—was properly kept.

10

Sinfonia Domestica

If you can fill the unforgiving minute
With sixty seconds' worth of distance run

RUDYARD KIPLING

*H*eifetz bought his house in Beverly Hills about forty-five years before he died. He considered himself a home decorator of good taste, and the decor in his house reflected his orderly and organized mind. Everything remained in its unchangeable place for decades, pleasantly displayed for the best possible use and view, in an order and position that were just as inflexible as his principles; he felt safe with his possessions only as they were positioned, and he immediately corrected the slightest deviation. He often admonished me that a home should be cozy and intimate instead of an exhibit of ostentatious opulence, and he did his best to achieve this goal. It was a man's home, though, lacking perhaps a feminine touch, yet I can't imagine his putting up with any woman who also had strong opinions about home decoration.

The house was atop one of the hills, strictly speaking a few yards outside the boundaries of Beverly Hills but still considered part of that exclusive settlement. His street was hardly detectable on the map; even taxi drivers, facing at most turns a "Not a Through Street" sign, would get lost in the winding maze of crooked streets leading up to Heifetz's lane. Arriving at his vantage point on top of the hill, one was rewarded on a smogless day with a magnificent view of the glittering Pacific Ocean not too far away. In the late afternoons the sun threw a golden bridge over the ripples of the sea, extending all the way to the horizon. This view, however, was mostly wasted on the inhabitants of Heifetz's house, which had windows toward the ocean only in the apartment above the garage, originally built for his youngest child, Jay. When I knew Heifetz, the magnificent view was available only to his housekeepers who occupied the garage apartment, often in quick succession. The property itself straddled the ridge of the hill. His street was also "Not a Through Street" with

only four or five houses occupying the space between the nearest intersection and the turnaround at the end of the cul-de-sac. Once he told me
that when he bought his house, it was the only one on the street.

Heifetz apparently also bought up the available vacant land around
his house, for the size of the parcel suggested the compounding of three
or four lots. During the forty-five years he lived there, he planted various
kinds of shade trees. He selected his trees wisely to suit the climate: his
favorites were pine trees, jacaranda, palms, eucalyptus, and sycamores. In
the spring the night-blooming jasmine around his property filled the air
with its heavy perfume. The trees grew huge in their time, and they
became his closest friends; they always responded to his thoughts, understood and inspired him while he sat for hours during the afternoons
underneath them, and above all represented the calm stability that he so
craved. His lot was flat, a quite valuable asset in Beverly Hills, where many
houses seem burrowed into the mountainside or anchored to the street
by only a concrete apron, jutting out on stilts over the void. His land must
have been artificially graded because it lay on four different levels with a
few steps leading from one to the next. His house was built on the lowest
level, and an empty lot occupied the highest one. On an in-between level
was a swimming pool which he had built to exercise his legs after he
broke his hip shortly before I met him, but during my time with him he
used it perhaps once a year to justify its existence. Next to the pool was his
studio, almost in the center of his property. A breezeway which sheltered
a ping pong table led from the house to the studio. The door to his studio was guarded by the famous RCA His-Master's-Voice dog, Nipper, cast
full-size in plaster, symbol of music recording for over half a century. On
the next highest level of the property was a paddleball court, and one
level higher, at the intersection of two streets, were a tool shed and a
huge compost pile on an otherwise empty lot. This lot also contained
some fruit trees, of which a peach tree gave Heifetz the most trouble. To
protect it from the squirrels and birds, his gardener talked him into cov-
ering it with a zippered net. However the squirrels and birds still got to
the fruit, and when Heifetz finally rescued one peach from the tree,
miraculously saved from the predators, he calculated that that single
peach cost him about three hundred dollars. After due consideration of
the possibility of even higher costs for another peach, he cut his losses,
had the net removed, and let nature take its course.

He had a beautiful garden with lots of flowers in front of his porch
that faced toward Los Angeles. The hill on this side of the garden dropped
off suddenly toward the property below in a steep grade, giving the

impression that one was walking on the edge of a deep ravine. This ravine was sort of a jungle, and it often had to be shored up with planks against erosion. The roots of his huge trees in time got into the pipes of the drainage and sewage system, so that backed-up toilets and sinks regularly intruded on his idyllic peace.

Nature sent her other representatives regularly visiting Heifetz's solitude; raccoons banged on the garbage cans at night, a family of quails ran for cover under the bushes during the day, and for some years, especially during the winter, a small family of deer came up from the bushy ravine, brazenly ate up all the flowers, and returned for another snack when the flowers were replanted. Eventually the neighborhood somehow got rid of the deer because they were a regular menace on the narrow streets; they never learned in the urban surroundings to fear humans and at night placidly gazed in the lights of approaching cars in the center of the street. In the summer a flock of escapee parrots came to rest on the trees and made an awful racket, which Heifetz tolerated with more patience than he would have had for human noises. Squirrels leaped from one tree to the other, birds sang in season, and owls hooted after dusk, but the noise of cars and trucks from civilization below didn't penetrate the natural sound barrier of Heifetz's trees. In this entire menagerie Heifetz cared the least for the squirrels because he thought they were destructive. The place was lost even for the standard star-gazing bus tours that plagued the vicinity where famous movie stars lived, and only a few determined violinists found it once in a great while, only to be politely turned away if they had no appointment.

The house itself was oddly positioned at a right angle to the street, with all its windows opening into the two courtyards and toward Los Angeles. On clear nights from the garden and the porch there was a dazzling view of the city lights below. The whole property was in the shape of a triangle with a blunted point at one end; the house itself cut through this blunted point and divided the property into two parts. The entrance was at the smaller side of this triangle, and the visitor could observe only a small courtyard upon opening the gate; the house itself cut off the view of the bulk of the property for anyone coming from the outside.

The visitor entered the first small yard through an ancient gate with an antiquated latch which was never locked. This courtyard, surrounded by a high palisade fence on three sides, held all sorts of native California vegetation, some of it planted next to the fence and trained over it. In spite of its beautiful emerald green grass, the yard imparted an uncanny feeling, perhaps because the closeness of the trees overhead and the carefully controlled vines on the fence gave the impression of a forbidding fortress.

Coming up a few steps into the semidarkness of this yard, the visitor had to pass the garage on the left, then make a sharp right turn to aim for the entrance. One passed under very wide overhanging eaves, wide enough to give the feeling of an arcade. Heifetz decorated the outside walls with special plants that tolerated the shade and put up colored Italian and Mexican tiles and pottery to break up any monotony. He also placed some colorful river stones on a small table at the angle of the two walls. The roof of the house was covered with several layers of wooden shingles, some so old that they crumbled away. When Heifetz wanted to get it repaired, no roofer would take the job, it seemed so hopeless. Heifetz kept insisting on repairing instead of replacing the whole roof as the roofers preferred. He considered the roof good enough to last his lifetime, and he was right. Eventually, to escape his badgering, I climbed on the roof and replaced the crumbling singles. Luckily the roof had a low pitch so that I was in no danger of sliding off. Heifetz watched me, partly with approval, partly with apprehension, but this time he was scared enough not to give me a time limit for the job. I had the advantage over most of the roofers that my light weight enabled me to crawl all over the ancient shingles without breaking them.

Both the kitchen and the main entrance doors were old fashioned, in the unpretentious ranch style, a most unusual phenomenon for California where expensive doors seem to be indicative of social and financial status. From behind the louvered windows of the kitchen or the curtains of the dining room, one could easily observe who the visitor was, and Heifetz often availed himself of these vantage points if he was alone in the house, to determine whether to answer the bell. I saw him often enough lurking behind one or the other when I rang the bell and there was no housekeeper in the house to answer it. To save himself the trouble of letting me in, Heifetz offered me a key to the house several times, but I refused it until the time that I came from another part of the house to find him unconscious on the floor. By not having a key to the house I had hoped to serve him notice that I still expected to be treated as a guest.

The layout of the house made the visitor feel lost and disoriented, perhaps because its main walls didn't line up with the street and there were no street-facing windows through which one could orient oneself in relation to a known point. From the entrance to the right one reached the guestroom, which also served as Heifetz's library; to the left the hallway led, at a slight angle, to a small sitting room on the right and a more spacious dining room on the left. The hallway then continued in a complicated maze of smaller passageways, one branch passing through the bar, which faced away from the kitchen entrance, another leading to Heifetz's bedroom, a third one to the "mezzo" room, as he called it, which had been his ex-wife's bedroom. The original plans by Lloyd Wright, Frank Lloyd Wright's son, had included a large open porch in front of the bar, but Heifetz had enclosed it to serve as his favorite living room. It had a continuous glass wall toward the garden and skylights in the ceiling, and in this porch–living room Heifetz kept one of his pianos and his most precious paintings. The place was full of light, and he enjoyed sitting there whenever he couldn't be outdoors. His pictures were lighted from above, and he kept the room's gas fireplace lit even in summer evenings when it was cool.

The house was loaded with memorabilia from his past, including some beautiful paintings. At the entrance the visitor faced two paintings by Georges Rouault which originally had served as studies for his great painting, *The Passion*; in the porch was a famous painting by Chaim Soutine, a picture by Raoul Dufy, and other paintings by well-known artists. Heifetz once described to me the amount of trouble he had gone to in putting up his pictures, trying out different lighting effects, looking at them from all angles for their most advantageous position, taking care that they wouldn't crowd each other and could be enjoyed from as many points in the house as possible without being ostentatious. He had good taste and did a very good job. Among his memorabilia was a set of stemmed drinking glasses in the dining room engraved with the emblem and imperial crown of the czar of Russia; the shelves were loaded with vases and decorative vessels Heifetz had collected during his concertizing years. Sometimes he talked about these objects and the circumstances under which he had received them. Apparently they meant a great deal to him because he strictly forbade his housekeepers to dust or move them an inch to the left or right.

Heifetz had enjoyed his professional world tours. He always had with him an accompanist, a manager, and a valet, and sometimes his family or an entourage of friends kept him company. In his lifetime, travel underwent dramatic changes: horses and buggy were still common when he was born, and astronauts were circling the globe when he died. Most of his tours were by comparatively slow trains and steamships; once he showed me the formidable footlockers he had used for traveling. To take care of several sets of social, leisure, and stage suits and to be prepared for heat and cold and rain with top and underwear, a valet went with him from one end of the world to the other. Heifetz's standard nightmare, even years after his tours, was to miss a train or boat, or have his boat held up by stormy weather and as a result miss an important engagement.

Another nightmare that haunted him even late in his life was the fear of losing his violins. He traveled with both his Tononi and Guarnerius, keeping them in a double case. Usually he didn't entrust his violins to anyone, not even to his valet. Once, however, while getting off a train, for some reason he thought that his pianist had the violins with him. They got as far as their hotel when he discovered that his violins were missing. After a frantic search for the violins, his manager called up the next station where the train stopped; his violins were found and returned by the next train coming back in their direction. Heifetz told me this story with such seeming indifference that he appeared to take it for granted. He never said in what country or year it had happened, but the temporary loss could not have been recent or the story certainly would have had a different ending.

As a young man Heifetz was a car buff, and he often showed me his pictures of antique cars, I presume to educate me. He knew quite a bit about old cars, and it didn't take much to start him on the subject. I don't remember how many cars he had in his younger years, but the collection must have been impressive. Heifetz had been a good driver and liked speed; he was fond of reminiscing about the trips he made regularly from New York to his Connecticut farm in the early morning hours after concerts or parties, driving as fast as the car would take him, even over icy roads. He took driving lessons from professional race drivers, and showed me the proper way to hold the wheel, how and when to shift while turning at high speed, and other tricks for controlling the vehicle in an emergency. I thanked him for the instructions, but I don't feel safe in a speeding car, so his teaching in this field went to waste.

When I first accompanied him to the beach, he always took the wheel and showed me how to drive in traffic. Sometimes his driving got on my nerves as he artfully dodged other ambitious drivers, shook his fist at poor or pushy drivers, told them off, and threatened them with a citizen's arrest for not following the rules of traffic as he perceived them. When the traffic was too heavy or too slow, he often drove on the shoulder or on the center turning lane and felt that the whole world was conspiring to hold him back or to force him to drive "by the book." When he got older, he wisely left the driving to me. He was a terrible backseat driver. Once, going to Malibu, he made me drive in the center turning lane because the beach traffic was too slow for his taste. His excuse, as usual, was that we didn't have to do everything "by the book." Of course, we were caught, and the police also had an opinion different from Heifetz's about doing things by their book. However, to my amazement, Heifetz was able to talk the policeman out of giving me a ticket. I think the policeman found a bit odd the combination of a young woman and a fast-talking old man driving together in the center lane, and that perhaps helped to give credence to the cock-and-bull story that Heifetz concocted under pressure. He also had an Auxiliary Policeman's badge which he had no qualms about flashing around under such circumstances. His impromptu show made my skin crawl, but he rather enjoyed it; he thought of it as just another successful performance. Another time I was not that lucky; he made me drive on the shoulder of the road, and I got a ticket for it. Instead of regretfully paying for it, Heifetz made me go to court to fight it; he wanted to see if I could wiggle out of it or at least reduce the penalty. He was right; I talked the judge out of a penalty and got a suspended sentence.

An honorary member of the Newport Beach Police Department, Heifetz even had his own badge, as well as a license that gave him the privilege of carrying it. Photo by Jack Nilles

HEIFETZ WAS NOT particularly impressed with technology, much of which he considered a waste of human intellect and energy. He observed and lamented the pollution of the environment as the most visible result of progress, and to do his share, at his own expense he had a small car converted to be electric battery driven when such technology was mostly just talked about. The car sat in his garage, up on blocks and useless. He tried to drive it to campus, but after several breakdowns along the way he gave up for good.

Recording, reproducing, and transmitting sound also made giant leaps during Heifetz's life. The year he was born, the first radio waves were sent across the Atlantic, and when he died spacecraft sent back pictures of distant stars. The technical quality of his own first recordings was a far cry from present sound technology, but when he was offered the opportunity to have them digitally transcribed onto compact disc and as much technical imperfection removed as possible, he listened to one sample and rejected the idea, as could be expected. At any rate, Heifetz didn't much appreciate "canned" music, which lacked the excitement of a live performance. For him music making meant taking chances and doing something different and daring at every performance. He told me that he preferred some takes of his recordings that were technically imperfect but musically more exciting. He listened to recordings only as a second choice for hearing music, for he rarely went to live performances in his late years. Still, he was too much of a professional not to know how recordings are made and how their perfection, fixed forever, is achieved.

He parted ways with television when he once caught himself sitting in front of it with his eyes glued to the screen. Suddenly the thought occurred to him that he must have looked like a rabbit. "I don't like to look like a rabbit," he told me and with great satisfaction smashed his set with his cane. Heifetz never had much regard for people sitting mesmerized in front of their sets. To watch television in his presence was unthinkable. The cult of TV must have contributed a great deal to his alienation from friends and society, for he found himself an outsider with people whose interest seemed to center on daily television programs.

Secretive as he was, Heifetz soon devised means to communicate with me when he didn't want others to know what we were talking about. He taught me some elementary Russian, and in turn I taught him some basic Indonesian. When in company, he would deftly use the words from the language that nobody present could understand. For fun I sometimes used a few Russian words in Russian-speaking company, which was always a great success because it was so unexpected and, I suppose, sounded funny with my Indonesian accent.

That he was a family man gone astray I learned from his odd desire to have somebody in the house when he came home by himself at night. When he had a housekeeper, he asked her to wait for him in the kitchen or to come down from her apartment when he got home, whatever the hour. When he had no housekeeper and wanted to go somewhere alone, he asked me to come to his house at eleven in the evening, just to greet him at the door. Far from considering it petulant nonsense, I always obliged. Coming home to a cold hearth, for a man who had all the success one's heart could desire, is indeed a failure of a sort, regardless of why and how it happened. I always made sure that the fire was on in the fireplace when he came in, and a drink, fixed exactly the way I knew he liked it for a nightcap, was waiting for him on the bar.

Heifetz read a great deal about art, as well as biographies of painters, musicians, singers, composers, and actors, and he religiously perused *Reader's Digest* and *National Geographic* from cover to cover. He considered these as down-to-earth magazines without scientific pretense, and he could remember most of their contents from trivia to stories about crafty politicians, pollution, taxation, popular psychology, and the future of humankind. He marked articles for me to read and to discuss with him, and he even subscribed to magazines for me so that I could do some of the homework by myself. Once, early in our acquaintance, he asked if I knew a famous actress of the nineteenth century, I think it was Eleonora Duse. With my education "from the jungle," I was hardly acquainted with Shakespeare, let alone with an actress. He took it upon himself to complete my education, for, as he said, "A musician must be familiar with other subjects of art, and with their artists. In order to be a complete musician, one should not be interested only in music." From then on, Heifetz supplied me with books on everybody and everything he knew, especially masterpieces of Russian literature, and I had to report to him in some detail about what I had read. If he was in a real family mood, he would read to me from whatever book he happened to be reading, pointing out the highlights of the story to make sure that I wouldn't miss anything of importance. At other times he would ask me to read to him, keeping himself busy by correcting my pronunciation and accent.

Reading books wasn't the only means Heifetz used to amend my backward education. Starting with explaining the paintings in his own house, he went through the history of art, not so much for style and detail in the painters' works, of which he probably didn't know much either, but rather to impart general information about their historical background, the life of the painters, the museums where the most famous paintings were, famous cities in America, Europe, and Asia, and well-known buildings and churches—the kind of information I had never received during my school years in Java. For me at that time Rome meant stinking toilets in the restaurants where I had to take my grandmother during the two days I had been there, and I knew Amsterdam only for its narrow and steep staircases, with their wooden rails slippery from coconut oil in my uncles' houses. I discovered from my conversations with Heifetz that the desire to see the wonders of the world must be implanted in most of us, just as the desire to hear good music is mostly a matter of exposure. I'm sure my grandmother and grandfather never expressed a desire, while staying in Amsterdam, to see the Rijksmuseum, the Van Gogh paintings, or even to tour the city for its sights; all they wanted was to talk to their children and relatives, carrying on an endless small talk that goes for conversation among family members, I presume, everywhere. I am sure Heifetz had his own crash courses in culture, and he was just too happy to pass on to me what he had learned; Vilna may be physically closer to Rome and Amsterdam than Yogyakarta, but beyond that, the level of cultural awareness in the neighborhoods we both came from wasn't that different.

I also imagine that Heifetz did not pick up his table manners in his Vilna home. Leopold Auer must have seen to it that his prodigies' success in the concert halls was balanced by proper behavior at the receptions and banquets that usually followed such events. Jaschinka learned well, for dinner with Heifetz was always a ceremony, lasting at least an hour; the table always had to be set the same way, which was his own elaborate version of a standard banquet table setting. He taught me how to do it— until that time I didn't know how to set a table formally—and then expected me to pass on this knowledge to the products of small Mexican and South American villages, women of various ages and mental capabilities, some of whom hardly knew which end of the fork to use. Such efforts were doomed to failure from the beginning, but Heifetz never gave up on his banquet table standards; if a new housekeeper couldn't learn the protocol within a week or so, this was just one more reason to fire another raw recruit.

Heifetz ate very slowly, pausing between courses; he made toasts and expected other guests to do so at regular intervals as well, always mentioning some pretense for the toasts, and he liked to clink glasses with everybody around the table. Among his favorite toasts were "Here is to general misunderstanding" (perhaps Heifetz thought of himself as often being misunderstood) and "Here is to a room with no corners." There had to be dessert, even if only a baked apple topped with heavy cream or a scoop of ice cream. Other favorite deserts of his were Baked Alaska, which I suspect he liked for its self-contradictory name and nature, and Danish pastries, which he liked to have around and look at but ate very little of. He was quite weight conscious and controlled himself in his eating habits. He always received around Christmas time a box of almond cookies from his favorite niece, Anne "the cookie," his sister Pauline's daughter. Much as he liked these cookies and appreciated them as a sign of attention, he ate only one or two before passing them to all around. Coming to my house for dinner, he often parodied children's cravings for sweets with a greeting at the door, "What's for dessert?" Coffee, strong and decaffeinated, had to be served, and light conversation on a limited list of subjects was expected from me or from others if guests were present. After coffee, if we were alone, we often played music together; he never played the violin in company as a social entertainment but sometimes was willing to play four hands at the piano in the presence of guests. He played the violin in company only in chamber music, and even that was always a planned event with carefully selected guests.

When Heifetz stopped teaching on the USC campus in 1981, he continued his master classes in his studio at his home. He even gave private lessons to several young violinists who did not live in L.A. but made the trip once a month. I took care of the financial arrangements and rehearsed with them before their lessons. By 1984 this stopped as Heifetz began to lose interest, although practicing with me at the piano was never a chore for him. We would spend the major part of the afternoons playing through his violin repertory. His music library was organized into four categories: concertos, sonatas, short pieces, and his own transcriptions, all kept in alphabetical order. I accompanied him through the whole of this considerable collection several times in a period of about five years. He seemed to want to teach me everything I should know as an accompanist by getting me acquainted not only with the pieces he had played in his life, but also with other compositions he considered worth knowing. Whether we were playing an old warhorse or a completely new piece, we always played in the correct tempo, and he never let me just play the notes; he always expected the spirit and style of the piece to be there from the first reading even if some notes were left out. Heifetz often emphasized that a good sight reader should be able to pick out the essential passages in any kind of piece and give the impression of reading everything, and an accompanist should pick out all essential melodies that support, counter, or contrast with those of the violin. These sessions were a challenge for both of us. I think he was saying good-bye to all that he lived for and lived with, and I was soaking up from him everything that he was willing to part with in the twilight of his life. As an old man he still got all excited over minute details, shouted and screamed at me, called me "bloody no good," then rewarded my work with the praise "not too bad." Once he told me that only music could make him cry. Music rejuvenated him, passion sparkled in his blue eyes, and when he played the climax of a piece, it always gave me an electric shock. To build up the details toward a climax and then to finish with a feeling of satisfaction left behind was a specialty that came to him instinctively without the labor of cerebral calculations. Eventually he told me that at my first audition he had seen more in me than just a violinist from the jungles of Indonesia, even though my violin playing wasn't exactly at the level he expected from a prospective student. And once, after a session, he looked at me and said regretfully, "I should have been born later or you earlier; imagine, we could have spent our lives giving concerts together." I felt honored and deeply touched.

One would assume that Heifetz's fingertips were covered with tough calluses from long and hard practicing. Strangely enough, this was not the case at all; his fingertips were very soft, and even after hours of playing, they never hardened but only developed a crease for a short time from pressing hard on the strings. The skin on his hands was thin and sensitive; he bruised easily, and big, mean-looking blood clots appeared around the bruises or cuts, especially on the backs of his hands, although he healed quickly. His back didn't bother him as much as could have been expected. He never sat in a slouching or sprawling position but always erect, preferably on the hard seat of a hard-backed straight chair. He had a special wedge-shaped hard board that he put behind his back if it bothered him.

If Heifetz wasn't in the mood to play the fiddle, he was always game for playing four hands at the piano. Once he said wistfully that the piano was really his favorite instrument, but circumstances and family pressure prevented him from making it his chief instrument. The fact that he knew the piano so well was bad news for his accompanists, for none could get away with imprecise work. Heifetz knew every single note in the accompaniment and all of them had to be accounted for. He always studied the accompaniment as hard as the violin part and tolerated no sloppiness in ensemble playing. As a rare witness of Heifetz's piano playing in his youth, an old friend of mine once reminisced that as a young person she was invited to a family which young Heifetz was in the habit of visiting, drawn there mainly by the girls in the family. The radio was playing some popular music when Jascha entered. He first asked one of the girls to dance, even before taking his coat off; then, when the piece was finished, he turned off the radio and continued playing the same popular piece at the piano.

When we began to play four hands at the piano, Heifetz complained that his fingers on the keyboard felt like "cooked spaghetti" from lack of practice. In spite of this handicap, he always kept up with me and with the spirit of the music, artfully dodging difficult passages or reducing them to the bare essentials and faking others, just to keep the music moving in the proper style and tempo. His favorite opera reductions were from three Puccini operas—*Madame Butterfly, Tosca,* and *La Bohème.* He could play the overtures to these operas by heart, and those to *Parsifal, Eugene Onegin,* and the Mozart operas. He had me study and play them as well. He also liked to play the Beethoven and Mozart symphonies, Strauss's *Till Eulenspiegel,* Mendelssohn's Overture to *A Midsummer Night's Dream,* Wagner's *Tristan and Isolde,* Bizet's *Carmen,* all in four-hand arrangements for one piano. We played these pieces so much that eventually we both knew all the difficult passages by heart. To get his fingers in shape, once he showed me a short warmup exercise in parallel and contrary motion that served for both stretching the fingers and for playing passages smoothly as well. The whole exercise lasted only a minute and a half, but it did everything that much longer exercises were supposed to do for your fingers. Characteristically he played the exercise only once and expected me to remember exactly how he did it. He never told me how he came upon this exercise, and I never saw it printed anywhere—he could have put it together himself.

With Heifetz, one was never far away from surprises. One night he surprised me by getting out his violin, tuning it, then motioning me to the piano: "Conus!" he said laconically and expected me to start instantly with the introduction. I didn't have the music in front of me, but that didn't really matter; he wanted to play right then without the slightest delay. I had to play the piano part of the violin concerto by Julius Conus from memory as best I could. From then on, whenever I played an accompaniment, I would try to memorize it. He later pulled the same trick on me with other pieces, but it no longer took me as much by surprise. I still don't know whether this was just a game with him or another way of testing my musical memory. Perhaps it was both.

Another time, after dinner, he played a recording of Edward Elgar's *Enigma Variations,* which I had never heard before. Experience told me that he was up to something. I listened to the music more carefully than usual, and surely enough, when it was over he sent me to the piano and asked me to play as much of the piece as I could remember. Some people have a special talent for this and can reproduce every note even after one hearing, but I am not one of them. Yet under pressure I was able to reproduce the main theme and several variations while faking the harmonies. "Pretty damn good imitation," he said when I could go on no longer.

It may sound peculiar, but it was Jascha Heifetz, the violinist, from whom I learned most as a pianist. He regularly went to his studio in the afternoon to do some work, perhaps to practice, and left me alone for a blessed hour or two when he didn't need my constant attention. I used those times to practice the piano in his living room. However, I would hardly finish a piece when I would hear his voice from behind a curtain or from the door behind me, telling me what I should or should not have done with certain passages. I never knew how long he had been hiding there. After a while he did this regularly and gave me piano lessons a few times. Heifetz knew a great deal about piano technique and suggested unorthodox fingerings to achieve certain effects or to get around the problems caused by my small hands, but he didn't bother with the usual stuff piano teachers focus on while correcting, underlining, marking and checking notes and whole passages, and generally fussing about how to do things "correctly," in the "proper" style and execution, and with the "right" pedaling. I've seen music practically illegible from these markings, always made with a soft, thick pencil that smudges over the music and eventually makes the score a disgusting mess. As he did with his own music, Heifetz never marked anything, but just as in his master classes, he expected me to remember everything he said.

Despite his insistence on knowing the score, he never bothered with technique and wrong notes during these sessions with me. He was concerned only about the character of the piece and the total effect that the music would have on the audience as the only valid aspects of music making. Timing was among Heifetz's well-kept secrets, rarely pointed out by his reviewers because of its subtle nature. Timing is an aspect of art that is almost impossible to teach without a sure instinct: notes, phrases, sequences, even a whole movement should be played in such proportions that the audience has time to absorb each part according to its importance. Heifetz often warned me never to rush into a new passage before the music played itself out, yet never to drag it on until listeners would be bored with it. He knew exactly when to move the music and when to stretch it, when to be just plain simple and when to be ornate; yet he always guarded the overall structure of the music from too much elaboration on details. He never gave me theories about how to execute anything. He was the ultimate "doer" who by instinct and long practice knew exactly what a particular piece wanted to say, recognized its weak points, covered them up, and strengthened its most effective aspects. He spent hours teaching me how to make cuts and transitions, and how to watch for the key relationships, all with an eye to avoiding yawning audiences. Above all he wanted it to be exciting.

After playing music in the evening, Heifetz liked to play cards, often way past midnight. He was a night person and could stay up to the wee hours of the morning without being affected by it. We always played for money, in small stakes, and when he won, he collected, and when he lost, paid up. He was a sharp player and kept track of the tricks and cards in hands; I had to learn fast if I didn't want to lose my shirt.

Heifetz still had friends and fans all over the world who knew he was an ardent stamp collector and sent him musical stamps wherever a new issue appeared. The volumes of photographs in his studio included many from his early life. He told me that as a young man he had enough equipment to become a professional photographer. Photography had been his second passion, next to driving fast cars, but when I knew him he didn't even have a camera. When I showed him pictures I had taken and he liked them, he always snatched them away and they all ended up in his album. "You have the negative. You can always make some more copies of it for yourself," he would say to justify this behavior. If one wanted to pho-

Heifetz sampled different liqueurs and found one he didn't particularly like, in Tacoma at the home of his friends Ann and Norman Tremaine, 1980. Photo by Norman Tremaine

tograph him in company, permission had to be asked, and he allowed only one or two pictures to be taken. He always looked a bit artificial in these pictures, and if he smiled at all, it was the "Say-cheese" smile; for these pictures he usually gave the "don't bother me" kind of look.

Heifetz liked to dress elegantly. His private tailor knew his exact measurements, and he could order a new suit without even appearing in person. Though he dressed for society and more or less accepted its conventions, he often made fun of its shallowness. In his early years, for a while life had been a continuous party, but later he rather liked to observe human folly in company: "What's more funny than people?" he often asked. He once showed me a suit made of expensive material, which he wore only a few times. He asked me to look at it very carefully. I noticed only after a second look that half the suit was made of dark blue material, and the other half was black. He had had it made to test people's power of observation. Nobody ever noticed it—or had the courage to make a remark about it. He also had shoes of these colors but wore one of each on the opposite sides from the colors of the suit.

Heifetz sometimes wondered what drove people to social gatherings. He often observed that no one pays attention to what the other one has to say, and people can hardly wait to bring their own two cents' worth into the conversation. He said that he had tested his theory that nobody really cares about the response to a hearty, if routine, "How are you?" greeting. To prove his point, Heifetz sometimes returned the greeting with "I'm sick in my stomach and my aunt just died." To his satisfaction, the invariable, standard, and expected response had always been "That's good."

11

Theme and Variations

If you can trust yourself when all men doubt you,
But make allowance for their doubting too

RUDYARD KIPLING

*A*lmost at the center of his property in Beverly Hills, Heifetz had his "Sanctum Sanctorum," as he called it, the holiest of all holies, his studio. There he practiced the violin and felt safe from intruders and unauthorized listeners; there he puttered around, arranging his files and music library and putting in order the volumes of photographs of his past. It was all an exercise in futility, the whiling away of his days, but he would not admit that to himself. Unless he gave instructions to the contrary, he couldn't be disturbed in his studio. Only his secretary had access to the place; anyone else needed a special invitation to enter, and he rarely gave one.

Although the studio was built in 1947 by Lloyd Wright, Heifetz obviously had a great deal to say about its design. It was an oblong building, nothing special from the outside. The largest room, used for rehearsing when he transferred his class there from USC, was hexagonal; a pantry, a bathroom, and an office surrounded the rehearsal room. In the office his secretary took care of his finances and correspondence. His files reached back to his earliest year in this country, all perfectly organized by subject. Heifetz spent countless hours organizing these files and could immediately locate anything without searching. A careless secretary's misplacing a file was a capital sin which called for immediate dismissal. Heifetz wouldn't even let his housekeepers enter his sanctuary; only the secretary was permitted to dust lightly once in a while and only under his watchful eyes.

The rehearsal room had a big window on each of two sides with the piano under one window and a large counter under the other. The counter held his students' violin cases or those of the visiting musicians in times past when he had chamber music there. At first I didn't pay much attention to the layout and organization of the studio since I had nothing to do with it. However, this changed when Heifetz wasn't teaching any more and his secretary came only once or twice a month. Although the need for dusting became increasingly evident as the days went by, Heifetz would say that he would rather put up with a little dust and dirt than let anyone come into his studio. The thought of being disturbed there or of anyone moving anything outside of his control positively frightened him.

I usually went to the studio to accompany him at the piano, but as time went on and needs arose, he entrusted me with the key and occasionally sent me there to fetch something for him. I didn't have to waste my time looking for what he wanted because he usually told me exactly where to find it, including the cabinet and file number. Old instruments, as his were, need a certain amount of humidity to keep them from drying out and developing cracks in their thin wood. People with precious instruments go to great lengths and use elaborate systems to maintain a steady level of humidity. All Heifetz did was to keep a big glass of water in the cupboard that held his Guarnerius and Tononi, with the door slightly ajar. When he sent me to the studio to check the water level in the glass for the first time, I took it as a sign of his ultimate trust. From then on I had to check it whenever I went into the studio.

Eventually I became quite well acquainted with the organization of his files. When I began to look around, I noticed that he had all kinds of drawers and cabinets, all full of music and all carefully cataloged, as well as his own complete collection of all his recordings. Files and shelves were organized by categories of miniature scores, full-size scores, manuscript scores, solo violin pieces, concertos for both violin and piano, accompanied pieces, chamber music, duos and trios for violin, and other scores for unusual instrumental combinations. Within the groups everything was in alphabetical order.

One afternoon after we had played through some pieces, I asked his permission to dust the place, and he reluctantly agreed. As always, Heifetz gave me the exact amount of time to do the job—as usual, a very short time—and he watched me while I dusted. I also didn't mind dust very much and could live without dusting for quite a while. But as I went through the motions, I noticed six cabinets with closed doors; he had never asked for anything from these cabinets in all the years I was with him. Pandora's curiosity took the better of me, and I asked him what was hidden there. To my surprise, he gave me a benevolent answer: "If you really must know, why don't you open them and find out for yourself? They are not locked." It was indeed like opening Pandora's box, though no evil emerged but rather a great deal of hope. The six cabinets contained the manuscripts of his unfinished transcriptions and his finished but unpublished ones, as well as piles of music by various composers, all bearing his notations, pieces he had considered but had never transcribed.

In still another part of these cabinets were the manuscripts of violin concertos dedicated to him but which he had never performed, although he found them worthy of preservation. I also found in one of those cabinets his own original compositions, some published, others in manuscript only; they were mostly songs in once-popular styles, but some were composed for piano solo. There I found the manuscripts of Grigoraş Dinicu's *Hora staccato* in all its published versions, including those for piano solo and for two pianos. Heifetz didn't think much of his own piano compositions; most were based on rhythmical patterns and variations in a jazzy manner. I played these pieces for him several times, but then he destroyed all that he considered unworthy of preservation. A piece for one piano, four hands, that he didn't destroy was a sort of paraphrase of José Padilla's *Valencia*, once a popular song. Heifetz used the opening theme from the first movement of the Beethoven violin concerto as an introduction to the song's own well-known theme.

As I pretended to be dusting seriously, I focused my attention on his unfinished transcriptions; they were all put together with their original versions as if he was ready to continue working on them right where he left off. Heifetz tolerantly let me go through them without interfering; I counted about fifty of these unfinished manuscripts. I knew this wasn't the time to press him further about these pieces; even talking about them would have been out of order. To his organized mind, we were dusting, the two of us, each in his or her own way, not working on music. "There is a time and place for everything" was a favorite saying and I knew that forcing the issue would have only met with stiff resistance.

Since he wasn't teaching any more, we spent a great deal of time playing music together; during the afternoons in the studio, either I accompanied him or we played violin duets. In the evenings we played four-hand piano pieces in the living room, or he would ask me just to play something for him, and then he would give me suggestions about interpretation. One day after we had finished playing a piece in the studio, he seemed to be in the right mood for my question: "Have you ever given a thought to those unfinished transcriptions in the cabinet, you know, the ones you saw me handling the other day?"

As always when he was caught by surprise, he became defensive: "What about them?" He sounded as if he wanted to tell me to keep my nose out of his business.

I summoned all my courage and continued, "Are you going to leave them as they are?"

"It is for me to know and for you to find out." Heifetz always retreated to such formulas when he could not or did not want to give a straight answer. Yet it was he who added, "If I wish them to remain incomplete, then they will stay incomplete."

I knew he was defensive only because he took my asking as a sort of criticism, but perhaps he also felt that those half-finished projects were crying for his attention. I tried to soothe him: "You know how much I love your transcriptions and how I admire your ability to bring out—"

"Don't flatter me," Heifetz interrupted me.

"I only want to call them to your attention since I know that you don't like leaving anything unfinished."

"Don't tell me what to think about those manuscripts." He sounded gruff, but I saw in his eyes a gleam of acknowledgment. I knew my timing was right and that I had put the wheels in his head into motion.

Days, perhaps weeks, went by without any mention of the transcriptions. However, one day while I was practicing the piano in his living room and he was in the studio, I heard his ancient buzzer. "There is something very serious I want to discuss with you," Heifetz said over the intercom.

The day was smoggy and overcast, and as I glanced at Los Angeles in the fumes below, I knew he would be in a foul mood. Heifetz liked only sunshine and clear sky, and I expected the worst. I knocked on the door of his studio, and he opened it only a crack. He had a very serious look on his face and seemed to be upset about something. I observed him as he watched me cagily, and when he saw that I looked worried enough, he opened the door and gave me a devilish grin. He was happy as a clam in mud to have fooled me again with his feigned seriousness. He went to his desk, opened the music card file, and asked me to pull out the number 18 and 22 drawers; I felt elated because I knew that some of his published transcriptions were there. Then he asked me to find in the drawers behind his desk the original works on which the top three transcriptions in the pile were based.

Heifetz took out his fiddle, and after we played through the three transcriptions for violin, he asked me to play the original piano works. What happened next baffled me at the time: he went on comparing the original piano works with his transcriptions and explained to me his working process, including how he made the original work sound more interesting and how he brought out the composer's hidden ideas by adding a few bars of his own. By following his explanations I learned to look at a composition from a great performer's point of view; Heifetz uncovered for me the hidden possibilities of a composition and showed me how to recompose an original piece to make it suitable for the violin and piano combination. I understood, then and there, that his transcriptions were no literal arrangements of the original material, but new creations that the composer himself could have written, had he conceived his composition for violin and piano as equal partners. I valued tremendously that Heifetz felt comfortable enough with me to explain this creative process and to pass on the principles of an art that has evoked so much spite from latter-day purists and music critics.

Heifetz meticulously compared not only the music notation but also the performance marks between the original works and his finished transcriptions, pointing out to me the changes required by his reinterpretation of the pieces. At the end of his explanations, he made me compare his original manuscripts with the published versions for mistakes or for possible editorial changes. I found none.

During the next years, in fact, from 1984 to the end of his life, we played through and discussed nearly all his approximately 150 transcriptions, both the published and the unpublished ones.

Heifetz's motives for doing transcriptions were several, most obviously to add new works to the violin literature. He once told me, "Ever since I began to know the piano literature, either by playing pieces myself or by listening to my sister [Pauline] practicing them, I often felt envious of the vast number of pieces written for the piano and I sometimes wished that some of them could be played on the violin." I presume that he also felt that the artistic merit of some pieces he had to practice as a child, especially that of the arrangements, was quite inferior to that of his sister's piano pieces. He was inspired by the importance of the piano in the violin sonatas of Mozart and Beethoven and discovered that these sonatas were no mere vehicles of a violinist's desire to show-off, as some works he played in his younger years were, but rather that they demand an equal partnership between the two instruments. I can even say with confidence that Heifetz's transcriptions were inspired in a backward way; from studying the piano parts in the Mozart and Beethoven violin sonatas, he discovered, from a violinist's point of view, the possibilities hidden in pieces written for piano and then began to study them with an eye to a violin-piano transcription.

Heifetz played plenty of arrangements throughout his career. It wasn't unusual in the early part of the century for recitals to feature complete violin concertos accompanied by the piano: the Mendelssohn violin concerto and Édouard Lalo's *Symphonie espagnole* with piano accompaniment were standard on his early programs. A far cry from its role in a Mozart or Beethoven violin sonata, the piano in these concerto reductions tends to be totally subservient to the violin, as it is in the original showpieces by Sarasate, Wieniawski, Henri Vieuxtemps, and Paganini. Heifetz's intent in his transcriptions clearly was to break this tradition and give the piano something more substantial than empty, oom-pah-pah accompaniments.

Heifetz changed the music he played to varying degrees. Once he put in front of me the piano part of Giuseppe Tartini's Violin Sonata in G minor, and as he began to play his part, he told me to watch out. He had pasted staff paper containing a new accompaniment over some of the original accompaniment, and further down, handwritten notes appeared between the printed ones with the proviso "2a Volta," meaning that I should play the handwritten notes instead of the printed ones when this section was repeated. In some Handel sonatas he changed the basso continuo in repetitions and added new figurations in the right hand, which was, after all, standard practice in baroque style. These changes were only for his personal use in his concerts; none were ever published and probably were not even noticed by critics.

The old warhorse that Heifetz was asked to play most often in his life was August Wilhelmj's arrangement of Franz Schubert's *Ave Maria*. Few if any listeners ever noticed that in Heifetz's recording the pianist sometimes plays more notes than appear in the score. When I played it with him, he wanted me to make the accompaniment denser by adding more notes within the harmony and at the climaxes, although he didn't specify which notes. He felt that these additions would make the piece more effective. Quite often he also changed a few bars of well-known romantic violin concertos if he felt that the music as written did not present the violin to its best effect. Only those who know the pieces with some precision are likely to detect the extent of his cuts in his own transitions or the way he exchanged movements from one sonata into another. Some of Kreisler's violin-piano compositions have interesting piano accompaniments, but the works are not as intricate as Heifetz's. These changes were made for brevity's sake, for redundancy is a sin not uncommon even to some of the greatest composers. Heifetz, the showman, knew exactly how much authenticity his audiences could take and always preferred an exciting performance to a boring but authentic one. It is a well-kept professional secret that Heifetz had a heavy hand in the violin parts of the concertos he commissioned in his lifetime, albeit most of the "corrections" were made with the composers' approval, which is a euphemism for twisting their arms.

No doubt some of his transcriptions, arrangements, and changes in the commissioned works were made to show off his virtuosity. He has often been charged with overdoing the silky tone that characterized his sound—like wearing silken underwear, as a puritanical reviewer sternly chastised—yet he soon recognized that the sweet cantilena idealized in the nineteenth century was not the only effect worth emulating. He spent countless hours not just perfecting the traditional sound of the violin but also working on new sounds and incorporating them into his expressive armor. For these experiments his transcriptions served as custom-made, ideal vehicles. Few violinists could achieve a perfect, genuine, up- and down-bow staccato, for which his *Hora staccato* was his ideal vehicle; in other arrangements he showed me how he used fake harmonics, which he achieved by manipulating the bow in ways that I had never heard or seen anybody do. He used the contrast between vibrato and nonvibrato sound to express musical ideas, as in the beginning of the Sibelius violin concerto. He often encouraged his students to play off-strings, attacking from above the strings, to begin or end a virtuoso passage, if that approach seemed necessary to create a rougher edge or to enhance excitement. He couldn't tell me often enough that besides playing as well as possible, one must exercise a visual effect on the audience by playing the instrument, not by body language. He compared the technique involved in some of his transcriptions to a magician's tricks: a hidden magic in them should be produced smoothly and at a speed that would seem fast but really was not, in order not to give their secrets away. Once he showed me how to play his arrangement for solo violin of Sergei Prokofiev's March from his *Children's Suite*, originally a piano piece for children. He made a difficult arrangement of it; one has to maintain a march rhythm and clear intonation while playing two or sometimes three lines at the same time: pizzicatos, double-stop chords, harmonic chords, grace notes, and passing chords have to be played in dazzling succession while keeping the melody going underneath it all. Heifetz was indeed the magician while playing it for me: he made me hear harmonics when none were played and gave the impression that a whole string section of an orchestra was playing. When he finished, he handed me his fiddle and said, "Here, you try these tricks with the harmonics, just as I showed them to you." I usually hesitated to accept such challenges, but this time I was eager to try and imitate his magic. Of course, I could not. Heifetz smiled at my futile effort, then gave away the trick: "Your finger is on the right place, but you don't strike the note with the correct stroke. You must attack from the air, and as soon as you draw the bow fast on the string, you must come off it in a dash up in the air." I tried the magic his way, and this time it worked, for the fake harmonics are found only high up on the fingerboard.

Heifetz wrote his first transcription on an impulse in Mexico City in 1927. As he told me the story, the night before his first concert there, he went to a cafe, and there he heard Manuel Ponce's popular *Estrellita*. (Ponce also used the melody of *Estrellita* in the second movement of his violin concerto.) He was touched by the graciousness of the Mexicans, by the service and respect he received there, and he decided right in the cafe to arrange this song as a tribute to the people of Mexico for his next night's recital. He went to his hotel room, took out a pack of cigarettes (he was a heavy smoker at that time), ordered several bottles of Coca-Cola to stay awake, and set to work. By the early morning hours he finished the piece and even clean-copied both piano and violin parts. "I felt sorry for my accompanist," he said, "for he had a tough time reading from my manuscript with six sharps in the key signature and everything else except the kitchen sink that I used in that first arrangement of mine." He played the piece the same night with rousing success. For his arrangement, with its jazzy chords and double sharps, he changed the key to F-sharp major from whatever key the cafe musicians had used, with the intention of bringing out the especially luscious, rich sound of Mexican songs. In F-sharp major there are no open strings, and one hears the least number of overtones. Heifetz felt that the lack of resonance in the open strings enabled him to produce a richer, more sonorous, silky sound that was more covered and closer to that of the human voice. This luscious sound is also supported by rich harmonies and modulations in the piano accompaniment: the thematic dialogue between the violin and the piano in the modulation to D major at the climax of the piece gives the effect of brightness and an open and happy atmosphere.

Another arrangement Heifetz made after hearing a cafe performance, this one in Romania some time before 1930, was his even more famous *Hora staccato*. *Hora* is a Romanian word for a round dance widely practiced in the villages of that country; Heifetz added *staccato* to describe its manner of performance. The original music consists of a quite unpromising scale-type melody, but it achieves its strength from a cascading

drive and unrelenting rhythm. Its difficulty lies in the up- down-bow staccatos that are necessary for its fluid performance, but few can execute
them as Heifetz did. Most performers can do only up-bow staccato, which
is easier to control, and some do not even have a real staccato at all, an
"honest staccato," as he called it, only a flying one, since staccato requires
a steady hand and a perfect bowing technique. Heifetz once told me: "I
don't often allow my students to play the 'Horrible Staccato,'" as he
called it in jest, "because in most cases the students only want my approval
of their tremendous, fast staccato, and are looking for my compliments
on their performances. They rarely can play down- and up-bow staccatos,
especially in different tempos; most of them are geared only to one speed
which they are unable to change. I don't want to discourage them too
much."

He told me a story of a talented student in his master class who
wanted to learn a trick or two whenever Heifetz demonstrated difficult
passages on the violin, but who also wanted to impress Heifetz. When
the student had the opportunity to play a short piece of his own choosing,
he proudly selected the *Hora staccato*. Heifetz replied without enthusiasm, "I wish you'd play something else, but if that is the only short piece
you have prepared for today, go ahead." The student proceeded to play
the *Hora staccato* at demon speed, and the class applauded loudly. Yet
Heifetz said only, "Your performance made me very nervous. Now I'd
like you to start again but at a slower tempo which I will give you. This is
the only way I will be able to tell whether you have an honest down- and
up-bow staccato." To everyone's surprise except Heifetz's, the student
could not play at the much slower tempo. A slow tempo is more difficult;
the faster, the easier.

Once he showed me his own down- and up-bow staccatos in different
tempos. He had perfect control over his bow no matter what speed he
took, even when he was over eighty years old. I noticed that he never
played the *Hora staccato* twice at the same speed; I played it with him several times and found this absolute control astonishing. He told me a
small secret—though not an explanation—of this control: "Don't you
ever let initial success, while playing a piece, get to your head, and con-
gratulate yourself before the job is done; always remember, be it a one-
minute or a twenty-five-minute piece, you have to concentrate on the
mood and the character of it all the way to the last note without ever letting your concentration lapse."

Hora staccato and *Estrellita* are unusual pieces among Heifetz's arrangements: they are the only ones he wrote following his impressions of

a live performance. In these two pieces the harmonization and compositional process were his creation; he only borrowed the melodies. All his other transcriptions, as far as I know, were based on published music: on piano pieces, songs, orchestral music, and even operas. Among the simplest Heifetz arrangements were those in which he merely transposed a piece for the violin. Of these, a favorite of his was the third movement of Sergei Rachmaninoff's Sonata for Cello and Piano, Op. 19, written for the Russian cellist Anatol Brandukov. In this case Heifetz simply transposed some of the cello parts one or two octaves higher, as the range and expressive capability of the violin required, but never changed a note and even used Rachmaninoff's original piano accompaniment. Heifetz liked to include this piece on his programs because the piano has a thematically important part; it introduces the main idea in a style reminiscent of Schubert and runs in canonic imitations with the violin. He never published this arrangement, but it was always on his music stand, and we often played it together in his studio.

Another transcription of particular interest is Heifetz's Preludio from Bach's Partita No. 3 in E major for solo violin. It is an interesting transcription because it wasn't inspired by Bach's original solo violin Partita, but rather by Rachmaninoff's piano solo arrangement of the same piece. Rachmaninoff arranged three of the Partita's seven dance movements. The Bach-Rachmaninoff Prelude for solo piano is a masterpiece in itself; Heifetz rearranged the piano arrangement for the violin as if it were an original piano composition. Neither Rachmaninoff nor Heifetz changed a single note in the original Bach composition for violin, but Heifetz ingeniously used the thematic material in Rachmaninoff's piano accompaniment to imitate the style of Bach's accompanied violin pieces.

Of all his transcriptions, Heifetz was particularly happy with his Gershwin arrangements. Among his contemporaries he felt the closest to Rachmaninoff and Gershwin; he asked each of them to write something special for him, but neither one complied with his request. Heifetz felt a certain affinity to George Gershwin's jazzy style, and as he told me, "That was perhaps the reason why the Gershwin transcriptions turned out to be something I am proud of. Besides, I always wanted to play something by Gershwin. I hope my arrangements are proof enough of my love and admiration for Gershwin." Another time he said, "I wish I had half of Gershwin's talent."

Heifetz himself had quite a talent for jazzy rhythms. He loved to improvise at the piano until the crack of dawn, with me as his private audience. We played jazzy musical games, in the course of which he would ask me to beat a steady rhythm on the arms of my chair while in between he would beat the craziest rhythmical patterns on the arms of his chair: off-beats, mixed rhythms with displaced accents between his two hands and my beat, fast runs in one hand and slow off-beats in the other hand, and syncopations of all kinds. He had the kind of rhythmic imagination and the talent to execute these rhythms that would have qualified him as a percussionist in any first-rate jazz band. This may explain his own jazzy violin obbligato contributions to his transcriptions of Gershwin's *Three Preludes* and of the songs from *Porgy and Bess.*

In general Heifetz stayed within the harmonic framework of the original composition and only made changes if he felt that the original work could use more colorful harmonic support. He changed the keys only if he knew that another key would be more advantageous for the sound of the violin. For example, in the transcription of *Navarra* by Isaac Albéniz, he changed the key from A-flat major to A major because A major, with its overtones from the open strings, makes for a brighter key. He also felt free to make the change because the work was completed not by Albéniz but rather by another composer, Déodat de Séverac. When Heifetz first heard me playing Albéniz's *El puerto* in its published version, he turned to me and said, "You know, I don't like the ending as it is in the score; do something about it." I got inspired and improvised an ending on the spot. Heifetz asked me to play it several times and declared that he liked mine better than the original. I never wrote out my version, but I have been playing it from memory ever since.

We had been playing through his transcriptions for several months when Heifetz began to question me about my studies in theory, analysis, orchestration, harmony, and counterpoint. I told him that I had taken some courses in composition back in Buffalo; in return he told me how he studied the same subjects at the St. Petersburg Conservatory, as a special student because he was so young. Then one day he surprised me by giving me the Romance from Rachmaninoff's Second Suite for Two Pianos, Op. 17, and told me to transcribe it for one piano, four hands. He gave me a week to do it. When I brought it back a week later, all finished, he looked at it and put it aside. But several days later he asked me to join him at the piano, and we played through my arrangement. He pointed out what was still needed in my arrangement to capture Rachmaninoff's special flair and drama. I was particularly happy to do this work because I needed pieces to play four-hands with Ada, who by the age of ten had become quite an accomplished pianist.

A few days later Heifetz asked me to go back to the same cupboard where I had first found his unpublished and incomplete works and bring them all out; I counted about fifty works. In the course of the following months he made me study and play through their original versions, and then we played through the parts he already had finished. We did this over and over again with each piece until he decided whether to complete or discard it.

I also found in the pile of finished transcriptions a number of works that he had often played in his recitals but which had never been published, among them Melody, a transcription of Christoph Willibald Gluck's *Mélodie* from the ballet *Orfeo ed Euridice*; a transcription of Chopin's Nocturne, Op. 27, No. 2, in D-flat major; one of Jacques Ibert's *Le petit âne blanc* from the piano suite *Histoires* and of Irving Berlin's "White Christmas"; two movements from Zoltán Kodály's *Háry János* Suite from the opera by the same name; and other pieces, most of them well known from his recordings.

Heifetz was a meticulous editor of his own arrangements. He wrote out the fingerings, bowings, and other performance marks in the smallest detail, not only in the violin parts but in the piano parts as well. These markings shouldn't be taken lightly; they are there for a reason, even if they seem unorthodox and odd for a less adventurous performer. Heifetz was never satisfied with a new transcription until he played through it several times with the piano accompaniment; he let it rest for several weeks and returned to it again and again until he was convinced that everything was right and that the performance markings served their intended effect. He sometimes asked what I thought about his piano writing, whether it was well-written and easily fingered for pianists, or if it needed some change or improvement. Being a pianist himself, he always wrote pianistic passages, and usually I could only admire what he did. Occasionally, though, I spoke up and suggested better ways to achieve what he intended to do in the piano part. Although he usually didn't take my advice at face value, rather seeming offended by my audacity, several days later he would bring the piece out again with my suggested changes written in, wanting to know if that was what I meant.

Heifetz demanded that his publishers include in the piano score every single marking in the violin parts; he wanted to make sure that the pianist would be conscious of what the violinist was doing and would be prepared to give the violinist enough time if a tenuto, rubato, glissando, or finger replacement was indicated in the violin part. He finalized his markings only after he was convinced that they conveyed fluency, dash, and energy, and that they gave more adventurous violinists an opportunity to display a certain visual flair in their execution.

The first unfinished work we began to work on earnestly was the Humoresque in G major from Rachmaninoff's Op. 10. Rachmaninoff himself made two revisions of this work and played the second version in his piano recitals. Heifetz asked me to memorize all three versions of the Humoresque and play them for him until he completely absorbed the mood of all three versions in his mind. He eventually decided to use in his transcription materials from all three versions, taking parts from here and there that he judged to be the most effective for the violin. When neither of the three versions lent itself to a good violin transcription, he let the piano part stand and wrote a violin obbligato over it in the same manner as he did in the middle section of Gershwin's Prelude No. 2. A similar technique appears in his transcription of Rachmaninoff's *Oriental Sketch.* Heifetz never considered the violin as the dominant instrument in these works; he always considered his transcriptions as enhancing the beauty in the original material by adding the violin as an equal partner to the piano. Sometimes he made considerable changes in the original piano parts; thus Heifetz's piano accompaniment to the *Étude-tableau,* Op. 33, No. 7. is more difficult than the original Rachmaninoff piano version.

Among the curiosities Heifetz taught me was how to make manuscript corrections in the old-fashioned way; he had a leaf-shaped knife, sharp on both edges and with an ivory handle, which he used to scrape off the notes he wanted to eliminate, exactly as codex scribes did it in the Middle Ages. He was as skilled as his medieval predecessors were; he never dug a hole in the paper, his scraping was hardly visible, and he could go over the same spot repeatedly without damaging the paper. The manuscript paper he used was of high quality, with clefs all preprinted, because it accepted the new ink on top of the scrapings without diffusion. Of course, when we did the first version of a manuscript, he always used pencil and erased his mistakes easily; he used the scraping technique only if he wanted to change something that was in ink in an already finished clean copy. It was characteristic of him that after he finished even a small section of his work, he always copied it in ink and had a photocopy made of it just in case something should happen to the original clean copy.

After the piece had taken its final shape and the piano-violin score was copied in ink, we would play through it several more times; sometimes Heifetz did a few more scrapings and changed a few notes, but if

Heifetz's pocket metronome and ivory-handled manuscript scraper, with a manuscript page from one of his unpublished scores. Photo by Jack Nilles

after repeated playing the piece didn't please him, he would tear up the result of weeks and sometimes months of work. Thus perished by his hands some thirty-eight of his 150 transcriptions, pieces representing roughly five years of work. He shredded his manuscripts with slow, deliberate motions, his face showing a queer pleasure, as a naughty child would destroy a favorite toy of which he had tired.

Eventually twelve pieces remained of the fifty that had been in the cupboard. Heifetz wrote out the violin parts after he decided that the pieces were worthy of his name as their transcriber. Four of these pieces were performed by two of his students in the spring of 1988 at the Chamber Music L.A. festival as a tribute to their master after his death. Heifetz was very proud of his arrangement of Moritz Moszkowski's *Sparks*, a devilishly difficult piece in its solo piano form, made even more difficult and effective in Heifetz's transcription. It's a masterpiece in the exchange of thematic material between the two instruments, requiring split-second cooperation between the violin and the piano. I played the piece with Yukiko Kamei, his one-time assistant, and we did a good job at it. In the first half of the transcription of Dohnányi's Romanza from *Suite for Orchestra*, Heifetz called for scordatura, lowering the G string to E to produce a deep, viola sound, followed by a return to ordinary tuning, by no means an easy feat within the short time allotted to the violinist.

In his studio's cabinets I also found many published scores that Heifetz had received as complimentary copies. We played through these pieces, and he commented to me as he carefully studied them with the eyes of a craftsman. He would invariably criticize their appearance and the publisher's printing technique: "Things have changed so much; people don't take pride any more in what they are doing. It is all business, to make the most money at the least expense." He complained about the poor quality of the paper, the inconsistent spacing of the printed staves, the wrongly placed performance marks in comparison to the way they used to be, the smudgy prints, an overall lack of sharpness on the printed page, and a host of other things only a professional would notice.

Heifetz decided that the last twelve arrangements we worked on together should be published. He asked me to contact some of the publishers he used to work with. To his chagrin, practically no one remained whom he had known and with whom he had had personal contact. Nevertheless, he made an attempt to publish his scores by sending them to various publishers. The publishers, however, sent him notices about their own editorial policies, telling Heifetz of necessary changes in his manuscripts to make them conform to modern printing techniques. Heifetz was adamant that not a note, not a mark, should be changed in his manuscripts, because they were placed where they were for a good reason. In the past, editors apparently were always willing to make exceptions for him and let him have his way. This wasn't the case any longer, and after exchanging correspondence, Heifetz asked for the manuscripts to be returned. He received apologetic letters stating that there was nothing unusual in their requests for editorial changes and that they were only exercising their general editorial rights. Heifetz remained obstinate, as one could have expected, and his last twelve transcriptions were never published. It is too bad, because they were exceptionally well done, and they constitute his *Schwanengesang*—his swansong—as a transcriber.

Two of the last transcriptions Heifetz completed in 1986 were of Rachmaninoff's Preludes, Op. 32, Nos. 7 and 12. He wasn't very happy with how the work progressed, but I encouraged and helped him finish as a labor of love. However, he never completed his very last project, his transcription and condensation of Gershwin's *An American in Paris*. All the sketches were laid out but with empty spots here and there; he crossed out a great number of false starts and made notes for the transitory modulations that would fuse the various sections, but when I would bring the piece out for him to finish, he always turned me down, saying, "Not now. Later." I had the feeling that he wanted me to finish it, and I began to question him about how he planned to do certain unfinished parts and what parts of the sketches to use and which ones to leave out. To my surprise he didn't turn me down, nor did he give me smart answers, but told me what I wanted to know. Because he never liked to be quizzed or pressed about anything, his willingness to talk about this piece indicated to me that my feelings about his intentions were right. Even though he didn't want to write anything down, he played the unwritten parts for me several times and commented that the whole thing was a bit too long. At that moment I felt as if I had been led through a secret door to a place of great musical wisdom. I felt fortunate and privileged, glad that I had not decided against his wanting me to become a pianist. Yet while I was working for Heifetz I had no opportunity to think things through. All I could do was to absorb what he was passing on to me and store it in my mind. To sort things out, to reflect, would take time.

Two years after death I admitted to myself that I had to complete *An American in Paris*. Heifetz had always said never to start something and not finish it. But even more, I had come to see this title as representing our long collaboration in our adopted country. I finally was able to take out the manuscript and attempt to finish it. One morning during my summer vacation in Switzerland in the most beautiful surroundings, I sat over it and tried to remember what he had told me. At first nothing came to my mind; the manuscript stared back at me, ungiving and unforgiving for my long neglect. Then, after two weeks, the notes in the manuscript began to make sense. They came together with the sounds as he had played them the last time, and it seemed to me that I heard his voice telling me where to cut, where to change, where to modulate, what to leave out, and what belonged where. I had to write a few transitional measures to connect some disjointed parts, but I felt that his hand was guiding mine. When I finished the transcription at the end of the summer, I had the feeling that he had written it, not I.

Heifetz liked to write cryptic dedications at the top of his transcriptions; they mostly consisted of abbreviated names, their meaning known only to him and perhaps to the persons to whom they were dedicated. I often felt that when Heifetz played his transcriptions he played them with these people in mind, and with his playing he reminisced over events that prompted their dedication; I also felt that this special feeling of his added something to these pieces that no one else could fathom or imitate, as if he had developed special sounds and techniques to perform them. For this reason I always feel, when someone else performs his "itsy-bitsys," that something is missing, something that represents the enigma of Jascha Heifetz.

12

Dies Irae

If neither foes nor loving friends can hurt you;
If all men count with you, but none too much

RUDYARD KIPLING

*I*t wasn't easy to be a friend of Jascha Heifetz; he superbly ignored his
enemies, thereby making them hate him even more, but his friends he
exposed to all kinds of vexations which he expected to be tolerated and
cheerfully endured in the name of friendship. He gave the impression to
outside observers that he owned his friends with a total disregard toward
their feelings; the thought of inconveniencing them apparently never
occurred to him, and their only privilege was to obey his summons. Heifetz was the picture of an absolute monarch stepping out of the past. As
behooves such a ruler, he surrounded himself with intrigues and fos-
tered unhealthy rivalries while viewing the combatants with glee and de-
tachment. In the process he sometimes poisoned the living waters of trust
and friendship, and by also allowing himself to become overwhelmed by
the agony of doubt and suspicion, he became embroiled in a perennial
hellfire on earth so vividly described in the Dies Irae for the hereafter. Yet
he was also willing to rationalize if someone else tried to poison his mind.
He told me that someone he had known for a long time suggested that in
spite of all the hardship he was exposing me to, I had an ulterior motive
in staying with him—namely, money. In reply to this challenge, Heifetz
took an easy way out. "At least I have something to offer," he said, "and
she doesn't suffer for nothing." It is not easy for me to turn this surface of
my searching prism on him, but unless I do so, my story will be a hagiography, and that would go against the principles of the very man who
prided himself on being difficult.

In his defense I can only quote Aristotle's saying that "There was
never a great genius without a tincture of madness" and add that Heifetz's childhood as a prodigy and the responsibilities that went with it
made almost everything understandable and forgivable. Heifetz often

showed that tincture of madness, and while spending his life rebelling against rules and models, he was also busy creating his own ironclad principles and precepts, thereby building his own trap with maddening inconsistency. Perhaps his childhood was paradoxical as well, for although his parents controlled his every move, his life lacked the guideposts that the usual rules and models can provide. Sometimes he revealed a dysfunctional mind; mutually exclusive thoughts and ideas ran simultaneously on parallel tracks, never meeting up with one another.

He had always been a shrewd observer of human nature, but since he had a natural tendency to concentrate on everything that was bad, his observations made him bitter rather than tolerant and forgiving. As do many musicians who spend their lives practicing the minutest details, Heifetz tended to take everything seriously. He knew no measure of big or small, and that included even small talk. His wry humor was mostly derived from real-life situations, and he had no appreciation of or talent for wisecracks. As a true performer who considered it his job to make his audiences emote without showing his own feelings, Heifetz never laughed at his own jokes or stories, only sometimes cracked a crooked smile. It was difficult for him to adapt to the formulas and assumptions of society, and he didn't have to look hard to find the false notes and the insincerity in his fellow human beings. He always had to probe and find the brute beneath the thin veneer of civilization, then prick the balloons of inflated egos and generally make a pest of himself. In turn, society looked at this strange person with apprehension and a jaundiced eye, always suspecting that Heifetz really didn't belong there, yet kowtowing to him because he was a world-famous celebrity. In his younger years he liked to believe in the sincerity of this adulation, but he wasn't surprised when he found himself more and more isolated in proportion to his exit from the limelight. After he retired and retreated into his own world, he had to come to the realization that some of those whom he trusted as his friends began to consider him a "has-been" and were reluctant to respond to his summons. In the past he had conditioned himself quite well to face the "two imposters," Triumph and Disaster, represented for him by success and failure, but he wasn't quite ready in his old age to face a new set of imposters, the most devastating ones, abandonment and despair.

With the years passing and his physical strength ebbing, Heifetz also had to face another imposter, as the inevitable thought of passing away began to crowd in on him. He was still full of zest for life and wouldn't give up easily; I once heard him walking up and down in his house and muttering to himself, "I don't want to die. I don't want to die." I presume that a clock built in our mind signals the time left for us, and in his last years he seemed to recognize that nature had taken its course and that the time was approaching to withdraw from life. The process of withdrawal began prematurely and surreptitiously, years before it should have happened, with the troubles surrounding his master class.

The troubles started as early as 1974 when the class had to move from the familiar, homelike atmosphere of Clark House to an efficient but sterile and cold new building that had been finished on the USC campus. It was a concrete and brick building with corridors barely wide enough for two people to pass each other, with pillbox classrooms and windows that couldn't be opened, a building where pumps circulated the air that hummed relentlessly in the occupants' ears at a low, yet maddening, noise level. It was Heifetz's frequent custom at Clark House to visit his friends on the faculty during his lunch breaks; in the new place he couldn't find anybody, and when he knocked on doors to look for a familiar face, all he got was a blank stare with a "What can I do for you, sir?" from someone who pretended not to know who he was. Heifetz always apologized in his bumbling way for disturbing a class, yet he half hoped for recognition and perhaps a civil invitation to come in, which, of course, he would have refused.

Heifetz had his private room in the new building, adjacent to his classroom. For a while he tried to adjust to the new surroundings and pretended that nothing important had happened, but his heart wasn't in the place and he didn't enjoy teaching there. Though all the windows in the building were fixed to save energy, he demanded that his classroom have traditional windows that he could open to hear the birds singing under his window just like in his old place, instead of breathing in dead silence the artificial, stale, recirculated air. His friend Dean Beglarian bent over backward to fulfill his wishes, and Heifetz got not only his open windows but even a fully grown tree transplanted under his class window, just as it was in his old place. However, instead of birds singing from the tree, only disturbing noises came up from the crowded courtyard of the campus below, and one day someone even practiced the trombone under his window while he was teaching. Against the backdrop of all these hazards, soon it became obvious that Heifetz was looking for excuses to leave campus.

Always on the lookout for his students' welfare, Heifetz started searching for a place in the building where they could spend their lunch hour. In the old Clark House there was a stately entrance hall, a homey kitchen, and a private garden with benches and chairs to use during recess and to eat one's lunch. In the new building there was no room for the students, and if they had to stay indoors, they had only the dank, windowless hallways, smelling of drying concrete and of the peculiar odor of dust circulated by air pumps. Heifetz went on a discovery tour of the new building and found that the flat rooftop would be an ideal place for student recreation. The university, of course, couldn't agree to sending students to the rooftop since no insurance company would tolerate such a risk. Heifetz couldn't or didn't want to understand that. He proceeded to fight for the establishment of a place for communication and contact between faculty and students. This became his priority and goal, and he gave the music school dean a sort of ultimatum, to get it done or else.

The next item on the list of his misfortunes was that Dean Beglarian, who protected and shielded Heifetz from academic and administrative backbiting and bickering, quit the university for a job in Florida. That left Heifetz defenseless against the envy of the faculty, which began to question his privileged position. Heifetz knew that Dean Beglarian was his only true friend on campus, once remarking in passing, "I wouldn't be surprised if Dean Beglarian left the school because of the mismanagement of the class funds. There was nothing he wouldn't do for me or for my class." Although Dean Beglarian had started a million-dollar foundation for the preservation of both the Heifetz and Piatigorsky chairs and Heifetz had donated the entire income from his concert of October 1972 at the Los Angeles Music Center—his last full-scale concert—to improve the salary of the music faculty at USC, the actual status of these funds was never made clear to him, and they apparently were diminishing at an alarming rate. When a new dean of the School of Music was appointed, Heifetz went through the motions of meeting him and his faculty at a reception in the new director's house, shaking hands with everybody and saying the usual, meaningless formulas, but he left as soon as he was introduced to everybody present. I was with him at this reception and knew that it took great effort for him to do even this much socializing, but he did it for the survival of his master class.

His efforts, however, were in vain, for the new dean died in a short time, and the search committee came up with someone whose job apparently was to wipe the slate clean in the School of Music. At the same time Heifetz had become tired of the hassle of traveling twice a week to the university. One of his principles was never to travel on the freeways of Los Angeles, and going through street traffic was no fun any more. He was eighty-one now and had accumulated enough excuses to abandon his uninspiring classroom in the new building. One day, without further ado, he told his students that from then on they had to come to his studio in Beverly Hills for classes. I don't know if he was aware that teaching classes outside of campus was highly irregular and needed special permission from the university; such acts could easily be construed as being destructive of institutional discipline. By that time, though, even if he knew it, he didn't care.

The new dean apparently decided either to make Heifetz comply with university procedures or to make an example of him. Heifetz was called to the dean's office to negotiate his yearly contract. As I understood it, his salary was in question. But he never negotiated with anyone except through his lawyer, and he refused the invitation. Heifetz was repeatedly asked to come to the dean's office to discuss the place of his teaching and his salary, but the real reason for the tough policy requiring him to teach on university property turned out to be that funds for running the class were down to nearly nothing. Claims were made that money pledged for the Heifetz-Piatigorsky chair was never paid into the fund and that the master class should come under direct management of the university. This would have resulted in the establishment of a minimum number of students for his class, a restriction to which Heifetz never would have agreed. He staunchly refused even to meet the new dean, either in his office or anywhere else. Heifetz knew that faculty members had a quite unfavorable view of his salary and that it had been discussed at faculty meetings, but the knowledge that not one of his "friends" raised a peep in his defense or tried to straighten out the facts made him even more obstinate. Before the second semester was over, he received a letter from the new dean with a statement of the financial status of the master class funds. There was just enough money to pay him, his assistant, and me for our services for the current semester. Heifetz tendered his resignation in the spring of 1983 before he was dismissed. After he resigned, he got just one letter from a faculty member, someone from whom he expected it the least, expressing his sorrow for the treatment Heifetz had received from the university. He showed me the letter, and from that I understood that he clearly knew the faculty's position against him. All he said about the letter was "It's too late."

Apparently Heifetz's lawyer saw enough evidence of one sort or another to start a lawsuit against the university. The school was hoping to settle out of court since Heifetz would have had to appear in court to make a deposition. This cut short the lawsuit because he would never appear in public and subject himself to questioning in a subsequent lawsuit on a subject that he considered nobody's business. It wasn't the loss of his contract with the university that hurt Heifetz the most but rather the conviction that his efforts to teach the violin following a great tradition had been rejected and that he was prevented from continuing something unique, something that nobody else could do. Here I must say that he never talked about his own rank among violinists, never praised himself, and never fished for praise from others, yet he knew his own value without false modesty, as a true professional craftsman knows the value of his artwork in comparison to that of others. I also must say that he didn't even like being called an artist; he thought of himself as "just a fiddler," as he often said, because he left esthetic judgments to others. In defiance of fate and perhaps privately even shaking his fist at it, he decided to continue teaching in his own studio, rehiring his teaching assistant and me as class pianist at his own expense.

But to go it alone wasn't that simple, as Heifetz found out soon enough. Prospective students applied as usual through the university, only to hear that he was not teaching there any more, period: no forwarding address, no advice about his whereabouts or his teaching at his home. Naturally the applicants looked for other teachers, and while some found out, too late, that he was teaching his master class at home, others never learned about it. The number of applicants began to peter out, and it was only a matter of pride on Heifetz's part that he didn't completely give up. Officially the master class never ceased, but with each passing year there were fewer and fewer applicants. By the end of 1985, the only applicants were those who were unacceptable or who wanted private lessons from him.

For all these years I was paid either by the university as the pianist for his master class or from his own funds when he started his private master class. As the number of his students diminished, he needed to find a new title for me to make my presence legitimate. Heifetz was in desperate straits for help when even his secretary of fifteen years left him to get married. Only then did he hire me officially as his house manager. A few months later, however, he realized that if he had to call me "manager," he was being managed again. He hated managers from his concertizing past, so he asked me what I thought my title ought to be. I told him that it would have to be a long one since I already had many different responsibilities, including those of his off-duty housekeeper, manager, chauffeur, whipping post, pianist, collaborator in music arranging, organizer, repairperson, and, above all, recruiter of new housekeepers and secretaries who changed sometimes by the week. To simplify matters, though, I said I would take any title he came up with. It was "unofficial private accompanist," which would sound appropriate on his payroll.

Heifetz may have been saddened by his troubles at the university, bothered by his ailments, and perhaps sorry to lose his friends and students, but none of these had such a profound effect on his personality as did the selling of his beach house in 1984. The necessity wasn't financial but rather came from losing his treasured privacy to strangers who he felt intruded on his neighborhood. He loved to spend his weekends and holidays there and enjoyed the peace and quiet which was broken only by the sound of the waves incessantly crashing over the sand. He used to take long walks on the beach with a stick in his hand, sit down in the sand at the end of his walk to gaze over the endless horizon, and then return to the house to take his daily nap. He had a nodding acquaintance with a few people living at the beach, but he rarely socialized with any of them; the neighbors respected his desire for privacy and left him alone. For stargazers there were plenty of celebrities walking on the beach—the Colony, where many of the famous film stars had summer homes, was a little over a mile away from his house. The house next to his on the north side was owned by Robert Redford, but it was always rented out and I never saw him there. Another movie celebrity lived on the south side, but he occupied his place most of the time.

All this peace and quiet evaporated when neighbors of long standing moved away and a younger, livelier generation moved in. Rock music blared all day from the radio, sometimes senselessly, because once when Heifetz sent me over to ask them "to pipe down," I found the house empty and the radio roaring away in the yard. Then a sailboat was hauled up on the beach and parked on his property for several weeks, right in front of his teahouse, cutting off the ocean view. The sheriff was called and the lawyer put into action, but they could do nothing because nobody seemed to know who owned the boat. Weeks later the boat disappeared as suddenly as it had come. In addition, the crowds on the beach became denser and more aggressive, some of them settling down in front of his gate, making lots of noise at a place Heifetz had so carefully roped off as his own. There was even more noise over the water: jet skis roared away in front of his property all day long during the weekends, helicopters cruised overhead in response to emergencies, and private airplanes buzzed the neighborhood, all providing the kind of background noise which modern society seems to depend on. Heifetz made my life miserable, too; almost every half-hour he made me call the sheriff's department or some other agency to complain about these nuisances, demanding that something be done about them. Of course, nothing could have been done, and nothing was done. No wonder that Heifetz began to feel uneasy in his own place, and he was at a loss to explain to himself how he had gotten into the middle of all this.

The final blow was a huge winter storm that wreaked havoc on the neighborhood, his property included. The raging waves smashed his fence on the ocean side, and the brick steps that led over the fence were demolished. The roof of his teahouse hung precariously on two posts, and even those were knocked awry by the waves and the whirling sand. The whole yard was thickly covered with sand from one end to the other. There was sand several inches deep in the living room of his house, and the water moved the furniture around like toys, but because most of it was made of wrought iron, the damage there wasn't too great. Some of the neighbors suffered even greater damage, and a few houses were virtually demolished. Heifetz's house, however, sat a little farther up on the shore and escaped serious damage.

I think this storm was the last factor that made him decide to sell the property. First, though, he wanted to restore the yard and the teahouse to their original shape, but the original drawings couldn't be found. Again I got the order to "Do something about it!" I wasn't without experience with architectural drawings, having seen enough of them in my father's office, and so from memory I was able to reconstruct on paper in detail how the yard and the teahouse looked before the storm. I even found a contractor who could read my sketches, and the yard was restored exactly as it had been before.

After his beach house was sold and Heifetz stayed in his Beverly Hills home most weekends, a quick deterioration set in, probably from a combination of aging and self-pity. The little happiness and good feeling that the beach represented for him were gone with all its pleasant memories. I think the fact that his beach property was small made him feel in control of everything around him. With its loss, his well-organized world came apart. He had shown irrational behavior in the past and had been destructive of himself and others, yet all that was nothing compared to what now came to the surface. Having alienated his friends and no longer having any students, Heifetz had all the time in the world to concentrate on me and torment himself with the question: Why did this girl stay behind, what are her motives, and why didn't she leave me with all the rest when I tried my best to make her leave? He had tested my motives in the past: to see if I sought money, he raised my salary, then a few months later reduced it to a ridiculous level and watched my reaction. When I

protested, he made sly remarks that money can buy everything. Pointing out to him that he couldn't even "buy" a housekeeper who could fulfill his expectations would have been useless; he would have blamed me
for not being able to produce the kind he really wanted.

To his senseless suspicions about me, he added a new one, that I
wanted to kill him, but this one, I found out later, wasn't completely the
product of his own mind, or if it was, he sought confirmation of it from
"friends" who had been close to him in the past but now never came to
see him any more. Even years after he had died, the story came back to
me as something deserving of serious consideration. Such was his power
over others that hardly anyone among his acquaintances would stand up
to him and disagree with anything he said. Their usual reply to him was
"If you think so, Jim, there must be something to it" or "Do as you think
is best for you." Yet agreeing with him or catering too much to him was a
sure way to lose his confidence; he craved contradiction, a chance to do
the opposite of what he was told to do.

This new suspicion broke to the surface not long after he sold the
house at Malibu. It happened early on a nice afternoon. He was standing
at the bar contemplating the drink in his hand when all of a sudden he
looked at me with cold, hostile, unseeing eyes, and out of the blue asked
in a strange voice: "Did you put some poison in my drink? What kind was
it? Was it rat poison?"

He was dead serious. The question wasn't the kind of joke that passes
between people who know each other well enough to amuse themselves
with such corn when there is nothing better to talk about. Past experience had taught me that contradicting him or denying his accusation
would have been useless. Instead I took the glass out of his hand, slowly
took a sip, and handed it back to him. It didn't taste any different from
what it should have, and I told him so. He looked at me suspiciously for
a while, perhaps waiting for the poison to take effect or wanting to ask me
what antidote I had taken before I drank it. Then he changed his mind
and went to his studio without saying another word.

It was a beautiful Sunday afternoon, and I knew he was thinking
about the beach and pitying himself for being here when he could be
out there, asking himself why he had given up the beach house rather
than fighting for his rights while he was still in possession of it. The poi-
soning incident was a first for me, and for a while I didn't know how to
cope with it. I had heard rumors that sometime in the past, Heifetz had
suspected one of his wives of being out to get him, which had brought
him near a nervous breakdown. Such rumors, true or untrue, serve at

best as cautionary tales, and I decided to find my way out of this corner with my own methods and preferably cut off further suspicions in his mind. I took the bull by the horns and confronted him with his own suspicion directly.

The next day he was in a rather contented mood and seemed to have forgotten the poison incident of the day before. When I brought up the subject, he innocently said that he remembered nothing at all. I decided not let him get away with it that easily and pursued the subject.

"Jim, I wish I were your mother," I said.

"Why?" he sounded surprised.

"Because after what you told me yesterday, I should now take you on my knees and spank you."

He looked at me and after a while struck a darker mood: "You're a fresh kid—I should do that to you." Then he thought about it for a few seconds and changed his mind. "OK, go ahead and spank me."

"I know you're kidding," I said, "but spanking isn't the solution. It's too late for that."

It was too late, indeed; Heifetz, in many aspects, remained the child who had missed the spanking, physical or figurative, when it was due. As he didn't play much with toys in his childhood, as an adult he played with people who were thrown his way by accident or necessity. His petulance toward his friends knew no limits; a last-minute invitation would be a command and declining it brought from him the caustic remark, "They are a stick in the mud." An excuse to get out of a previous engagement had a standard answer, "Ditch it." With this attitude he surely lost to attrition the number of people whom he could invite, because he rarely gave his friends a second chance; there were no rain checks if his invitation was once refused. Indeed, the word *friend* has to be understood, in his case, in the most superficial sense of the word. I don't know if Heifetz ever had a friend whom he could take into his confidence and with whom he could have passed the ultimate test of friendship—mutual tolerance for one another based on equality; tolerance between him and his "friends" seemed to be rather lopsided as he expected them to be subservient to all his whims.

In company Heifetz set the tone of conversation, and I often watched guests dancing on eggshells, especially those who didn't know him too well. Sometimes he talked a lot of nonsense, and I watched his guests biting their tongues rather than contradict or correct him. I suspect Heifetz knew he was talking nonsense, but he was on the lookout for an honest reaction; a respectful "I don't think so" or "I have a different opinion" often would have set the record straight, and Heifetz would have had a higher opinion of his guest. He never locked horns in arguments but always accepted a reasonable, short, and easy explanation on about the *Reader's Digest* level. After an explanation, like a child, he would drop the subject without feeling a need to get deeper into it. In company he didn't like to talk even about music deeper than just on the surface, and he never went beyond discussing some performers of the past, never of the present, and even that mostly with his students and professional musicians. He had read enough reviews of music and appraisals of his performances to know that "deep" explanations often laughably miss the point. If a musical question was pressed on him by an inexperienced guest, he would shrug it off as "Shop talk" or try to be funny in the days when he could skillfully parry the question: "If I answer this, I would have to send you a bill for it."

After his housekeeper of many years quit, his friends and eventually I were entrusted with finding new ones for him. They were invariably fired, some within a very short period of time; some lasted longer, but his way of firing and hiring often had nothing to do with competence. Some didn't even last long enough for us to find out what they were made of. Here are some samples from the list of his housekeepers: the one from Turkey who brought her boyfriend to kill Heifetz because he didn't pay her for the hours she didn't work; the one from Scotland who sued him in small claims court because she was fired within a week with no reason given and without advance notice; the one from Yugoslavia who wanted to marry him and started a smear campaign against me in order to get me out of the way; the one from Mexico who lasted one hour, for when Heifetz laid eyes on her the first time, he said, "Get rid of her; she has the evil eyes." Then there was the one who drove a Rolls Royce and called him a bastard SOB, threw a kitchen towel in his face, and stomped out. Another one lasted for almost five years, but eventually Heifetz made me fire her because she was too good to be true; he suspected that she was spying on him when she noiselessly moved around in the house so as not to disturb him. "She gives me the creeps," he said. "Get rid of her."

This last housekeeper, Maria, was a rather good-humored, charming character, and we became quite friendly. She was a smart Hungarian peasant woman, but her peasant-style cooking contributed to her downfall in the eyes of the master of the house. After Heifetz passed away, she told me a story about what had happened to her on one of my rare days off. Heifetz had asked me to buy lobsters since Maria didn't drive and he had invited an old lady friend for dinner. Maria heard Heifetz talking to the lady about the exceptionally good dinner she was about to receive, but he never mentioned the word *lobster*. Such cryptic information enhanced the guest's expectations yet didn't kill the surprise, as Heifetz's mind went.

As it happened, Maria had never cooked lobster before. She frenetically tried to call me at home for instructions, but I was out. As dinner time approached, she put the lobsters in the broiler and checked on them several times as they were sizzling, but having no idea how cooked lobsters should look, she always thought that they still could use more broiling. She really had never left the village she came from: everything she cooked on her own was overcooked and on the heavy side, as if it was for the peasants who had just come home from working in the fields from daybreak to sunset.

As she was contemplating the lobsters, she heard the bell from the dining room. When she entered, Heifetz asked her whether it wouldn't be a good idea to call the fire department, and he pointed to the smoke swirling out of the kitchen into the dining room. Maria made a silly excuse but took the smoke as a sign that the lobsters were done. She brought them in with their shells black and crackling, deposited the "exceptionally good dinner" on the dining table, and, smelling something similar to a rat, retreated in a hurry to her kitchen. Heifetz wasted no time in calling her back. He looked furious. He cut a piece off the lobster, put it on his fork, stuck it out, and ordered her: "You eat it!"

Maria obediently swallowed the first piece of lobster in her life and wondered what made people pay sixteen dollars a tail for such awful, rubbery stuff. The lady guest came out after dinner and consoled Maria for having cooked a very good lobster, but Maria suspected something must have been wrong because Heifetz didn't talk to her for several days.

I had to bring candidate after candidate to the house for the housekeeper job. For a while Heifetz interviewed them, but soon he decided that I should do the hiring and he would do the instant firing. This system surely eliminated some of his problems, because one housekeeper, after being fired, brought her boyfriend to my house to kick my door down. To her mind, I owed her the money she claimed she didn't get, because I hired her. I had to try to learn Spanish, Turkish, Serbian, and a few other languages, since none of them spoke passable English. As a reward for my efforts, Heifetz held over my head forever that I was unable to find a housekeeper who could pass muster. This was just another way, I suppose, to pass on responsibility and assert his control over me. In the last couple of years of his life, we just talked about getting a competent housekeeper; the ones I found even seemed hopelessly incompetent to me, yet Heifetz tolerated them as long as I supervised the way they worked, which meant that I did the crucial parts of the job and they got paid for it.

The housekeeper merry-go-round was just an innocent sideshow compared to the effects of the depression that took possession of him after he sold his house in Malibu. He had always had periods of depression, but for about two years these periods came with regularity: he was all right for one or two months, then hit the bottom to the point of insanity. Each period would last for a week or two and sometimes longer. I always saw the warning signs: first he became cantankerous, finding fault with everything, then picked on things that made no sense and insisted on doing things that couldn't be done. When I succeeded in doing the impossible, he suspected my motives, doubting why I tried so hard to please him. At such times he looked at me as if I was a complete stranger and raved at me: "What do you want? What are you doing here? What are you waiting for?" While formerly he would not let me play in concerts, assuring me that my time for that would come, now he accused me of neglecting my talent: "What keeps you here? You should be out there playing concerts." Then he would repeat accusations and quote "authentic" sources about my evil intentions, repeating that "two million Frenchmen cannot be wrong." Once when I asked him what he meant by that, he said, "Everyone I know agrees with me about what I think of you." I could only answer, "Well, I didn't know that I had that many odds going against me." My flippant remark calmed him down for the moment. Heifetz was always for the underdog, and to be the underdog against his two million Frenchmen was, indeed, a formidable load to carry. He was so much for the underdog that, as he once told me, he picked his Guarnerius violin as his permanent instrument over his Strad not only for the different tone colors it could produce but also because he considered the Guarnerius an underdog against the more famous Stradivarius.

Even as he sought confirmation of my wickedness from what he called the majority, the self-destructive side of his nature was fighting with his reason to completely possess his mind. Heifetz' reasoning worked on crooked logic: everybody either left him or he got rid of them, he visited nobody, and nobody came to his house—what, then, is this Indonesian jungle girl doing here even though he did everything possible to get rid of her? What does he have to do to destroy his last contact with humanity? When such thoughts overpowered his mind, Heifetz flew off the handle as if possessed by an evil spirit bent on his own destruction.

One time, right in my presence, he called a friend and complained that he was unable to make me leave him however hard he tried, but he could not fire me because he needed me. "I gave her all the rope she needed to hang herself," he moaned, "but she wouldn't do it." A few days later I told him that no matter how many strands he spun into that rope, it would never be long enough for me to hang myself. I would have to be fired to be gotten rid of. That, fortunately, he was sane enough not to do. At such times, telling him as some of his friends did, "Jim, do what you want," was the worse thing to do, for indeed he didn't know what he wanted. Sometimes I used his crooked logic to make him do something that had to be done, but eventually he would discover the strategy and call me devious. There were times when he made me sit down in front of him and kept on raving for hours, calling me all sorts of names, counting all the evil I had done to him, repeating charges that he must have heard or that he had put into the mouths of others, and when I said that I would rather not listen to all this, he would push me back on my chair and continue to scream at me, "Oh yes, you will listen to it until I'm finished."

When I lost my temper and screamed back at him in the same tone he used, he seemed to recover his reason temporarily and either kept quiet or hushed me up saying, "You know, there is room for only one temper at a time. Now it's my turn and I will let you know when your turn will come." Even with this he strengthened his hold on me, because the thought of my "turn" coming made his ravings more tolerable. Strangely enough, he sometimes remembered that my turn was still coming to me, and a couple of days later would ask me what I wanted to say on a particular day. Although the elapsed time would have taken the anger out of me, at least I would have the satisfaction of having a chance to say what was on my mind.

In order to survive and to be at peace with myself, I looked for all kinds of excuses for his behavior. I explained to myself that Heifetz had spent the better part of his life, including his childhood, in an occupation that only people with the strongest will and determination can carry out successfully. He had an enormous talent and an enormous will to succeed on an almost superhuman level. When the object of this fantastic combination of talent and will was gone and he didn't concertize or teach any more, this all-consuming will, looking for an object and not finding one, turned to self-destruction. This problem must be common in people of great drive and little education whose will cannot find another object to latch onto except the self and its immediate surroundings. He found me standing in the way of his self-destruction, and he directed all his willpower toward getting me out of the way. Amateurish as my explanation may have been, it gave me a measure of understanding to hang onto. I also took consolation in Heifetz's favorite poem, Kipling's "If," and especially the part that reads, "If you can accept compliments and verbal abuse in the same manner, you will be a man, my son!" The irony of this situation was that Heifetz often and at great length discussed this poem with me and apparently drew as much strength from it as I did—except for him it served to support his point of view.

That I read his state of mind correctly was confirmed for me as he kept to his daily schedule with an iron will even throughout his worst depressions; this determination perhaps kept him from going off the deep end altogether. He expected me, too, to control my emotions, and regardless of how I felt or of what had passed between the two of us during the day or just a few minutes before, I had to do my job as if nothing had happened. When he didn't feel physically ill, he got up on time, went through the motions of his daily chores, went to his office to practice or to check the mail and his bills, ate his meals as usual, and even watched me practicing the piano and gave advice. Even at those times when he felt that I was out to kill him, we kept on playing music in the studio during the afternoons and in the living room during the evenings and afterward played cards, all as if nothing had happened. Music was the only remedy that temporarily brought him back to his senses. When we sat together at the table, he expected conversation of a sort. He tolerated no sulking on my part, no show of anger; we had to do everything convincingly, including making music, which had to be up to his standards. I couldn't help but admire his superhuman self-control. By being forced to control myself, too, I went through the oddest, most unusual, and most nerve-wracking schooling that I had ever had, an education that I would not have taken from anyone else.

As time went on, his depression was sometimes so deep that even music couldn't snap him out of it. Once I was sitting there helplessly listening to his endless mad monologue, and in my despair I remembered a story he had told me some time before. He was in Indonesia playing in several towns, and he happened to be caught alone on New Year's Eve in Jakarta. As he recalled the story, he had gone alone to a bar to celebrate. Upon returning to his hotel, he found a small Javanese houseboy waiting for him at the door of his hotel room, shaking himself out of sleep as Heifetz appeared; the boy politely opened the door for him and asked if he needed anything for the night. The moment this story occurred to me, I also recalled how important it was for Heifetz not to come home to an empty house, and I understood why he was so touched by the little Java-nese boy waiting for his return. I didn't explain to him that in Indonesia he could have had a host of people waiting for him at his door, all day and night, for just a few pennies. Such a mercenary explanation would have destroyed the idyllic and personal meaning of the scene for him. How-ever, recalling this story gave me a sudden inspiration: what would hap-pen if I sat down at his feet by his chair as he was angrily denouncing my machinations against him, and just stay there as that little boy had stayed by his door in Jakarta? After all, I'm also an Indonesian, and perhaps it wouldn't be too far fetched to wonder whether he would make the con-nection between me and the good feelings another Indonesian had given him. Heifetz even liked to believe that I looked and behaved more as a Javanese than as a Chinese, which I thought could work in my favor. With-out saying a word, I brought him some tea and sat down on the floor close to his chair. Heifetz was totally taken aback. He looked at me suspiciously, then calmed down, and as the evening wore on, a feeling of contentment spread over his face and his depression temporarily ebbed. I tried the same cure on several other occasions, and it usually worked.

Regardless of how bad the day was and how angry he had been with me, when I left at night I always kissed him on the cheek because I could never let anger harden and fester overnight against anyone whom I loved. He always submitted to this kiss, even if he was railing at me just at the moment when I was ready to leave, for in the bottom of his heart, he also knew that I was his last hope for sanity. Going home late at night I often cried in the car and drove around the block several times to com-pose myself before entering the house. I wanted no questions from my husband and no sensible advice.

At one point, obviously acting on an ill-conceived suggestion, he actually fired me from all my duties in his house. I accepted the dismissal but told him to call me if he needed anything. Two days later he meekly called with a ridiculous problem—that he couldn't turn the stove on or that it didn't work properly—and asked me to come and call the service to repair it. When I arrived, he was in pretty sad shape; he hadn't shaved for two days and hadn't eaten much either. I don't know what would have happened to him if I had left him for good. Heifetz had come to the point in his life where he could not do without service yet behaved antag-onistically toward it, as many old people do. Once he made me shave his face, and my protests that I had never shaved anyone were of no avail. I had to lather his face and try his safety razor on an easy spot; he touched it with his fingers and declared me a barber graduate. Next he asked me to cut his hair, in which art I had a little more practice. He found the result not too bad.

Once, on a particularly bad day as he was trying to make life difficult for me and for himself, Heifetz suddenly came up with the question "Why don't you quit?" He had tried this tack before, but a satisfactory answer had always evaded me. Now I felt that I was ready with a proper answer, and it stopped him cold.

"If you would like me to be out of your life you must say so and fire me," I said. "I am not a quitter, neither am I a deserter; therefore you will never have my resignation. You are doing your damnedest to make it impossible for me to make your life easier for you. All I need from you is to give me a chance to do it right. All I need from you is time. I want nothing else from you."

I knew that with this answer I threw the ball back in his court, and it made him think of the responsibility he had for his own life. Perhaps he wasn't that much out of his mind either, because he understood perfectly well what I meant. He became silent and for a change had no answer or objection to what I had just said. I must have touched a sane part of his mind, because from then on he gradually became less and less abusive and began to treat me again with respect. I never knew all through this period of his life whether he was pretending or had actually lost control over his reason, for sometimes in the middle of his raging against me, he suddenly would become tender, say a few loving words with no connection to what he had been saying before, and then go back to his previous raging. One does not have to be a psychiatrist to suspect that he suffered from a form of malaise that perhaps could have been cured, had he permitted himself to be treated.

I told Heifetz the truth when I said that I was not a quitter, but I must admit that it was his music and our music making together that kept me there, even at times when my husband and my friends advised me to leave him and save my own sanity. I did not tell anyone that I had a secret fortress where I retreated to restore my energy, a technique that kept me coming up again no matter how often I was knocked down. During his worst ravings and name-calling, I would recall the Jascha Heifetz of my childhood, the one whom I always imagined to be the most perfect person in the world. For my childish mind only the most perfect person could play the kind of music I heard on his records. Back then I had built for him an eternal shrine in my heart, and now as an adult I retreated into this place, and while he was screaming at me, I worshipped the beauty and perfection engraved there forever, shutting the present

Jascha Heifetz out. In my fortress I felt perfectly safe from everything except physical violence, because here I was immune to the man I knew could not be real, who couldn't destroy me or his image in my shrine however hard he tried.

I don't know what made him snap out of his period of severest depression. Perhaps his rational self realized that he could not count on outside help if he wanted to survive, or perhaps the process of aging just took something out of him that changed his attitude toward life. Perhaps, also, the few days I left him to fend for himself also helped. I might have been too willing to cater to all his whims, sometimes anticipating his wishes even before he uttered them. That convinced him that we were "on the same wavelength," but the sobering truth was that I just knew him too well, and I was ahead of him in figuring out from a sequence of events, from his changing moods, half-expressed thoughts, even from the seasons of the year or the time of the day, what would be triggered in his mind. My willingness to anticipate his wishes eventually worked against me: predicting what he wanted became impossible when he himself didn't even know what it was; yet he expected me to divine it. At such times he became upset and belligerent because he was convinced that I stubbornly blocked our common wavelength and sabotaged the anticipation of his wishes which he himself couldn't even express in words. When this happened, he could only stutter, "You know what I want—you are just an obstinate mule and don't want to know it," as he incoherently searched for words to express his desires. Quite often he never found the words because there was nothing behind the search, just the infantile "You of all people should know it."

Even after he snapped out of the depression that had come on and off for two years, his wants often were like a child's shopping list. When his old tube radio of 1920 vintage broke down, he expected me to find a repairman who could fix it. I had to go through the process of finding one, even though there was no hope of finding replacement parts. When the intercom between his studio and the house went on the blink, he wanted me to get it fixed but wouldn't let the equipment out of the house. I had to find an old telephone repairman, and he told me what to look for and how to rig up the wires. While I worked on it, Heifetz stood by and gave me a time limit to fix it. I think he was jealous of the telephone's taking my time away from him, but he also was convinced that a certain amount of pressure always brought better results. Unfortunately his intercom's Stone Age parts wouldn't hold together, and parts were no longer made for it. He wouldn't let me have a new system installed because the old one was much better. I put the old one together with spit and mud, and it even worked for a while. Then there were the lights on his paddle-tennis court. The court hadn't been used for decades, the metal light poles were all rusted out, and the wires, laid under the concrete surface, couldn't be located, but the old lights were supposed to be restored because "they were there."

In the last four years of his life Heifetz's mental condition "improved," if that's the word to use for a person who has given up. Perhaps he had finally accepted his own shortcomings and those of the people around him, truly a feat that had taken him many years to achieve. He seemed finally to accept me as a person who really loved him for himself, and to accept his life's verdict, old age. The violent scenes stopped— he stopped fighting and retreated into his shell. We spent more and more time working on his transcriptions and playing music together. He couldn't tolerate the thought of letting me out of his sight, and whenever I mentioned that I had an invitation to play here or there, he would object and repeat, "Don't worry, your time will come." Perhaps it was just plain old selfishness, or perhaps he wanted to save me as long as possible from the encounter with his two "imposters," success and defeat.

As with so many simple, unsophisticated souls, success, like his struggle for perfection and the fault-finding that went with it, defeated Heifetz. Success put him on a pedestal where, as an intensely private person, he felt unsafe and uncomfortable. Such a position can be trying even to a person of more extensive education, more sophistication, and a less suspicious nature than Heifetz was endowed with. Outside his art world he liked to brush off problems that should have concerned him with the statement: "My mind is too full of other, more important things than to be concerned with this." However, the world did intrude on him, and against this intrusion he invented his principles as a bastion behind which he could safely retire when cornered. As time went on and he got old, his bastion became a trap from which there was no escape. While it worked, it saved him from the fate of others with similar positions and similar backgrounds; Heifetz kept track of musicians who committed suicide under the pressure of success or degraded their lives with drug and alcohol abuse, and of those who squandered their talent before it was fully developed. Though not an altogether happy man, Heifetz survived by hanging on to his defenses against a world full of admirers, camp followers, sycophants, promoters, pushy fans, and a host of other people who tried to tear him apart and have a piece of him for their own purposes. He paid a heavy price for success, enriching the world by emptying himself.

13

Threnody

Yours is the Earth and everything that's in it,
And—which is more—you'll be a Man, my son!

RUDYARD KIPLING

*B*y all musical formulas this chapter should bear the title "Finale."
Finale it would be for ordinary mortals, but Jascha Heifetz did not
exit from life with the same finality as common people do. His legacy will
live just as long as any monument of lasting value is destined to live. Perhaps it will even escape the fate of ordinary monuments and survive as
long as recordings can be preserved and recopied. The title "Threnody"
—dirge—has multiple musical connotations, including a connection to
Gluck's opera, *Orfeo ed Euridice.* Heifetz made one of his favorite transcriptions from this opera using the mournful melody in which Orpheus
laments losing Euridice to the Underworld. Heifetz never published this
transcription but had it recorded and often played it in his concerts. I
often accompanied him playing this melody, which he did with so much
feeling that I always felt that he had his own passing away in his mind.
When I play it on the violin I still have the inexplicable sensation of his
presence. With this chapter I'll partially shed my role as an observer of his
character and take on the role of historian, inasmuch as this chapter contains some unknown details of Heifetz's last days.

   In the last years of his life, Heifetz became more and more haggard,
and his usual slow and deliberate movements were even slower and more
deliberate. He needed something to steady himself when he walked and
never let his bamboo stick or the Auer cane out of his reach. To shut the
world out, he pretended to be hard of hearing if what was just said didn't
interest him or wasn't to his liking. Strangely enough, when it came to
music, he always heard everything just as keenly as ever. He never missed
a note, and when I played for him or we played together, he continued to
comment on everything down to the finest details. By 1986 he rarely left

the house, brooded a great deal while sitting in his garden, and periodi-
cally rewrote his will, sometimes in the presence of his lawyer, sometimes
all by himself. He seemed to have made peace with himself and to acqui-
esce to living on borrowed time. It is evident from his will that he wanted
to be remembered by those who worked for him or whom he loved, but
the fate of the bulk of his estate didn't seem to concern him any more. I
am convinced that he had a definite intention with his estate, but either
out of modesty or for reasons known only to him, he only hinted about it
in his will, a style consistent with the ways he often expressed his wishes.
Perhaps he wanted others to discover what he wanted and to take responsibility for its execution. Yet he made sure that everyone was remembered
in his will, either by name or by hinting at their function in his life, which
he wanted to be remembered, and left them something. He was still in
reasonably good health, his mind was clear, and apart from stomach
aches, backaches, and occasional dizzy spells, he wasn't plagued with anything unusual for a man in his eighties.

Despite his physical strength's ebbing away, he kept to his daily routine as strictly as if he were to give a concert the next day. Music still kept
him going, sometimes in a heartbreaking way. One day as I came to his
house, I heard him practicing at the piano the difficult accompaniment
to a Rachmaninoff song (the title translates as Spring Flood or Spring
Waters) that he particularly loved. I stopped outside the door so as not to
disturb or perhaps even embarrass him in his romantic communion with
music. After all those years of music making and perfecting his art, he was
still trying new interpretations of the same old song, stopping here and
there, playing it slowly, then in tempo, always somewhat differently as if
looking for something new in it. I waited in front of the door for a while,
even after he finished playing, and came in pretending that I had heard
nothing. Later that day I brought out for him the unfinished Gershwin
transcription, since he seemed to be in the mood. He was willing to discuss it for a while, but when I urged him to put down some notes, he gently brushed the manuscript aside: "Not now," he murmured.

A sure sign of the breaking down of his spirit was that he didn't even
fight my efforts to have a live-in housekeeper, although he did get back
at me by hardly acknowledging her existence and talking to her only
through me. If he didn't feel well, and he often didn't or pretended not
to, he wanted me to stay overnight because, he said, he didn't feel safe
alone. I had to fight my feelings between staying with him or going home
to my husband and by now eight-year-old daughter who needed a
mother. Even if I couldn't stay overnight, he always asked me to come

before breakfast so that he wouldn't come out from his bedroom in the morning to what he felt was an empty house.

His doctor recommended daily walks, which he was willing to endure for a while. He even joked sometimes before our daily walks by bringing out an old leash and saying, "Here, hold the other end of it and take the dog for a walk." But eventually no persuasion could make him move out of the house, and the farthest he went was the swing in the garden where he could sit for hours. As a result of giving up physical exercise, Heifetz became weaker by the day.

He fell several times in his house and was found unconscious, his face red. Losing consciousness must have preceded the falls, for Heifetz apparently fell like a log and didn't even have a chance to break his fall with his hand or body. He must have hit the floor with his head quite a few times, and it was only a matter of luck that he didn't fall on a concrete floor or hit his head on something sharp and hard. He fell a few times when I was in the house, and at those times I was able to help him get up. One day, however, I wasn't there when he fell, and as I came in, I found him unconscious on the floor. I became quite frightened, for he didn't respond to my efforts to revive him. However, before I had a chance to call for help, he came around and told me not to call anybody, including his family. I made an appointment with his doctor for the next day and had to be with him during the examination to describe the state in which I had found him. Heifetz must have had a very strong constitution, because, despite all these falls and head injuries, his doctor could find no noticeable effects on his body. While falling Heifetz suffered a few bruises on his legs and hands, but they all healed without serious consequences. Yet these falls were not entirely harmless; it turned out that some caused serious injury to his brain.

In spite of his reservations about organized religion, Heifetz did believe in God, perhaps even in an afterlife, and on occasion he explained to me in his bumbling and roundabout way that there is no effect without a cause and the world would not exist unless somebody had made it. This was as far as he ever got in a philosophical discussion. The only practical result of his belief in a Supreme Being was that of all the Jewish holidays, Yom Kippur, the Day of Atonement, was the only one he faithfully observed. In the past he had liked to spend this day by himself but in the last two or three years of his life he asked me to stay with him even that day, although all day long he never said a word and demanded total silence from me, too. Heifetz told me that, as far back as he could remember, he always fasted on this Jewish holiday according to the religious prescriptions and celebrated the passing of the fast with dinner at the house of one or another of his Russian Jewish friends.

In 1987 Yom Kippur fell on 3 October. Heifetz was eighty-six, four months short of his eighty-seventh birthday. I spent the day with him and observed that, in spite of his age and weakness, he abstained from food and drink all day long, beginning with the night before, faithfully following the rules, "going by the book" for this one. After sunset at the holiday's end he asked me to take him to the house of his very close and dear friends of more than forty years' standing to break the fast with them. He also asked me to stay with him throughout the evening. During dinner he made toasts, as was his custom, on all kinds of subjects, but he wasn't quite as lively as he used to be at such occasions. He looked quite pale and didn't have much appetite, not even for the challah, the sweet bread that he would tear with his hands at such times in the traditional way instead of cutting it. Drinking usually didn't affect him to any great measure even at eighty-six, and this night was no different. He never even once mentioned, as he jokingly used to say after a few drinks, that he felt a little "shiker" or "squiffed." We played a couple of hands of gin rummy, and he was just as sharp as ever.

I drove him home in his car that night somewhat earlier than usual. He got out of the car and went inside the house to push the button that opened the garage door since I didn't have the automatic garage door opener in the car. He was standing by the garage as I drove the car in, and I rolled down the car window to tell him to wait for me and I would help him up the steps at the side of the garage. He often got angry with such suggestions; this time he pretended not to hear me and went to the steps by himself. They were built next to the garage wall on one side, but the other side was open and without railings. I had begged him for years to let me have railings installed on the open side, but Heifetz considered railings unnecessary and would not hear of it.

He started up the steps without difficulty and nearly reached the top when he lost his balance. By good luck or by instinct, he fell with his back toward the garage wall, hitting the wall with the top of his head as he fell backward. Had he fallen with his back turned straight down the steps or to his left toward the open side, he would have died instantly from hitting the concrete floor. As it happened, he hit the wall with the side of his head, slumped backward, and then slowly slipped down the steps to the garage floor. He passed out and didn't respond to my efforts to revive him.

I ran into the house and called 911, the emergency number, and let it ring for a while, but there was no response. I didn't dare to leave him alone longer as panic crept up on me. Suddenly I recalled that there had been an earthquake the day before not far away, and the 911 switchboard must have been jammed with emergency calls. As I came back with a hastily prepared ice pack, I was relieved to hear him moaning. I held the ice on his head, and he slowly regained consciousness.

He lay on the concrete floor about fifteen to twenty minutes before he was strong enough to get up. I was still holding the ice on his head with one hand, but he insisted on walking up the stairs on his own. We went into the house, I led him to his bedroom, and he lay down on his bed fully dressed. I took his shoes off and stayed with him all night, sitting in a chair next to his bed. I renewed the ice pack as needed and put some ointment on the bruise. Neither of us had much sleep because he wanted fresh ice packs all through the night. By morning the swelling began to disappear, and Heifetz said that he felt much better. He didn't want anybody to know anything about the accident.

On 4 October he got up late, as usual. It was a Sunday, when he always had brunch instead of breakfast. He had a good appetite, ate well, and went to his office in the studio, as usual, without my help. To get there he had to climb some steep steps, of course without railings, but that didn't seem to worry him. We practiced some violin-piano pieces together as usual, until four o'clock in the afternoon, then came out to sit on the swing-chair at the side of the swimming pool, which was the usual thing to do on a nice Sunday afternoon. He asked me to sit next to him. There was nothing strange in his behavior, nor did he ask unusual questions. We ate dinner at eleven in the evening, which wasn't an extraordinary thing with him. He ate very little and then wanted to play cards. We played for an hour, but he still didn't want to go to bed. He was in his dressing gown the whole day, but that wasn't unusual for a Sunday. By one o'clock in the morning, having been exhausted from the vigil of the night before, I excused myself and left him alone in the living room. I didn't dare to go home and stayed in the guestroom for the night.

He seemed to be all right for a whole week, but at the end of that week something prompted him to ask me to stay overnight. I complied with his request. I woke up at three in the morning hearing strange noises and saw the lights on in the living room. I went out to investigate and was surprised to find him there, all dressed, puttering around as if trying to find something. He seemed to be a bit disoriented and asked me for his dinner. He wouldn't listen to me when I told him what time it was but insisted that it was dinnertime and he wanted food on the table. I set the table for him, gave him what he wanted, and told him again what time it was and that I was worried. None of this seemed to make an impression on him, but he let me go back to bed instead of playing cards or doing other after-dinner activities.

The bruise on his head healed beautifully. Virtually all signs of the accident disappeared, and I had high hopes that the big fall had no effect on him. Once he even made me bring out his unfinished transcription of Gershwin's *An American in Paris.* He played the finished parts over and over again on the violin, shouted instructions to me at the piano, and wanted me to take notes about changes that he felt were necessary at certain spots. Then he tired of the project and didn't want to work any more. I didn't know then that I had just heard Jascha Heifetz playing the violin for the last time in his life. Even in his playing there was nothing unusual, no memory loss, no stumbling of the fingers: apparently those parts of his brain that control musical and hand-muscle activities were not damaged. All this time since the accident he never complained of pain, but with iron will continued his daily program of going to his studio, opening his correspondence, and doing everything as if nothing had happened. However, from the time when he asked for his dinner in the middle of the night, he showed signs of disorientation. I had to convince him to make an appointment with his doctor to have his head examined. I quoted his own line to him, that it would be better to prevent something more serious from happening than to suffer from the consequences of neglecting his health. I also had to threaten him with staying in the hospital, which always worked.

His doctor, Ed Shapiro, noticed that the wound on his head had almost healed. The scab was dry, and the black and blue marks around it were fading away. He gave him a thorough examination and then suggested that a CAT scan should be taken to detect the extent of damage to his brain. Heifetz, as in the past, staunchly refused to submit himself to newfangled methods of medical examination. He also gave me strict instructions not to notify his family about anything that had happened. Yet I couldn't take this responsibility on myself and got around his instructions by notifying his close friends, hoping that the message would filter down where it should. I was right: his son Jay, a few close friends, and his lawyer came to see him after the news spread that Heifetz wasn't feeling well.

On 12 October his disorientation became worse, and his doctor ordered a CAT scan regardless of Heifetz's objections. However, no machinery was available until 15 October. During the three intervening days at home Heifetz was sometimes lucid, other times disoriented. But regardless of his state of mind, he gave signs that the end was coming.

It has been observed that a sure sign of the end of one's life is a sudden loss of taste for favorite foods and drinks. Heifetz began to behave in a most peculiar manner toward his usual drink, bourbon. I would pour it for him at the usual time in the early evening, but after a sip he would declare that it was no good and that I must have done something to it. One day when I said that it was as usual, he asked me to add some gin to it. That mixture didn't meet requirements either, and I had to pour out in different glasses various combinations of bourbon, Scotch, gin, vodka, vermouth, and whatever else was available in his bar. He took a sip of each one and then asked me to make another kind for him. Sometimes there were six or seven glasses on the bar, all full of these various concoctions, and he would taste one after another, at the end rejecting all of them. It seemed that he went through all the drinks he had ever had in his life and found none of them to his taste, singly or in combinations.

He always kept an orderly series of monetary units in his pocket, ranging from one penny to a twenty-dollar bill, and made sure that he had at least one piece of each denomination. This was his way of preparing himself for all kinds of emergencies. In his last days he began to hoard money under his pillow, which he had never done before. I would not have noticed it, but he pointed out the bills to me and said that this money was there for the poor, especially for his poor students. He also had a gold chain from an old-fashioned pocket watch with a number of charms on it. He wanted to be sure that it would be saved for him when he came back—he didn't tell me from where.

Although he must have felt the end coming, he took his glaucoma drops every day in the most careful manner, as he had been accustomed to do for as long as I had known him: he would ask me to come to his medicine cabinet, have me take out all his medicines, ask me to pick out the one he was supposed to use, carefully check it and read everything on the labels, and watch me measure out the appropriate number of drops before I put them in his eyes. His routine and iron will for order never changed as long as he was in control of himself. Only his meals took quite a bit longer than before.

The day after the CAT scan was taken, his doctor called and reported that it showed a subdural hematoma, which I understood was a mass of clotted blood that had formed somewhere on his brain. Immediate surgery was indicated, and his doctor even sent an ambulance to his house. I was surprised that Heifetz didn't balk when I told him that he had to go to the hospital. I can only guess that he felt the seriousness of his situation. As for myself, I wishfully convinced him and myself, too, that it would be only minor surgery and that he would soon return home. It took all my willpower, however, not to break down when I helped him out of the house to the ambulance; he stopped for a moment at the door, looked at me with his sad, fading blue eyes, and said softly, "Darling, this is not the way to go."

It wasn't his reason, it was his life instinct that made him come along. Instead of resisting leaving the house and dying with the kind of dignity he had wanted for his last hours, he meekly let himself be led to the ambulance. Often in the past, in the dark moments of his deep depressions, he would talk about the futility of life, even of doing away with himself, or about the necessity of someone's mercifully doing it for him if he became incapacitated and could not do it for himself. Yet when the moment of truth arrived and the question arose whether to fade away on his own or to seek medical help, he left this decision to others.

The operation revealed a severe hemorrhage on his brain where he had hit his head during his last fall, but it also showed other blood clots, some of them near his most recent injury. By the time of the operation these old injuries were all in a membranous, semi-hardened state, pressing on various parts of his brain, apparently the results of his previous falls and perhaps the causes of his fainting spells.

As the saying goes, the operation was successful, but the patient didn't survive. The operating lesion on his head healed beautifully and even his hair grew back, but Jascha Heifetz never recovered. He regained consciousness one week after the operation and superbly ignored all his doctors and nurses, who with their tools and instructions tried to probe his awareness of the world around him. The second week after the operation Heifetz whispered in my ear, "Let's go home." He tried to communicate this same message to his nurses and doctors; I don't think he realized the situation he was in and the care he needed to survive from one day to the next. All I could do was to hold his hand, read to him, and talk about plans for the future, about our playing music together and the transcribing projects. I also played on a cassette player some of his own recordings which seemed to please him and calm him down. On 4 December—I will remember the exact date forever—as I leaned over his face to wipe it off with a damp cloth, he looked at me and I saw that he wanted to say something. As I put my ear to his mouth, he whispered to me, "I love you." He had tried to formulate these words with his lips before, but that was the first time I clearly understood what he said. After that he said it every night when I left him in the hospital and kissed him goodnight.

The miseries of being in a hospital, helpless and immobile, are appreciated only by those who have seen the humiliation or were part of it themselves; being handled as a baby is tolerable only if one is not aware of it. Proud and private person as Heifetz was, he reached Sheol, the biblical Hebrew equivalent of Hell, in that hospital, descending into its deepest depths still alive. As far as I know, no clergyman of any denomination visited him during his stay in the hospital. Once a close friend came and read in Hebrew the Prayer for the Dying, beginning with the familiar opening, "Sh'ma Yisroel Adonai Elohenu." At first Heifetz gave no sign of recognizing the meaning of the simple ceremony, but then I saw in his eyes the moment of realization that in death awaited for him the much-desired peace.

True to his secretive nature, Heifetz successfully concealed all the time in the hospital whether he was conscious or not, and no one could ever be sure how much he was observing of what was happening around him. Sometimes when visitors came to see him and he wasn't ready for them, I detected a signal in his half-closed eyes: "Get them out of here." The life-long habit of never receiving visitors unannounced stayed with him even on his deathbed. While I was with him, he never said a word to his doctors, nurses, or visitors; nobody was the wiser whether he did or did not care what they were telling him. Aside from the few words he whispered to me, he seemed completely to ignore the world around him.

On 10 December Heifetz suffered a brain-stem stroke early in the morning. On the same morning the hospital's Bio-Ethics Committee had a session to determine the validity and legal aspects of his irregular living will. He had written a statement some years earlier, expressing his wish that if worse came to worst, he wouldn't want to be a vegetable tied to life-sustaining machinery, but the hospital administration did not consider his statement binding and proper because the legal requirements for such a will had changed since the time when he wrote it. I was called in to face the committee and to make a deposition concerning Heifetz's true wishes, and the committee had to explore all legal aspects before letting his living will stand. I told the doctors the truth, that although Heifetz would not respond to them, the responses that I received when I was alone with him suggested that he didn't respond to the doctors on purpose. At that time I still believed that Heifetz would recover and would be able to continue a normal life. I believed in miracles. He had such a tremendously healthy constitution, such a powerful zest for life that, as I told the committee, I truly believed in the necessity of trying to save him by all available means. Yet I didn't keep from the committee that Heifetz had told me, as he had told other friends, that he wanted his life be terminated if he could not function as a normal human being. To determine whether Heifetz could still function as a normal human being was up to his doctors and the committee, however, and at this point their decision veered toward the negative. The members of the committee were gentle and considerate toward my opinion and me, and tabled their decision to make further legal explorations about the validity of Heifetz's living will.

But there was no need for a decision to be made: Jascha Heifetz died on 10 December 1987 at 11:10 P.M. He beat the committee and his doctors to the decision-making. I remember saying to myself, "Good for you, Jim. I'm glad you had the last word, as you always had."

I was at home the evening of his passing away, exhausted from the emotional shock of participating in the committee's life-or-death decisions and from spending every day and sometimes whole nights at his bedside for almost two months. I took a nap that evening and planned to return later to the hospital and spend the night with him. I floated into one of those unreal, semiconscious dreams that often happen when one is overtired: I saw Heifetz in a beautiful blue suit, standing afar; I was sitting in the same room with him, dressed in a long gown and looking at him. He came closer and closer, and when he got to me, he gave me a big hug and said, "I will be gone for a little while, but I'll return to get you. Wait for me." I could still feel the warmth of his hug when the telephone rang. His private night nurse called me before she called anyone else, with the news that Jascha Heifetz had passed away. Heifetz had died completely alone, peacefully and privately as he wished it to be; not even his nurse was present. She just happened to have stepped out looking for his medical chart. Finally Jascha Heifetz was free from all physical pain and illness, free from the torments of his quest for ever-higher achievements, and free from the loneliness at the summit. The bird of passage—to paraphrase the Kurt Weill song—flew into the dark again from the dimly lit hospital room.

His will specified that there should be "no funeral ceremony, no flowers (white or otherwise), no speeches, and a minimum of expense . . . to be kindly fulfilled." He also wished to be cremated and that his ashes be scattered over the Pacific Ocean, off the house in his beloved Malibu. His wishes were respected and fulfilled by his family.

I felt lost after his death, like being jarred out of a well-worn rut. After fifteen years of daily tests and trials, awakening every morning with the thought, What will he have for me today to make my life miserable or perhaps pleasant and joyful? What new musical or mundane challenges will he put me up to? What is going to break down in his old house that he will want to have repaired in less than five minutes? There was nothing to look forward to, and I felt as if I were floating in a vacuum without aim or purpose. A day or two after his passing away, people came out of the woodwork, some of whom Heifetz hadn't seen for ages, along with his family, including some of his grandchildren, and together they held a sort of memorial gathering in his house, some making speeches, others noises, all so irrelevant and useless. I couldn't help but cringe at the sight; the invasion of the privacy of his home was so contrary to what Heifetz believed in and had wished for.

Having been accustomed to knowing where Heifetz was for at least the last ten years, I decided to look for his body at the hospital the morning after he passed away. I thought for sure that the body should still be there, perhaps moved to the morgue. I am really convinced, like the Hindus and the Buddhists, that it takes quite some time, days, perhaps weeks, for the spirit of a person to leave its temple. It all depends on the kind of life a person led. Most cremations in my country take place a week or two after the person has passed away. At the hospital, however, I was informed that on the instruction of the family, the body had been taken away earlier that morning, nobody knew where to. I returned to his house and was told by members of his family that I should stop worrying about anything connected with Heifetz. I was kindly told that my duties toward Heifetz were over. I even asked one of Heifetz's close friends, but she didn't know where he was either.

I vaguely remembered Heifetz's telling me that he wanted his body cremated the same way as the body of his first wife, Florence, had been. When Heifetz married Florence, she already had a nine-year-old daughter from her first husband, King Vidor. Her name was Suzie, and Heifetz raised her as if she were his own. He often spoke of her with fondness, and we became good friends. It occurred to me that perhaps she could tell me where her mother was cremated. I guessed right. I called the crematorium and Heifetz's body was there. I had to ask the family's permission to attend the cremation.

It was to take place that very day. I didn't quite understand why everybody looked at me strangely when I said I wanted to be present. In spite of some open and some half-expressed discouragement, I managed to get to the crematorium on time. I was told only later that being present at a cremation is highly irregular in the unwritten American ritual of such events, and even so, only relatives would be permitted to be present. All others, friends and fans, are supposed to ignore such events, and relatives are ordinarily expected to pick up the ashes of the deceased, or whatever is given as such, whenever convenient. There is no drama in a cremation, since the bereaved ones would be hard put to shed tears when an electric switch is turned on, unlike the thud of the first shovelful of dirt on the casket in the grave. Perhaps Heifetz considered the drama of the burial, with its inevitable eulogies, as a hypocrisy, and that prompted him to request that his funeral should be a nonevent.

The journey to the crematorium, which should have taken two and a half hours, took longer than I expected. Several entrances to the freeway leading there were closed for one reason or another. The Heifetz spirit was still around making tasks more challenging than they should have been. "Everything worthwhile is accompanied by challenges" was one of his favorite sayings. As I drove through the city trying to find an alternative freeway entrance, I said aloud, "Jim, you are still consistently placing obstacles in my way—thanks a lot."

I was the only one present grieving for him when the cremation was performed. The attendants didn't want me to be present when the actual cremation took place, but I told them that I needed to say a private prayer before they opened the gate of the oven. At first they were reluctant to let me alone with the body, perhaps being afraid that I might faint. When I insisted that I would be all right, they left the room and I was permitted to say my personal eulogy with no one present. "Good-bye my dearest, for the last time. You treated the two imposters, Triumph and Disaster, just the same. Now you are returning earth to earth, ash to ashes, dust to dust, but you were a man, and you gave a good account of all that was in you." I said this aloud, and I didn't care if the attendants heard it; I knew Jim would have not objected to that much eulogy. Then I touched the skin of his face for the last time; it was smooth, pink and peaceful, without wrinkles. Then I read to myself the "If" poem, the talisman of his life, and thought of his laconic autobiography that he once gave to an interviewer (even though by most accounts his debut was at age six): "Born in Russia, first lesson at three, debut in Russia at seven, debut in America in 1917." Now I could add to it: "Died 10 December 1987, 11:10 P.M., all alone, and buried without fanfare, as he was born."

The attendants came in and asked me if I wanted to stay while they slid into the oven the paper carton in which he was lying. I stayed to the very end.

The events that followed his passing away, if of any importance, should be for another historian to recap. Death is the greatest equalizer, but we don't all leave the same marks behind. Some leave nothing, not even a memory, others leave the memory of love, still others only money to the laughing heirs, but Heifetz left the greatest treasure to all mankind in his records and in the legacy of his teaching. Jascha Heifetz had been a household name with musicians, especially with violinists, for the better half of the century in which he lived. Though his name was synonymous with perfection, he often said with desperation, "Perfection—what is it? Aiming for perfection is OK, but don't ever claim that you have reached it because you will tempt the gods." Indeed, what is perfection in our imperfect world of relativity and comparisons? Heifetz could be considered a violinist more perfect than most others, but to be perfect, in an absolute sense of the word, is not a possibility for humans. As part of the bargain, he and other geniuses of his kind are easy prey to incessant unhappiness because they set their standards so high as to make them hopelessly unattainable. High standards and a high level of creativity are coupled with insecurity and isolation, as if one were left alone on a high mountain, unable to see another being and not knowing how much higher one is allowed to go. He may have sounded cynical, yet he was being truthful when he often told me, after a party, that he had given "a good imitation of having a good time" or that he had made it believable that he was happy to see someone. He was alone in the midst of all that noisy admiration. Heifetz was constantly searching for meaning in life in his own nonphilosophical ways, but the best he could come up with was that we were all on a stage and that although we were playing our roles with more or less conviction, we had to give a convincing performance if we wished to keep our self-esteem reasonably high. As a fatalist he saw in nature alone the force that is unbendable, real, and superior; he bowed down before its powers and saw God in it or perhaps saw in it the only tangible manifestation of His powers.

Heifetz had no real competition during his career and probably never will; all violinists know at the bottom of their hearts that Jascha Heifetz set the bar so high that they can only look at it without hope of reaching it. As Fritz Kreisler allegedly said in the presence of other eminent violinists after hearing the young Heifetz play, "Well, gentlemen, shall we all now break our violins across our knees?"

The marks Heifetz left on individuals are just as complex as his personality was. He was best admired from a distance, which was much easier than putting up with the daily aggravations and tests to which he exposed everyone who was within arm's length. I was able to put up with him not only because of my admiration for him as a musician but also in no small measure because of my upbringing and a certain obstinacy in my nature. I was brought up to respect the elderly, and I found that Heifetz's irrationality was not without precedent in the tyrannical Chinese elders of my earlier years. Somehow these irascible, irrational elders reminded me of the God of the Bible who gets angry at His people, punishes and rewards at will, and gives and takes without having to justify His actions. However, my obstinacy was rewarded and Heifetz found me worthy to carry on, in my small way, the legacy of his musicianship. As fate would have it, we met at the right time and under the right conditions: he needed someone whom he could trust as a person and respect as a musician, and I needed a father figure both musically and emotionally who could give me what I never got from my family. In my youth I could escape my family only by making music; playing music was my only private time at home, and my mother fiercely protected my practicing from any intrusion by the rest of my family. Heifetz, in a sense, took away from me even that much privacy; I could make music in his house only when he didn't need me or when he wanted to make music. Yet it was music that kept me from running away from a person who wanted to have his cake and eat it, too.

Perhaps Heifetz made me depend on him too much, for when he was gone, I had to rediscover myself as a musician and as a person as well. Since I let him absorb me totally in his ways of music making, for a while I had to ask myself, am I playing this piece as I feel it, or am I playing it the way he would have expected me to do?

In my personal life I had to rediscover what my family meant to me, how to handle a daughter who needed a mother, and how to adjust to a daily schedule without Heifetz telling me every second of the day what to do. However, the uncertainties of the first years after his death have passed, and I no more feel as Euridice in the reversed role of Orpheus crying, "Orpheus, where are you?" Now I feel that whatever he taught me, I have absorbed as my own. All the hardship to which Heifetz exposed me made me a stronger woman with strong convictions and beliefs. I still get a bit sentimental when I recall the times when he asked me, "Have you ever forgiven me for taking charge of your life and deciding for you whether you should be a violinist or a pianist?" I always gave him the same answer: "There is nothing to forgive; if anything, I should be grateful to you for making this decision for me. I trust your musical judgment above everyone else's."

I'm glad that at times Heifetz also let me know his gentler side, which he wasn't exactly famous for. Once I felt quite ill in his house with the flu, but I didn't breathe a word about it. Late in the afternoon he asked me to go with him to his studio. He took the Louis Gruenberg violin concerto from the cabinet, spread it on the piano, and with violin in his hands was ready to play. I had never seen the piece before. To my horror, it was not only a manuscript in hardly legible handwriting but also an orchestral score. I could hardly see the notes, they were swaying so in front of my eyes, and I told him that I didn't feel well. "You just want to get out of it," he said gruffly, "but excuses will get you nowhere." I pleaded with him that I had a fever and the flu, but he didn't believe me. When Heifetz wanted to play, nothing could come between him and his music. He touched my forehead but pretended that it didn't feel warm. Eventually he sent me for his thermometer and stuck it in my mouth. I had a fever of 103 degrees. Heifetz got a bit scared, put me in bed, made tea for me, covered me up, and sat down and read to me. He would have made chicken soup, too, had he known how. I had to stay overnight, and he checked on me several times during the night.

Am I sorry to perhaps have wasted fifteen years of my life with Heifetz? I would be, had I received nothing in return. Time casts its veil on all that was bad or unpleasant, and his absence makes my heart grow fonder as the years pass by. Now I more often remember the good, the unique musical experiences that nobody else could have given me, the education he lavished on me. I feel that I hitched a ride to a star, and however rocky that ride was, I absorbed as much of its light as I was given to absorb. I also feel that my speech is too shallow to transmit all that he had given; his legacy can only be fulfilled by fighting showy superficiality in music making and by accepting his message to reach as high as one can reach.

14

Postludium

*I*n churches that carry on the great traditions of the past, the organist usually signals the end of the service with a postludium. This is the last chance of the day to play a shorter fugue, perhaps one of Bach, Pachelbel, or Buxtehude, and by gradually pulling out more and more stops, to urge the congregants to flight (*fugue* derives from the Latin for *flight*). The congregation is already happily heading toward the main portal of the church in a state of general contentment, being sure that now they are permitted to smile at one another, exchange greetings, and start a worldly conversation even before reaching the street. They are happy to know that thenceforth nothing stands between them and a sumptuous lunch but the pastor at the gate waiting to be congratulated on his sermon, which for some may faintly recall sermons delivered on Sundays past. On the last chords of the fugue, the bass is supported by the bombard register to signal the sexton to close the gates for another week.

Though organ music is not part of traditional Jewish ritual, the postludium can serve as a reminder that people are instinctively ceremonial by nature. Our life, no matter how primitive or advanced, is interwoven with religious and lay rituals which we accept without question. A thin veneer of social rituals provides a time for cooling off when anarchy threatens, and it keeps us from jumping at each other's throats at the first provocation. This basic need for public ritual haunted me every time I thought about my private burial act in the crematorium. I had difficulty accepting that this should be the final act that bound me to Jascha Heifetz's memory. When he passed away I knew that out of respect for his last wishes a memorial service was not planned, but I had thought that by going to the cremation and thus following through all the way to the end of his journey on this earth, I might be able to put my life with Heifetz behind me and start over fresh. Yet his body was laid to rest but my mind was not. After four years of struggling with this feeling I decided to do something about it.

The solution to such a simple problem as finding an appropriate memorial service came to me during a relatively common event, the funeral of a friend's father. Until that time I had never been to a Jewish funeral service. Its touching simplicity in the unadorned synagogue, intimating but not pushing the feeling of the sacred, revealed to me that this was the place to lay Heifetz's memory to rest.

In Indonesian folk mythology, after death the spirit stays around the body for a while, unwilling to leave its comfortable, well-worn place, and people believe that ceremonies are needed to tell the spirit that it is time to go. Perhaps my being an Indonesian had something to do with Heifetz's presence and influence still haunting me, not only in music making but also in the ordinary ways of life. A simple turn in my kitchen would remind me of his face peeking in and his asking, "Is there anything I cannot do?" Now it was my turn to tell him to let me go. I needed a final celebration of death to regain my peace of mind. I knew it was the typical insincerity of eulogies that made him put "no ceremonies" in his will. He was also afraid, he once told me, that an uninvited violinist might turn up at his funeral and take the opportunity to perform. Dead or alive, he would not put up with a performance that was forced upon him. Once he told me, "I would not want anyone to reap glory abusing my funeral ceremony."

Although this would not be a funeral ceremony, I soon found out that, like all ceremonies, a memorial service would have its own protocol, and trying to go against it would bring resistance. Having discovered what I had to do, I also wanted to go through with it as soon as possible. But this was only the fourth year after Heifetz had passed away, and I learned that nothing should be done until a traditional, sacred anniversary, the earliest being the fifth, and on the anniversary of the day of his death. I added insult to injury by insisting that the ceremony should take place on Heifetz's birthday, 2 February 1992, the nearest memorable day, and I persisted until everybody who had anything to do with the idea relented. I had to remind them that Heifetz never liked to do things the usual way. To make sure that my intentions were legitimate and would not incur the wrath of God, a zealous friend asked the advice of an ultraorthodox rabbi. This rabbi was the first sane person in the whole affair, and he kindly confirmed that no harm could come from holding a ceremony, for peace of mind, to honor the memory of the dead. The next sticking point in the affair was my insistence on reciting the kaddish, the traditional mourners' prayer, during the ceremony, for in Jewish tradition when a person is cremated this prayer is not said in the synagogue but only in a private home or in the cemetery. The orthodox rabbi thought about the dilemma and concluded that everyone is born good and therefore deserves the kaddish. Heifetz's error in ordering the cremation of his body must have come from his not knowing better, and therefore God might look the other way, forgive, and permit the recitation of the kaddish for him within the walls of a synagogue. Interpretation is a great art, and Heifetz always admired those who knew how to make the most of it. As he often said, it all depends on how you look at it.

The wise rabbi's opinion notwithstanding, I had a hard time finding a rabbi within a reasonable distance willing to perform a funeral service for a man who had been cremated. After a lengthy search I found a woman rabbi who was willing to do the ceremony on 2 February, which happened to be a Sunday. I told her of my sense of incomplete closure and of my desire to have Heifetz honored inside a sacred sanctuary before loved ones. She was understanding, warm, accommodating, and sympathetic to a fellow female in her day of need. Her only condition was that a quorum, or minyan, which consists of ten Jewish-born persons, be present at the service. As I understood from my more intransigent Jewish male friends, a male rabbi would have asked for ten males of the same specification. I'm sure Heifetz would have raised an eyebrow or two at the idea of a lady rabbi, considering his uneven and sometimes combative attitude toward women's roles—the woman's place is in the kitchen and her role in the family is to serve her husband and raise her children. But a woman rabbi was also out of the ordinary in traditional Jewish religious practice, and that would have pleased him. I invited to the ceremony the requisite number of Jewish-born people, plus a few more friends and loved ones, but the rabbi didn't ask for anybody's birth certificate.

Nothing was ever easy with Heifetz. As I was going to the service, this time—his birthday—it was my exit from the freeway which was blocked, and I had to make a long, roundabout trip, arriving in the synagogue at literally the last second. The woman rabbi was already at her pulpit with the required number of participants intently staring at her. The women seemed nervous, while the men had disapproval written all over their faces as they waited for my unintended grand entrance.

Yet during the ceremony I felt peace descend on me for the first time since Heifetz had passed away. The rabbi delivered a warm, touching sermon based on the metaphor of a ship sailing away while we on the shore see only its dimming lights from an ever-increasing distance. While she worked on her metaphor, I floated away toward the lights of that slowly moving but never-quite-disappearing ship. In quickly changing flashbacks I remembered Heifetz, the artist, who from our first meeting made my provincial mind vibrate with the excitement of endless challenges. Soon he had transformed me from a local Indonesian star to a bottom-rank student, often planting my feet firmly, not gently, on the ground. His powerful presence and superior musicianship could make me feel like nothing, so that although I did not understand at first, I found that he cared more for me than had anybody else with whom I had studied. Whatever his means, he never gave up and always brought out everything of which I was capable. That symbolic ship also took away Heifetz, the mensch (he liked the word, using it sparingly and only when it really had meaning for him), who had taught me never to cave in, not even to him, but to stand up for what I thought was right. He let me close enough to observe a basically shy man who was never at ease with his own fame and longed to be understood while even he could not understand himself, a person who never learned to relate to another person, not even as a child; a man who had no tolerance for cant and pretense and wanted to write a book "on the sham and hypocrisy in the world, about the upside-down things in the world, the things that pretend to be one way, but they aren't." Known as a hard man, he sometimes cried when we made music together, a little embarrassed about his emotional display. He demanded unconditional, ever-caring love, often without returning any of it, because love should be given freely, without ulterior motive. This expectation was the most difficult for me despite my unemotional upbringing.

The ship also took away that very fallible person who made the mistake of thinking that money could buy everything but eventually had the courage to admit that money-mindedness only made him a passenger on the ship of fools. Perhaps this had something to do with his pampered childhood, which he never really grew out of, remaining forever a restless imp sticking out his tongue at the world that tried to discipline him. Like an immature adolescent, he forever longed for freedom only to tie himself up in knots with his own innumerable principles so that even his iron self-discipline served only to make him its slave. Managed to death, he lost touch even with his own feelings. A musical messiah whose message as a performer was admired but unwanted, stamped with the stigma of genius before he could measure up emotionally to its meaning, trimmed to unnatural shape and form by parents, managers, and even by women, he was forever lost between self-centered willfulness and a search for the object of his will. An immensely proud and private person, he tried to hide the physical debilities that ultimately caused his death. When he let himself be free from his accumulated burden, he was a warm and wonderful person who preserved his enthusiasm for playing music to the very end, for "Loss of enthusiasm is deadly for musicianship." As we played almost every day together, he would debunk the idea of the delicate, sensitive artist, for as he said, "I assure you that it takes the nerves of a bullfighter, the digestion of a peasant, the vitality of a nightclub hostess, the tact of a diplomat, and the concentration of a Tibetan monk to lead the strenuous life of a virtuoso."

Thus was my silent eulogy while the rabbi gave hers, and I am quite sure Jim would not have minded my truthfulness.

I found myself thinking that most of the rabbi's funereal ships disappear forever, their passengers leaving not a trace, while those on other ships may leave an impressive imprint on history. Some of these imprints may remain vital, but others ossify into canons that are not touched for centuries. Since Heifetz had passed away, I had already met a few of his former students for whom his playing was the final word, a perfection that could perhaps be sought but never achieved. Yet to keep alive what Heifetz left behind, we must recognize that while technique can be learned to a certain degree, creativity cannot, and if one has the talent to create, a master is only a necessary stepping stone to reach one's own summit. As he once oversimplified it, "One does not need to be educated musically. We simply need to guard against musical miseducation. Our own ears, unless they have grown so used to mediocrity that they lose their keenness, will do the rest of the job for us."

With that ship getting smaller and smaller on the horizon, I could not help but to count my blessings: I was among the lucky ones, because for me the ship took away a major burden of my life as an artist, a burden that Heifetz would have mercilessly characterized as my being "a stick in the mud." Before this final ritual I always felt during my music making that he was looking over my shoulder, and I would face the uneasy question of whether he would have liked the way I played the piece or would have pounced on me for an interpretation with which he momentarily disagreed. As the ceremony went on, a feeling of freedom came over me, a feeling that from now on I could do what I wanted to do, the way I wanted to do it, without his imagined supervision. Now I understood the feeling refugees must have when, after crossing a forbidden border, their guide says, "You are free now; alas, you also must fend for yourself." With Heifetz there was never a single correct way to perform a piece: although there were many wrong interpretations, there was never just one correct one, and what was acceptable one day sometimes was cast aside the next. As he often said, "When I play a piece well I always hope that tomorrow I will play it even better." Just because Heifetz's performances are frozen in his recordings, one needn't hang onto them as the only authentic way to play these works. His message was just the opposite: be free to play as you feel, but feel sincerely and say something with your music, something that is your own. And therein lies the rub, in that "something" that he contributed to make the difference. Now I felt more than ever that it was this huge and ever-changing "something" which irretrievably sailed away on that ship and which no recordings or written or spoken words could replace.

After the rabbi finished her elaboration on the ship metaphor, Sherry Kloss, Heifetz's last assistant, read "If" by Kipling followed by Heifetz's personal interpretation of it, explaining why this poem had become the talisman of his life. The service concluded with the reading of the kaddish, proudly and in full voice by those who knew it in Hebrew and somewhat timidly by those who read it in English translation, perhaps for the first time. Reading the kaddish seemed at that moment to be my release from bondage; I felt I had done what he may secretly have wished but never expressed, to be honored decently and unpretentiously before his God within the walls of the sanctuary.

Driving home from the synagogue, I thought of the death of cellist Gregor Piatigorsky, Heifetz's close friend, some sixteen years earlier on 6 August 1976. Heifetz had specifically asked me to be with him for the day of the Piatigorsky family's memorial service. The death of Grisha, as he called Piatigorsky, was not unexpected, and Heifetz was composed enough to recollect for me the times they had spent together. From what he said I eventually gathered that we had held a private memorial service together, for he did not attend the official one held by the Piatigorsky family, nor the Piatigorsky memorial concert held at the University of Southern California where they both held chairs. Heifetz talked to me about the futility of all eulogies. In the somewhat incoherent manner that was his way of speaking when he got himself all excited, he said that the purpose of the funeral service was to make the survivors feel good and that, as a recognition of the merits of the dead, it should come much earlier when it still could mean something. Furthermore, those who attend usually do so just to see who else is attending; the dead becomes secondary to social gossip and vain bragging about who knew whom or what in connection with the one who had just passed away. I felt a tinge of self-pity in his voice, and perhaps his experience with funerals in his life colored his emotions. Then he firmly stated that he could never think of a greater praise for a man than stating that "he had died in his boots." He rambled on about how envious he was of an artist who had died onstage, and if he wanted to be buried, which he did not, he would have ordered a tombstone for himself with the inscription, "He died playing flying staccato."

I took a different road home to avoid the barricades on the freeway. We had music at my house for those who attended the ceremony. Sherry played Heifetz's Tononi violin, which she inherited, and I accompanied her at the Steinway piano that used to be his. We played some of his transcriptions; then I played the original piano version of Mendelssohn's *Sweet Remembrance* and other piano pieces that he liked so much and transcribed for violin and piano. Other close friends of Heifetz's who had missed the service at the synagogue drifted in, now participating in this final, wordless eulogy. Sherry and I did not rehearse for this occasion, and that, too, I think, would have pleased Heifetz.

Selected Sources

ABOUT JASCHA HEIFETZ

There is no definitive biography of Jascha Heifetz. Two books broach the subject; though they are unfortunately out of print, they are available in libraries.

Heifetz: An Unauthorized Pictorial Biography of the Professional Life of the Greatest Violinist That Ever Lived (Herbert R. Axelrod, ed. Neptune City, New Jersey: Paganiniana Publications, 1976; third revised edition, 1990) seems to take great pride in the fact that Heifetz, through his lawyer, Marvin Gross, strongly objected to its distribution. Despite threats of legal action, however, none was taken. I presume Heifetz was afraid that he would have to appear in court, which he avoided at all cost. The book's greatest virtues are its discography and a collection of Heifetz concert reviews. Among the clippings in the revised edition is that of 5 November 1952 in which Heifetz commented on the important Henderson review of 1921 (pp. 419–420). Some photographs in this book are mislabeled.

Both the Axelrod volume and Artur Weschler-Vered's *Jascha Heifetz* (New York: Schirmer Books, 1986) were savaged by Dennis Rooney in the December 1988 issue of *The Strad.* Yet in spite of Weschler-Vered's sloppiness (he mixes up Albany, New York, with Tirana, Albania, for example), this is the only coherent biography of Jascha Heifetz. It uses a great deal of material from the Axelrod book without giving proper credit.

Henry Roth's *Violin Virtuosos: From Paganini to the 21st Century* (Los Angeles: California Classics Books, 1997) contains a well-revised, condensed version of the Roth article that appeared earlier in Axelrod's *Heifetz.* A collection of articles by Samuel Applebaum entitled *The Way They Play* (Neptune City, New Jersey: Paganiniana Publications, 1972) includes an appraisal of Heifetz's violin playing.

Innumerable newspaper reviews covered Heifetz's concert perform-ances. He had a complete collection of these reviews, but he left it, along with the volumes of music and photographs, to the Library of Congress, where it is now in storage perhaps never to resurface for the perusal of the public.

Elaine Dutka's story "Inside the Master's Retreat," *Los Angeles Times,* 28 March 1999, describes the detailed, authentic reconstruction of Hei-fetz's hexagonal studio at the Colburn School of Performing Arts in Los Angeles. The studio still holds Heifetz's 78 rpm recordings. The Stan-ford Archive of Recorded Sound at Stanford University also houses re-cordings from Heifetz's personal collection, including a rare recording of Leopold Auer, according to archive founder William R. Moran.

A few magazine articles are worth mentioning. Roger Kahn, "Fiddler on the Shelf," *Life,* 31 October 1969, is well written, apparently based on personal contact with Heifetz and his family. *The Strad* dedicated its Feb-ruary 1986 issue to Heifetz and also included several articles about him in the January and December 1988 issues. The now-defunct magazine *Wis-dom* had a short, uncredited article in its June 1956 issue.

Myra Cohen Livingston was contracted to write a biography of Hei-fetz, based, apparently, on her interviews with people who knew him in a significant way. I was interviewed for this book. Myra had published several volumes of poetry and children's books and was expected to do a creditable job, but the publisher changed hands before the manu-script was finished, and it was subsequently turned down. A horn player and a close friend of Heifetz, she often helped out in his office in a pinch and had access to otherwise unavailable Heifetz material. She passed away before further efforts could be made on behalf of the manuscript.

There have been rumors of other prospective writers scouting for Heifetz material, but to date I am unaware of any published results. Leo-pold Auer's *Violin Playing As I Teach It* (New York: Frederick A. Stokes, 1921) was reprinted by Dover Publications in 1980. I have quoted from the introduction, p. xii. *The Heifetz Collection,* the complete commercial recordings remastered and edited by Jack (John) Pfeiffer, was released on sixty-five compact discs in forty-six volumes in 1997 by BMG, successor to RCA Victor, with an introduction entitled "The Heifetz Legacy" and works list by John and John Anthony Maltese. The jackets of the original LPs contain a great deal of information and interesting stories, written mostly by Jack Pfeiffer. Jack was a long-time close friend of Heifetz and the producer of his records. Miscellaneous information about Heifetz is available on BMG's website, bmgclassics.com, including Jack Pfeiffer's preface to the complete collection.

The Heifetz master class videos to which I refer in chapter 4 were part of the Library of Master Performers series of the National Educational Television and Radio Center, University of Southern California, Institute for Special Musical Studies (Homevideo Exclusives, 1962). Volumes 1 and 2 were reissued on videocassette as *The Heifetz Master Class* (Kultur Video, 1998). The Claremont College film mentioned in chapter 5 was first released in 1952 by World Artists, Inc., under the series title *Meet the Masters*. The film shows Heifetz answering questions in a classroom and playing works by Mendelssohn, Brahms, Gluck, Prokofiev, Wieniawski, as well as his famous arrangement of Dinicu's *Hora staccato*. Heifetz's appearance in 1970 with the French National Orchestra mentioned in chapter 8 was released as *Heifetz in Performance* in 1971 by Critics' Choice and reissued by Video Arts International. In addition to Bruch's *Scottish Fantasy*, it includes short works by Mozart, Bach, Gershwin, Debussy, and others.

About Indonesia

Because this book refers often to Indonesia, suggestions for reading about that country may also be helpful. Bill Dalton's *Indonesia Handbook*, sixth edition (Chico, California: Moon Travel Handbooks, 1995), is a useful travelers' guide, with extensive historical and political information. It was banned in Indonesia because of it anti-Sukarno attitude.

Java, A Garden Continuum, by George A. Fowler Jr., Roggie Cale, and Joe C. Bartlett (Hong Kong; Tulsa: Amerasian Ltd., 1975), is well-informed, written by authors who lived in Indonesia and looked at the country with compassion. In the Insight Guides series is Hans Hoefer and Scott Rutherford, *Indonesia* (London; Boston: APA Publications, 1997, distributed by Houghton Mifflin).

Works by Jascha Heifetz

*T*his list of Heifetz's completed works includes published and unpublished transcriptions for violin and piano, original compositions and transcriptions for various instrumentations, and songs published under the name Jim Hoyl. This list may not be complete, but it represents the best information available to date from Heifetz's labeling of his autograph and printed scores and from library databases. Note that Heifetz's titles sometimes vary from the titles of the original works.

Composer, Heifetz transcription, original work	Place, date	Publisher, date
PUBLISHED TRANSCRIPTIONS FOR VIOLIN AND PIANO		
Achron, Joseph		
From *Children's Suite*, Op. 57, eight pieces originally for piano	London, 1934	C. Fisher, 1937
Aguirre, Julián		
Huella from the song in *Canciónes argentinas*, Op. 49	Redding, CT, 1940	C. Fischer, 1942
Albéniz, Isaac		
Navarra from *Suite española*, Op. 47, No. 3, originally for piano (finished by Déodat de Séverac)	San Clemente, CA, 1933	C. Fischer, 1936 C. Fischer, 1937
El puerto from *Iberia*, originally for piano	n.a.	
Sevilla from *Suite española*, Op. 47, No. 3, originally for piano	Narranganset Pier, RI, 1930	C. Fischer, 1930

Composer, Heifetz transcription, original work	Place, date	Publisher, date

Alkan, Charles-Valentin (Morhange)
  Barcarolle, Op. 65, originally for piano
	Beverly Hills,
	  CA, 1956
		C. Fischer, 1958

Arensky, Anton S.
  Tempo di valse from Violin Concerto in
  A minor, Op. 54
	n.p., 1958	C. Fischer, 1959

Bach, J. S.
  Air from English Suite No. 3, originally
  for clavier
	San Clemente,
	  1936
		Harms, 1946

Preludio from Partita No. 3 in E major,
  originally for unaccompanied violin
	Hollywood,
	  CA, 1938
		C. Fischer, 1939

Prelude from *The Well-Tempered Clavier*,
  No. 8, originally for clavier
	Harbor Island
	  [Newport
	  Beach],
	  CA, 1942
		C. Fischer, 1944

Sarabande from English Suite No. 6, originally for clavier	n.a.	C. Fischer, 1937

Sarabande, Gavotte, and Musette from
  English Suite No. 3, originally for clavier
	San Clemente,
	  1933
		C. Fischer, 1933

Bax, Arnold
  Mediterranean, originally for piano
	San Clemente,
	  1933
		C. Fischer, 1935

Beethoven, Ludwig van
  Contradance, originally for violin and
  piano
	Harbor Island,
	  1943
		C. Fischer, 1946

Folk Dance from *Twelve German Dances*,
  No. 6, originally for piano
	Harbor Island,
	  1942
		Harms, 1943

Minuet, originally for piano	Harbor Island, 1943	Harms, 1944

Borodin, Alexander P.
  Serenade from *Petite suite*, originally for
  piano
	Harbor Island,
	  1943
		C. Fischer, 1944

Brahms, Johannes
  Contemplation from the song "Wie
  Melodien," Op. 105
	San Clemente,
	  1933
		C. Fischer, 1937

Castelnuovo-Tedesco, Mario
  Ritmo di tango from *Media difficolta*,
  originally for piano
	San Clemente,
	  1933; revised
	  1948
		C. Fischer, 1949

Composer, Heifetz transcription, original work	Place, date	Publisher, date
Sea Murmurs, an adaptation of "Arise" after William Shakespeare's *Cymbeline* from *Shakespeare Songs,* Op. 24, Vol. 6	Rome, 1932	C. Fischer, 1937
Tango, an adaptation of "Two Maids Wooing" after William Shakespeare's *A Winter's Tale* from *Shakespeare Songs,* Op. 24, Vol. 8	Cape Town, 1932	C. Fischer, 1933
Chopin, Frédéric		
Nocturne, Op. 55, No. 2, originally for piano	Harbor Island, 1943	C. Fischer, 1944
Debussy, Claude		
L'après-midi d'un faune from *Prélude à l'après-midi d'un faune,* originally for orchestra	New York, NY, 1940	C. Fischer, 1940
Beau soir from the original song	San Clemente, 1933	C. Fischer, 1933
La chevelure from the songs *Chansons de Bilitis*	Harbor Island, 1945	C. Fischer, 1947
Gollywogg's Cake-Walk from *Children's Corner,* originally for piano	Harbor Island, 1941	C. Fischer, 1942
La puerta del vino from *Preludes,* Book 2, originally for piano	Beverly Crest, CA, 1965	C. Fischer, 1965
Deep River (see Original Compositions and Transcriptions for Various Instrumentations, below)		
Dinicu, Grigoraş (see Original Compositions and Transcriptions for Various Instrumentations, below)		
Dvořák, Antonín		
Humoreske, originally for piano	Detroit, MI, 1935	C. Fischer, 1937
Foster, Stephen		
Jeanie with the Light Brown Hair from the original song	Redding, CT, 1939	C. Fischer, 1939
Old Folks at Home from the original song	n.a.	C. Fischer, 1939
Gershwin, George		
From the opera *Porgy and Bess*		
Bess, You Is My Woman Now	Harbor Island, 1944	Gershwin Pub., 1946
It Ain't Necessarily So	Harbor Island, 1944	Gershwin Pub., 1944

Composer, Heifetz transcription, original work	Place, date	Publisher, date
My Man's Gone Now	Harbor Island, 1944	Gershwin Pub., 1944
Summertime and A Woman Is a Sometime Thing	Harbor Island, 1944	Gershwin Pub., 1946
Tempo di Blues (There's a Boat Dat's Leavin' Soon for New York)	Harbor Island, 1944	Gershwin Pub., 1944
Three Preludes, originally for piano		
No. 1	Harbor Island, 1940	N. W. Music, 1942
No. 2	Harbor Island, 1940	N. W. Music, 1940
No. 3	Harbor Island, 1942	N. W. Music, 1942
Gluck, Christoph Willibald		
Sonata, originally for two violins and continuo	Harbor Island, 1943	C. Fischer, 1944
Godowsky, Leopold		
Alt Wien, originally for piano	n.p., 1931	C. Fischer, 1932
Halffter, (Escriche) Ernesto		
Danza de la gitana, originally for piano	Narranganset Pier, 1930	C. Fischer, 1931
Haydn, Joseph		
Adagio and Presto from String Quartet, Op. 54, No. 2	Redding, CT, 1939	C. Fischer, 1940
Hummel, J. Nepomuk		
Rondo, Op. 11, in E-flat major, originally for piano	n.p., 1931	C. Fischer, 1931
Khatchaturian, Aram		
Dance of Ayshe, originally for orchestra	Beverly Hills, 1948	Leeds, 1948
Sabre Dance from the ballet *Gayane*, originally for orchestra	Beverly Hills, 1948	Leeds, 1948
Krein, Alexander		
Dance No. 4 from Dance Suite, Op. 44, originally for piano	Harbor Island, 1941	C. Fischer, 1945
Medtner, Nicolai		
Fairy Tale, Op. 20, No. 1, originally for piano	Beverly Hills, 1949	C. Fischer, 1949

Composer, Heifetz transcription, original work	Place, date	Publisher, date
Mendelssohn, Felix		
Scherzo from Overture for *A Midsummer Night's Dream*	Beverly Hills, 1943	C. Fischer, 1943
Scherzo from Piano Trio in D minor, Op. 49	Harbor Island, 1942	C. Fischer, 1943
Sweet Remembrance from *Songs Without Words*, Op. 19, No. 1, originally for piano	Beverly Hills, 1945	C. Fischer, 1945
Milhaud, Darius		
Brazileira, No. 3 from *Scaramouche*, originally for two pianos	n.a.	Salabert, 1953
Modéré, No. 2 from *Scaramouche*, originally for two pianos	n.a.	Salabert, 1953
Mozart, Wolfgang Amadeus		
Allegro molto from String Quartet in C major, K. 465	Harbor Island, 1941	C. Fischer, 1946
Divertimento in B-flat major, K. 287, originally for orchestra	n.p., 1943	C. Fischer, 1944
Divertimento in D major, K. 334, originally for orchestra	n.p., 1943	C. Fischer, 1944
Menuet from Divertimento in D major, K. 136, originally for orchestra	n.a.	C. Fischer, 1940
Menuetto from String Quartet in D minor, K. 421	n.a.	C. Fischer, 1946
Menuetto from String Quartet in B-flat major, K. 458	New York, 1936	C. Fischer, 1940
Paradies, (Pietro) D.		
Toccata, originally for alte klavier	Roanoke, VA, 1937	C. Fischer, 1938
Ponce, Manuel		
Estrellita from the original song	Mexico City, 1927	C. Fischer, 1928
Poulenc, Francis		
Mouvements perpétuels, originally for piano	Narragansett Pier, 1930	C. Fischer, 1931
Presto No. 1, originally for piano	On board *Galatea*, 1939	C. Fischer, 1940
Prokofiev, Sergei		
Gavotta from *Four Pieces*, Op. 32, originally for piano	New York, 1935	C. Fischer, 1937

Composer, Heifetz transcription, original work	Place, date	Publisher, date
Larghetto and Gavotta from Classical Symphony, Op. 25	Roanoke, VA, 1937	C. Fischer, 1939
March from the opera *The Love for Three Oranges*, Op. 33	Baton Rouge, LA, 1937	C. Fischer, 1939
March from *Ten Pieces*, Op. 12, No. 1, originally for piano	Harbor Island, 1941	C. Fischer, 1943
March amoureux from the ballet *Chout*	n.a.	Boosey & Hawkes, 1961
March and Promenade from *Children's Suite*, Op. 65, originally for piano	Hawaii, 1978	G. Schirmer, 1978
Masks from the ballet *Romeo and Juliette*	Harbor Island, 1941	C. Fischer, 1942
Rachmaninoff, Sergei		
Daisies, Op. 38, No. 3, originally for piano	Harbor Island, 1945	C. Fischer,
Étude-tableau, Op. 33, No. 7, originally for piano	Beverly Hills, 1972	C. Fischer, 1974
Étude-tableau, Op. 39, No. 2, originally for piano	Beverly Hills, 1945	C. Fischer, 1947
It's Peaceful Here from the original song, Op. 21, No. 7	Beverly Hills, 1965	C. Fischer, 1968
Melody from the original song, Op. 21, No. 9	Beverly Hills, 1956	C. Fischer, 1958
Oriental Sketch, Op. 2, No. 2, for piano	Beverly Hills, 1945	Ch. Foley, 1947
Prelude, Op. 23, No. 9, for piano	St. Louis, MO, 1935	C. Fischer, 1937
Prelude, Op. 32, No. 5, for piano	n.a.	C. Fischer, 1947
Rameau, Jean-Philippe		
Rigaudon from *Pièces de clavecin*	Constantinople, 1928	C. Fischer, 1929
Ravel, Maurice		
Forlane from *Le tombeau de Couperin*, originally for piano	Harbor Island, 1941	C. Fischer, 1942
Valses nobles et sentimentales Nos. 6 and 7, originally for piano	San Clemente, 1941	C. Fischer, 1932
Rimsky-Korsakov, Nikolai		
The Bumble Bee from the opera *The Legend of Tsar Saltan*, Op. 57	n.a.	C. Fischer, 1931

Composer, Heifetz transcription, original work	Place, date	Publisher, date
Saint-Saëns, Camille		
The Swan from *Carnival of the Animals,* originally for orchestra and two pianos	Harbor Island, 1945	C. Fischer, 1947
Scarlatti, Domenico		
Selections from sonatas, originally for harpsichord		
Book I		
Molto Moderato (No. 71)	Harbor Island, 1943	C. Fischer, 1944
Allegro (No. 74)	Harbor Island, 1943	C. Fischer, 1944
Presto (No. 77)	Harbor Island, 1943	C. Fischer, 1944
Pastorale (No. 88)	Harbor Island, 1941	C. Fischer, 1944
Non Presto (No. 93)	Harbor Island, 1942	C. Fischer, 1944
Fuga (*The Cat's Fugue,* No. 100)	Harbor Island, 1943	C. Fischer, 1944
Book II		
Andante (No. 7)	Harbor Island, 1943	C. Fischer, 1943
Allegro (No. 19)	Harbor Island, 1942	C. Fischer, 1943
Minuetto (Supplementary Vol.)	Harbor Island, 1942	C. Fischer, 1943
Allegro (No. 21)	Harbor Island, 1942	C. Fischer, 1943
Andante (Vol. 14, No. 38)	Harbor Island, 1943	C. Fischer, 1943
Allegro (Vol. 15, No. 38)	Harbor Island, 1943	C. Fischer, 1943
Sonatina, originally for harpsichord	n.a.	C. Fischer, 1935
Schubert, Franz		
Impromptu in G-flat major, Op. 90, No. 3, originally for piano	New York, 1933	C. Fischer, 1934
Schumann, Robert		
Prophetic Bird from *Waldscenen,* Op. 82, No. 7, originally for piano	n.a.	C. Fischer, 1933

Composer, Heifetz transcription, original work	Place, date	Publisher, date
Turina, Joaquín		
La oración del torero for String Quartet, Op. 34	San Clemente, 1933; completed 1941	C. Fischer, 1942
Valle, Francisco		
Ao pe da fogueira (Preludio XV), originally for piano	n.a.	C. Fischer, 1945
Vivaldi, Antonio		
Larghetto from Double Concerto in B-flat major, originally for string orchestra, RV 547, Op. 22, No. 2	n.a.	C. Fischer, 1929
Weber, Carl Maria von		
Rondo from Violin Sonata, Op. 10, No. 3, in D minor	Chicago, 1933	C. Fischer, 1934
Wieniawski, Henri		
Caprice, from the original violin solo etude	Balboa, CA, 1939	C. Fischer, 1940

UNPUBLISHED COMPLETED TRANSCRIPTIONS

FOR VIOLIN AND PIANO

Berlin, Irving
  White Christmas from the original song   n.a.

Buchardo, Carlos Lopez
  Jujeña from the songs *Seis canciones al estilo popular*   n.a.

Chopin, Frédéric
  Nocturne, Op. 27, No. 2, in D-flat major, originally for piano   n.a.

Dohnányi, Ernst von
  Romanza from *Suite for Orchestra*, Op. 19   1974

Fauré, Gabriel
  Aubade, from Song No. 12 of *Morning Serenade*   1975

Composer, Heifetz transcription, original work	Place, date	Publisher, date
Gershwin, George		
An American in Paris, originally for orchestra	1978; completed in 1990 by Ayke Agus from Heifetz's notes and oral instructions	
Gluck, Christoph Willibald		
Melody from *Mélodie* from the ballet *Orfeo ed Euridice*	1949	
Ibert, Jacques		
Le petit âne blanc, No. 2 from the piano suite *Histoires* (also arranged for piano duet)	Mexico, 1934; revised 1958	
Kodály, Zoltán		
Two movements from *Háry János* Suite from the opera	n.a.	
Moszkowski, Moritz		
Sparks (Étincelles) from *Selected Piano Works*, Op. 36, No. 6	n.a.	
Poulenc, Francis		
Promenade à pied from *Promenades*, originally for piano	n.a.	
Rachmaninoff, Sergei	n.a.	
Second movement from Sonata for Cello and Piano, Op. 19	n.a.	
Humoresque from *Seven Pieces*, Op. 10, for piano	1973	
Prelude, Op. 32, No. 7, originally for piano	1953; revised 1984; completed 1986	
Prelude, Op. 32, No. 12, originally for piano	completed 1986	
Strauss, Richard		
Along the Silent Forest Path from the song Op. 9, No. 1	n.a.	

FOR PIANO

Padilla, José		
Valencia for one piano, four hands, based on the original song	1958	

Composer, Heifetz transcription, original work	Place, date	Publisher, date

ORIGINAL COMPOSITIONS AND TRANSCRIPTIONS FOR VARIOUS INSTRUMENTATIONS

CADENZAS

Brahms, Johannes		
Cadenza to Violin Concerto in D minor, Op. 77	n.a.	C. Fischer, 1947
Mozart, Wolfgang Amadeus		
Cadenza to Violin Concerto No. 4 in D major, K. 218	n.a.	C. Fischer, 1937

ORIGINAL TRANSCRIPTIONS FOR VARIOUS INSTRUMENTATIONS

Deep River for violin and piano (original theme from the Negro spiritual)	Boston, 1938	C. Fischer, 1939
Dinicu, Grigoraș (original theme)		
Hora staccato for alto saxophone and piano	n.a.	C. Fischer, 1937
Hora staccato for cello and piano	n.a.	C. Fischer, 1930
Hora staccato for clarinet and piano	n.a.	C. Fischer, 1937
Hora staccato for orchestra (arr. A. Schmid, ed. Heifetz)	n.a.	C. Fischer, 1945
Hora staccato for piano solo	Mexico City, 1940	C. Fischer, 1944
Hora staccato for tenor saxophone and piano	n.a.	C. Fischer, 1937
Hora staccato for trumpet and piano	n.a.	C. Fischer, 1938
Hora staccato for two pianos	Harbor Island, 1942	C. Fischer, 1942
Hora staccato for viola and piano	n.a.	C. Fischer, 1930
Hora staccato for violin and piano	1930	C. Fischer, 1930
Hora staccato for xylophone and piano	n.a.	C. Fischer, 1947

WORKS PUBLISHED UNDER THE NAME JIM HOYL

"Hora Swingato" (song)	n.a.	n.a.
Samba Diablo (for piano solo)	n.a.	Emery Music
"So Much in Love" (song; Marjorie Goetschius, lyricist)	n.a.	Emery Music
"When You Make Love to Me" (song; Marjorie Goetschius, lyricist)	n.a.	Emery Music, 1946